OZ CLARKE'S
REGIONAL WINE GUIDES

THE ENCYCLOPEDIA OF
SPANISH AND
PORTUGUESE
WINES

KATHRYN McWHIRTER
CHARLES METCALFE

A Fireside Book
Published by Simon & Schuster Inc.
New York   London   Toronto   Sydney   Tokyo   Singapore

A Fireside Book
Published by Simon & Schuster Inc.
Simon & Schuster Building
Rockefeller Center
1230 Avenue of the Americas
New York, NY 10020

Originally published in Great Britain by
Webster's Wine Price Guide Ltd,
Axe and Bottle Court, 70 Newcomen Street, London SE1 1YT

Typesetting by Dorchester Typesetting Group Ltd, Dorchester, England
Color Reproduction by Scantrans (PTE) Ltd, Singapore
Printed and bound in Singapore

10   9   8   7   6   5   4   3   2   1

Library of Congress Cataloging in Publication Data

McWhirter, Kathryn
   Encyclopedia of Spanish and Portuguese wines / Kathryn McWhirter,
Charles Metcalfe.
       p.   cm. -- (Oz Clarke's regional wine guides)
   "A Fireside book."
   Includes index.
   ISBN 0-671-75955-8
   1. Wine and wine making -- Spain. 2. Wine and wine making -- Portugal.
   I. Metcalfe, Charles. II. Title. III. Series: Clarke, Oz. Regional wine guides.
TP559. S8M34 1992
641.2'2'0946--dc20   91-27872
                                                                              CIP

CONTENTS

INTRODUCTION
OZ CLARKE

It used to be so easy making sense of Spanish and Portuguese wines. There was so little to make sense of. Spain was where you looked for your sherry. It might be where you looked for some cheap sparkling wine if your wallet didn't feel up to Champagne. And it had one good table wine – Rioja. Everything else, as far as we were concerned, was simply cheap and cheerful for when we couldn't afford anything better. And that was Spain – the country with the world's largest acreage of vines brushed aside in a few sentences.

Portugal didn't fare much better because it was perfectly possible at one time to say that apart from the fortified wines of port and Madeira – yes, Madeira is Portuguese, I'd almost forgotten – there was only one Portuguese table wine of any consequence – Mateus Rosé. Maybe a few intrepid travellers would return with tales of the sharp, low alcohol *vinhos verdes* they drank to wash down their salt cod – but that didn't appeal much to us in the chilly north of Europe. So is that all, from a country which has been demarcating its best wines since the thirteenth century, which set its own *appellation contrôlée* system in motion almost 200 years before the French, from our oldest ally, for goodness sake?

No it's not all. Certainly sherry, Rioja and *cava* sparkling wine are important in Spain. Port and Madeira, sparkling rosé and *vinho verde* are important in Portugal. But there is so much more to be discovered. Both Spain and Portugal have a wine culture as historic as those of France or Italy, and Portugal in particular offers a most startling variety of wine styles and grape varieties.

Until accession to the EC, the Pyrenees had constituted a remarkably efficient barrier between the Iberian peninsula and the rest of Europe. They weren't that interested in us, and our interest in them was strictly limited. Now, however, the Common Market, with its insistence on more free trade and the opening of frontiers, is exposing the Spanish and Portuguese wine producers to competition from their more sophisticated neighbours, in particular France and Italy. The effect on their industries has been electric.

There had always been regional differences, often very marked, throughout Spain and Portugal, because conditions differ dramatically across the countries. The temperate Spain of Rioja and Penedés in the north-east, the damp Atlantic acres of Galicia in the north-west, the stark barren plains of La Mancha in the centre, and the remarkable coincidence of intense heat with the moisture-preserving chalk soils of Jerez in the south-west couldn't possibly produce the same sorts of wines. Of course they don't. And will Portugal's various landscapes yield wines that are equally different? Of course they will.

But we'll need someone to tell us why all these wines are different and how they're different, because it is only in the very recent past that these countries have woken up to the need to explain themselves to a wider public.

Charles Metcalfe and Kathryn McWhirter were the first British writers to see that our knowledge of these two major wine-producing countries was woefully inadequate and so they set out to become *the* experts on Iberian wine. In the last few years whenever I've tried to contact them, one or the other is either in Spain or Portugal, just back, or about to set off. They have criss-crossed the two countries, minutely exploring the well-known areas as well as delving into the unknown. They've returned home with the most comprehensive understanding of Spanish and Portuguese wines of anyone writing today and I am proud and excited that they have written this book for us.

I've learnt a whole host of new facts about regions and grapes, wine styles and producers whose identities were hazy in the extreme. But not only that. All the famous regions are covered in much greater depth than is usual, and with far greater personal involvement. We get a real living picture of these two great but very different wine-producing nations, and if I can't get down there myself to check out all the new developments as well as all my old favourites, thank goodness I've got Charles and Kathryn's book at hand.

▶ A vineyard near Laguardia in the Rioja Alavesa, backed by the craggy Sierra de Cantabria. This is a traditional stronghold of the Tempranillo grape, Spain's finest red, now being planted throughout much of the country.

MAKING
WHITE WINES

A decade ago, you could rely on practically every Spanish and Portuguese white wine being yellow, rough and extremely alcoholic. Drinking them young was no solution; avoiding them completely was the only sensible procedure. Then, gradually, modern wine-making techniques began to percolate around the peninsula.

Modern white wines are made from grapes that have been picked early, before they become overripe. The grapes have enough acidity to make the resulting wines taste sharply fresh. They haven't become too sweet, so there isn't excessive sugar to be converted into excessive alcohol. And the sun hasn't burnt up all the attractive, aromatic substances that give white wine its character.

Modern white wines *can* be made even in fairly primitive equipment, given a little knowledge and skill. What is essential is that the fermenting juice should be chilled. Otherwise all the aromatic substances bubble off furiously, and all sorts of undesirable flavours begin to form. The traditional fermentation vessel in both countries is the *tinaja* (Spain) or *amfora* or *talha* (Portugal), a huge, earthenware Ali Baba pot, its top covered after fermentation with a wooden board, or nowadays more often with a sheet of plastic tied on with string.

A common alternative is the square concrete tank, sometimes lined with epoxy-resin or ceramic tiles. It is possible to keep the juice coolish in any of these basic containers, either by occasionally pumping the wine out, through a cooling system, and then back again, or by filling the fermenting vessel very gradually, adding a little cool juice every now and then to the boiling mass. The really modern way is to ferment in stainless steel tanks, automatically drenched with water if the temperature gets too hot, or sometimes equipped with their own outer cooling jacket. The other advantage of stainless steel is that it's easier to clean. To clean an empty *tinaja*, an unfortunate worker, brush in hand, is dangled inside on the end of a rope. And the bits he inevitably misses can easily turn the next wine bad.

Sadly, although the fresh white wine revolution is still on the march, such wines remain in the minority in both countries. Spain and Portugal are lands of small-scale grape-growers who, resisting change, are often reluctant to pick a month earlier, and forsake the pleasure of boasting that their wine contains 15 or 16 per cent alcohol.

Whatever the style of wine, the grapes have to be de-juiced on arrival at the winery. The very best juice simply runs out under the weight of the mass of grapes, and top wineries then use very gentle apparatus to squeeze out a proportion more. Wineries that aren't aiming for quality may use rough, continuous screw presses and/or centrifuges, which mangle the grapes and extract harsh and bitter substances as well as the juice. A fairly recent technique, used by some leading winemakers in Spain and Portugal, is to leave the grape pulp in contact with the squeezed juice for a few hours to extract more aroma from the skins.

The next step is to remove all the gunge before fermentation. (Solid particles in the fermenting juice can cause nasty flavours to develop.) This is traditionally done by leaving the juice in a tank to settle for up to two days then running the clean juice off the dregs. Nowadays, various substances such as enzymes can be added to speed the process. Really well-off wineries sometimes use special filters or centrifuges.

Once cleaned, the juice goes into the fermentation vessel. Some wineries rely on the action of natural yeasts, others use special cultured yeasts, which can be more efficient and give more predictable flavours. Left to itself, fermenting juice bubbles briskly and becomes very hot, well over 30°C. Ideally, fermenting white wines should be cooled to between 16°C and 18°C. The yeasts absorb the sugar in the juice and produce enzymes, which then release alcohol and carbon dioxide from the sugar, along with a lot of energy in the form of heat. After the first few days, the wine-to-be continues to bubble gently until all the sugar has been used up, or until the yeast dies of alcohol poisoning. The whole process might last a week if the fermentation became too hot. Ten to fifteen days is more usual, but really cool fermentations can go on for weeks or even months before they are finished.

In the very coolest parts of the Iberian peninsula (the Vinho Verde country of northern Portugal, and Galicia in northern Spain), white wines sometimes undergo a secondary fermentation, the malolactic fermentation. This is much more common further north in Europe because it happens only to wines from less ripe grapes that contain malic acid (the sharp taste in apples). In most parts of Spain and Portugal, the sun burns up all the malic acid before the grapes are picked. But wines made in cooler areas are likely to re-ferment gently – at some stage after the first fermentation – when bacteria get to work on the malic acid, converting it into mild lactic acid. Because this creates a softer taste, some winemakers encourage the malolactic fermentation but many, including most of the best *vinho verde* producers, take steps to avoid it. Either they filter their wine to remove the bacteria, or dose it with preservative.

Once fermentation is finished the wine is run off the left-over sludge of dead yeasts, then 'fined'. Fining clears the wine of hazes caused by minute particles that haven't settled out. It is usually done with a powdered clay called bentonite, which is added to the wine and then sinks down, dragging any impurities with it. Most modern white wines are chilled before bottling to encourage crystals of tartrate salts to form so that they can be removed – they might otherwise appear in the bottle and worry customers (though they are quite harmless). The wines are then filtered, and most modern, well-made wines are bottled for drinking young.

This wasn't the traditional way, however. The Spanish and Portuguese have historically enjoyed their white wines aged in wooden barrels. Sadly, to modern tastes, this left them dark, dull and fruitless, because few of the grape varieties used have the guts to withstand this sort of treatment. Nevertheless, many traditional winemakers persist in barrel ageing their whites. Only in a very few cases in Spain and Portugal does wood ageing add positively to a white wine's complexity.

SPARKLING Still wine can be made fizzy by a number of methods: the best – big business in Spain particularly – is that used in Champagne, and this is the method used for practically all the Spanish and Portuguese sparkling wines exported to Europe and the USA. The wine is re-fermented inside the final bottle by means of a little extra sugar and yeast. The snag is that once the fermentation is over, a deposit of yeast cells remains, and this must be removed to prevent the wine from looking cloudy and unattractive in the bottle. Because it is so fine, the deposit has to be shaken very gently and gradually down the side of the bottle until it rests on the cork, ready for removal. Usually in Spain this is done in large crates mounted on rockers or hexagonal bases, which are periodically rocked or shifted around until the sediment rests on the cork. A recently developed alternative is to use special 'agglomerating' yeast for the bottle fermentation. This sticks together when it has done its work, and can be shaken down the bottle much more quickly. The bottle necks are then plunged into freezing brine so that a plug of wine and sediment forms which can be quickly ejected when the bottle is de-corked, topped up and re-corked ready for sale. Other methods include gasification (pumping in carbon dioxide) and second fermentation in a tank, then bottling under pressure.

▲ Unloading Airén grapes at the winery of Señorio de los Llanos in Valdepeñas. Spain's most planted white grape, the Airén sadly has little flavour, but it can be made into fresh, gently fruity wine using modern methods.

MAKING RED AND ROSÉ WINES

Red and rosé wines are made from black grapes. But if you squeezed the juice out of those grapes and fermented it, you would almost always end up with white wine, because very few black grapes have red juice. All the colour is in the skins, so these (plus the pips – and occasionally the stalks) are left to ferment with the juice. As the fermenting juice becomes more alcoholic it gradually dissolves the red pigments, for alcohol is a strong solvent. Skins, stalks and pips also contain bitter, astringent substances called tannins. And the great skill in modern wine-making lies in extracting the desired amount of colour while limiting the extraction of tannins.

The first step in this direction is to remove the stalks before fermentation. Traditionally, producers in Spain and Portugal threw everything into the vat: crushed grapes, stalks, even

▲ Racking red wine clear of the solids left after fermentation at Cellers de Scala Dei in the spectacular Priorato mountains of Catalonia. It is astonishing to find such a modern winery in so remote a setting.

the odd rat if it got in the way. This was all brewed up together, with harsh and bitter results. The best winemakers have long given up this practice, however, and others, even backwoods co-operatives, are gradually following.

The other main way of limiting harsh tannins is to remove the skins and pips before fermentation is complete. Again, the Iberian tradition was to leave the solids soaking in the wine often right to the end of fermentation, and even after. But modern, softer wines are now drained off the solids after one or two weeks, then left to finish fermenting without the skins. However, this doesn't mean they are pale: most colour is extracted in the early stages of fermentation and, after two weeks, the wine is about as dark as it will ever be.

With rosé wines, the approach is a little different. Crushed black grapes go into the vat as for red wine, but the juice is run off the solids after no more than a day, while it is still just pink. Spain in fact has another category of wine, somewhere between red and rosé: *clarete* is usually made from a mixture of black and white grapes, crushed and fermented together for between three and four days.

To extract maximum colour in the shortest possible time, skins, pips and stalks (if there are any) – which tend to float to the surface – need to be regularly mixed back into the fermenting wine. This floating 'cap' is known as a *sombrero* in Spanish, *manta* (blanket) in Portuguese. The traditional way, still used by growers who make their own wine in open troughs or *lagares*, is simply to poke the skins down periodically with sticks or paddles, or, more basic still, to leap into the trough and stomp around! Nowadays it is more usual to pump liquid from the bottom of the tank through a pipe and spray it back in at the top. This is done at least once a day.

The Portuguese, especially port producers, often use autovinificators, rather like coffee percolators, which do this automatically. The pressure of carbon dioxide gas produced during fermentation periodically pushes wine up through a valve to spray back over the skins. Elsewhere, the most modern equipment resembles a huge washing machine. The inner drum is set by computer to rotate at intervals and churn up the juice and skins.

Temperature is also important. For most

grape varieties, the ideal temperature to extract colour but preserve fresh fruit flavours is somewhere between 26°C and 28°C. If temperatures shoot above 30°C, the wine generally tastes jammy. Some wineries have sophisticated equipment to cool their fermentation vats, some simply resort to spraying hosepipes on the outside. The worst simply allow the wines to boil away under the hot Iberian sun.

In Rioja there is another method of red wine-making, very similar to that used in Beaujolais – with similar, gluggable, super-fruity results. Small-scale growers, and some co-operatives and commercial companies, still make reds in this way. The grapes are loaded intact into the fermentation vat but inevitably some squash and the juice that escapes starts fermenting at the bottom of the vat. The carbon dioxide given off during fermentation rises up and envelops all the uncrushed grapes in a blanket of warm gas. These grapes then start to ferment inside their skin, gradually swell up and burst. The result is a delicious, fruity, deep-coloured wine – with minimal tannin.

Whatever the method, when fermentation is over the wine is run off; next the grapy residue is pressed, gently first, then more roughly, to squeeze out the final drops. The very final pressings go to the distillery, but the first pressing from the mush of skins may get blended back into the wine, either through thoughtless habit, or because the winemaker wants a tougher, more tannic effect.

Tannin isn't all bad: a fair amount of tannin is necessary in any red wine destined for ageing, as tannin and acidity are the two major components that keep a wine alive. The astringent taste of tannin softens with age.

Wood ageing is a strong tradition in both countries – but there is a widespread tendency to age wines too long. If a red wine starts out with enough concentration and substance, such a course of ageing can (and does) yield some of Spain's greatest reds, but these are exceptions. In France, Australia or California, wines are put into small oak barrels for a maximum of 18 months, then into bottle. In the Iberian peninsula, by contrast, wines are usually aged first for a year or so in large wooden vats, then in small barrels, sometimes for several years.

How much woody flavour the wines draw out of the barrels depends on the age of the barrels. New oak quickly gives wine a strong aroma and flavour – like vanilla and freshly sawn planks – but after about five years' use, a barrel has no flavour left to give. Wines stored in older casks simply age a little faster than they would in metal or concrete containers (and much faster then they would in bottle), first becoming more mellow then gradually less fruity. Official Spanish ageing regulations stipulate, for instance, that a red *reserva* should be aged for one year in oak, but without specifying what sort of oak. So there's no predicting whether a *reserva* will taste overwhelmingly oaky, or simply mellow.

While in vat or barrel, during the early months, practically all red wines in Spain and Portugal undergo a second, malolactic fermentation. This is provoked by naturally present bacteria which convert sharper acids to more gentle ones, and so give the wine a rounder, softer character. The wines are also cleaned or 'fined' with some substance such as gelatine, isinglass or, traditionally, beaten egg white. These substances capture stray particles floating in the wine and drag them down to the bottom of the barrel or tank. Some modern wineries centrifuge their wines instead. At various stages during barrel ageing, the wines are 'racked' – transferred to another container, leaving behind any solid deposits. Limited racking is necessary, but the more often it is done, the more subdued and finally fruitless the wines become. Apart from port, Spanish and Portuguese wines hardly ever throw a deposit in the bottle (unlike great French wines), because the lengthy wood ageing gives the deposit time to precipitate out before the wine is bottled.

The winery's responsibility for ageing the wine doesn't end once the wine is bottled – or so Spanish and Portuguese winemakers believe. In France, most wine producers sell their wines as soon as they are bottled, and expect the customer to keep them until they are ready for drinking. Spanish and Portuguese wines, however, are almost invariably sold ready for drinking, having been aged in bottle – sometimes for several years – in the winery. Bottle ageing gives a wine distinctive pruny, slightly mushroomy flavours, which can add the final touch of perfection or – if the wine was not gutsy enough in the first place – the final kiss of death, before it ever reaches a glass.

MAKING FORTIFIED WINES

Fortified wines are wines to which extra alcohol has been added at some stage during their production. There are two different reasons for doing this: and port illustrates one, sherry the other. In the case of port, alcohol is added during fermentation while quite a lot of the grape sugar still remains in the hot, bubbling juice. This dose of spirit kills the yeasts, stops the fermentation and so retains some of the natural sugar. The resulting young port is therefore sweet, tastes very spirity, and needs a few years in wooden casks to soften and mature. This is the basic method used also for Madeira, Moscatel de Setúbal and the fortified red Garnacha *generoso* made in co-operatives in many parts of Spain.

With sherry, by contrast, the juice is left to ferment until all the sugar is used up. Even sweet sherries start out life bone dry. It is only after fermentation is over that the spirit is added, different measures for different types of sherry. If a sweet sherry is required, the dry base will simply be sweetened up at a later stage with concentrated or fortified grape juice.

Before the spirit is added, simple sherry wine is one of the world's least impressive white wines. But the spirit enables it to mature for years in oak barrels – into one of the world's greatest.

PORT If you're keen to see wine being trodden by foot, the port country of the Douro may be your last chance. Up in these remote hills, some of the grapes are still foot-trodden in ancient, shallow stone troughs called *lagares*, accompanied by songs and fearsome local brandy. For a wine as dark and toughly tannic as port, it's vitally important – after the treading is over – that the skins and pips should periodically be mixed in with the fermenting juice to extract as much colour as possible. Traditionally, this is done by pushing down the 'cap' of floating solids with long poles.

More often nowadays, the grapes are fermented in autovinificators – large enclosed tanks in which the pressure of the gases produced by fermentation acts as a natural pump to spray the juice up over the skins. Other wineries use modern electrical pumps, and stainless steel tanks have also appeared in the last decade. Some producers even control the temperature, which is necessary if the results are to be consistently good. The wine ferments until it has reached about six or seven per cent alcohol, still containing more than half the natural grape sugar, before being fortified with raw grape spirit. This brings the alcohol level up to 19 per cent, the yeasts die, and the infant port is run off into a clean container, pressed from the skins, and left to settle.

The young wine is usually brought down to lodges (warehouses) in Vila Nova de Gaia early in the year following the harvest. First step is to analyse and taste every batch, assessing its quality and deciding how it should be matured. Batches of similar style and quality are blended together and put into wooden barrels of varying sizes for varying periods. The wines are 'racked' – run off any solid deposit and into a clean cask – about once a year for the first few years, then less frequently. The cheapest ports (basic rubies and tawnies) are aged in wood for only about three years, but the finest old tawnies may remain in barrel for up to 40 years.

As they age, the wines gradually mellow (though they remain spirity as the spirit level is kept topped up) and turn from dense, bright red to a lighter tawny colour. Vintage Character and Late Bottled Vintage, the next cheapest categories, age for four to six years before bottling. Of the wines that started out a finer quality, the best are blended together in the best years to make Vintage Port, which is aged for just two years in wood, but needs many more years in bottle before drinking. It keeps its colour much better in bottle than in wood and ends up redder and richer. Crusting ports are less-than-vintage standard but blends of good wines, wood-aged for three to four years.

MADEIRA Unlike the port grapes, the different Madeira varieties are kept separate in the wineries. Sercial, Verdelho and Tinta Negra Mole grapes are pressed like grapes for ordinary white wines, and the juice ferments without the skins. With Bual and Malmsey, however, skins are usually left in the fermenting juice for a couple of days in order to extract more colour, tannin and aroma. The wine ferments at anything between 18°C and 35°C in tanks or large wooden vats. Most companies add alcohol, as for port, to stop the fermentation when the required sweetness level has been reached, sooner for the sweeter styles, later for the drier. Young Madeira is fortified slightly less than port, to around 17 per cent alcohol. But some firms take the other route, ferment all their wines to dryness, then sweeten them up with fortified grape juice.

Now follows Madeira's unique 'cooking' process, which gives the wines their characteristic caramelly, tangy, slightly bitter flavour. The cheaper wines go into special kettle-tanks called *estufas*, in which coils filled with hot water heat the wine up to between 45°C and 50°C for a legal minimum of 90 days. Fine wines are left in casks for years either in hot attics above the *estufas* or in warehouses heated to between 35°C and 40°C. Even the cheapest Madeiras must spend a minimum of 18 months in wooden casks after their *estufagem*. Reserves have to be aged in wood for at least five years. Special Reserves for 10, and Vintages for 20 years.

SHERRY, MONTILLA-MORILES, RUEDA AND CONDADO DE HUELVA These wines – of similar style – are made in two basic ways, one of which leads to *fino* type wines, the other to *oloroso* type. Whatever the ultimate style, the juice is pressed from the skins, left to settle, then fermented right out to dryness.

Once the wines are dry and completely fermented, they are racked and fortified with grape spirit. This is where the big distinction is made between *fino* and *oloroso* styles. *Finos*-to-be are fortified to no more than 15.5 per cent alcohol, future *olorosos* up to 18 per cent. *Finos* then develop in a totally different way thanks to an unusual yeast called *flor*, which occurs naturally in all the areas that make this style of wine. The barrels for all types of sherry are filled just five-sixths full. The surface of the wine in *fino* barrels then grows a film of squidgy, oatmeal-white *flor*. While protecting the infant sherry from the air and keeping it pale in colour, *flor* feeds off the wine and affects its composition and flavour in various ways. The most marked changes in flavour are a new, sharp tang and a delicious pungency. *Flor* never grows

▲ The traditional way of sampling *fino* and *manzanilla* direct from the cask. The whippy *venencia* is plunged down through the film of flor, then whisked rapidly out again, before the film has time to re-form, and deftly poured from a great height.

on *oloroso*-style wines because it will not tolerate alcohol levels over 16.2 per cent. *Olorosos* gradually develop in contact with the air, taking on a rich, nutty aroma and flavour.

The third major sherry style, *amontillado*, develops out of *fino*. After *fino* has been in barrel for six years or more, the *flor* begins to fade and die, and the wine comes in contact with the air, turning amber-coloured and nutty-flavoured while still retaining the pungency and tang of a *fino*. These are true, fine, dry *amontillados*. The cheaper, sweetish wines sold as *amontillados* are fourth-rate *finos* darkened and sweetened up with concentrated grape juice. Similarly, creams are sweetened-up, low-grade *olorosos*.

All sherries have to be wood-aged for a minimum of three years, but the finest are aged for much longer. During this time, they pass through a *solera* system, a traditional means of gradual blending. When sherry is needed for bottling, only about one-quarter of the wine from the most mature barrels is run off at a time. Those barrels are then filled from slightly younger ones and so on until the last barrel receives a top-up of the youngest wine. This is vital for *fino*, as the nutrients in the younger wines keep the *flor* alive.

11

CLASSIFICATIONS

SPAIN *Denominación de origen* (DO) is the Spanish wine classification that fits into the EC's top 'quality wine' category – like *appellation d'origine contrôlée* in France. To qualify for this grand title, wines have to conform to specific regulations defining the DO boundaries (within which the grapes must be grown and the wines made), permitted grape varieties, vineyard practice (such as density of plantation and pruning), maximum yield (in weight of grapes per hectare), winemaking procedures, and minimum levels of alcohol.

But, sadly, DO on the label doesn't guarantee quality in the bottle. (Nor, indeed, do the equivalents in France, Germany and Italy, but it must be admitted that these other countries do have consistently higher standards.) Just over half of Spain's wines qualify for DO status, and many of the DOs thoroughly justify their quality title. But some of the (currently 36) DO regions, including a few of long standing, are producers of nothing better than basic plonk, with only the odd wine-making star to prove that the potential for better things really exists.

This seems to be more than ever the case with the new DOs declared in the past few years. The latest recruits are Chacolí (a sop to the Basques), Calatayud (extremely rustic), Conca de Barberá (home of Torres's magnificent Milmanda Chardonnay – except that it says Penedés on the label), and El Bierzo (tiny and remote). An uninspiring lot, with more than a whiff of politics to their promotion.

Within a couple of years, Spain also hopes to have an additional, higher category of quality wine with tighter rules, *denominación de origen calificada* (DOCa). Rioja seems likely to be the first candidate.

Further down the scale, below DO but in the upper echelons of table wine, there already is, theoretically, a category called *vinos de la tierra* – country wines, the EC-speak equivalent of French *vins de pays*. In preparation for joining the EC, Spain announced 12 of these in December 1986 and added another 21 a couple of years later – unknowns such as Pozohondo and Salcedón-Mondéjar. Well, the bureaucrats in Madrid and Brussels may possibly have cleared a filing cabinet or two in order to accommodate these new names, but take a trip to Pozohondo and you are unlikely to find a winemaker who has heard of *vino de la tierra*, never mind one who actually labels his wine with these mysterious words. In any case, little of the potential *vino de la tierra* is even graced with a label.

The other type of classification used for Spanish wine defines its age and, in principle, drinkability. *Crianza, reserva* and *gran reserva* are terms used to describe wines that have been matured in certain ways for certain lengths of time. The idea behind these is to present consumers with an instantly drinkable wine, rather than selling them a bottle that they may have to keep for years until it is ready.

There is a certain flexibility in the definition of *crianza* (which means 'ageing') wines. It is up to the individual *consejo regulador* – the governing body of a DO – to make the final decision on the rules but, in the absence of any local peculiarities, a *crianza* wine must have had a minimum of two years' ageing, whether in tank, barrel or bottle. For *reserva* wines the rules are more precise. They must be of good quality, and red *reservas* must have at least three years' ageing (of which one must be in oak barrel), and white *reservas* at least two years' ageing (of which six months must be in oak).

▲ The two Rioja labels both show the *denominación de origen*, and illustrate two types of age classification, *crianza* and *gran reserva*. Raimat, from Costers del Segre, does not bother to use *crianza*, though entitled to it.

Spain's finest reds are often released as *gran reservas*, wines of top quality from extremely good vintages; reds are aged for at least two years in oak barrel and three in bottle, whites for a total of at least four years (of which six months must be in oak). All this time in barrel does not *necessarily* mean that the wine will taste oaky. If old barrels are used, the effect is to mellow and soften the wine; only barrels under five years old impart an oaky taste.

PORTUGAL The Portuguese basis for wine classification is very similar to Spain's. There are rules defining a quality wine region (*região demarcada*) and how the wines from it should be made, and rules defining *reservas* and *garrafeiras* – the Portuguese equivalents of the Spanish *reservas* and *gran reservas*.

But the whole of wine-making Portugal is in a ferment at present over newly-established wine regions and changes to the rules. When Portugal joined the EC in 1987, Brussels gave them four years to come up with suggestions for new *regiãoes demarcadas*. At that point, there were 11 RDs (two of which were in the Douro, one for table wines, one for port, with different boundaries and regulations). But outside these regions there was an abundance of wines – some of them very good – in the Alentejo, Ribatejo, Oeste and Setúbal peninsula (up to then demarcated only for its sweet, fortified Moscatel). So the Portuguese hurried to nominate another 26 regions for demarcation.

These included just about anywhere in the country where half-way decent wine could be made. These regions were given the title of *vinhos de qualidad produzides em região determinada* (VQPRD) – roughly corresponding to VDQS in France – and also referred to as having *indicação de proveniência regulamentada* (IPR). Each one was told to set up a *Commissão* (committee) to supervise the control of wine quality. These committees have to be in place by 1991, and the hope is that under their guidance the 26 areas will ultimately reach RD status.

But no one really expects that all these regions will become RDs (confusingly, to be known at some time in the not too distant future as DOC – *denominação de origen controlada*). So Portugal, too, will probably end up with a two-tier classification system. There

has been no further news about a 'country wine' category (similar to *vino de la tierra*) which was to have been called *vinho regionão*, but it may yet suddenly spring into life. Only recently, without any warning to the outside world, the Algarve RD was sub-divided into four different RD regions. And, since the IPR regions were nominated in 1988, one has sunk without trace, two have changed their names, and another two have been added. In this atmosphere of restless change, anything can happen.

Some of Portugal's best red wines still hide behind the bald terms *reserva* and *garrafeira*, with only a company or brand name and no hint of origin. While frustrating for those who like to know precisely where what they are drinking comes from, these two descriptions do give some basic information about the wines. *Reserva* (not a term much used by Portuguese winemakers) can be applied to outstanding wine from a particular vintage that has an alcohol level at least half a per cent higher than the minimum required. *Garrafeira* has the same stipulations about alcohol level and outstanding quality plus ageing requirements. Red *garrafeira* must have had at least two years' ageing in vat or barrel, plus another in bottle. White *garrafeira* (in practice hardly ever found) must have had a minimum of six months in vat or barrel and six more in bottle.

▲ The Borba co-op is the first company to print the new VQPRD classification on its label. Garrafeira TE 1982 is typically Portuguese in its vagueness over origins, but the Bairrada label states the *região demarcada* clearly.

13

A–Z OF WINES, GRAPES AND WINE REGIONS

This section is divided into two parts: Spain and Portugal. For each there is an introduction giving an overall picture of wine-making in that country together with a map of the main wine areas. This is followed by an A–Z list which covers the demarcated wine regions – *denominación de origen* (DO) in Spain, *região demarcada* (RD) and *indicação de proveniência regulamentada* (IPR) in Portugal; often a wine is called after its demarcated region. There are also profiles of wineries that are significant either in terms of quantity or quality, as well as entries on grape varieties.

The wine region entries all follow the same format. The left-hand column contains the name of the region with its classification (DO, RD, IPR) and the relevant autonomous region (Spain) or province (Portugal). Where appropriate, there is then a check list of wineries in that region which have their own A–Z entry. Finally, the main grape varieties are given (up to a maximum of four and usually in order of importance). Grape varieties are shown separately for red, rosé and white wines. For regions making single-variety wines, all the permitted varieties are listed. The right-hand column gives a description of the region's wines with recommended producers.

The winery entries also have their own format. The left-hand column gives the winery name (sometimes the producer's) together with the relevant demarcated region. As before, this is followed by the autonomous region/province and the principal grape varieties.

If you cannot find the wine you want in the A–Z, consult the index as it may appear under an alternative name in another entry.

Some of the most interesting wine-producing areas of Spain (Andalucía, Catalonia, La Mancha, Rioja) and of Portugal (Alentejo, Douro, Vinho Verde) have their own spread with a map and list of wines, wineries and grapes found in that area. The names in these lists appear in their appropriate place in the A–Z.

The wine region and classification. Bairrada is RD (*região demarcada*), Portugal's 'quality wine' category.	**BAIRRADA RD**	
	BEIRA LITORAL	The province (Portugal) or autonomous region (Spain) where the wine is made.
These Bairrada wineries are listed separately in the A–Z in their appropriate place.	*Winery entries:* Aliança, Fonseca Successores, Pato, São João, Sogrape, Velhas	
The symbols stand for red 🍷, rosé 🍷 and white 🍷 wines.	🍷 Baga, Periquita, Tinta Pinheira 🍷 Bical, Fernão Pires (Maria Gomes), Rabo de Ovelha	The main grape varieties, up to a maximum of four. Where a variety has a local name, this appears in brackets; the grape Fernão Pires is known in Bairrada as Maria Gomes.
The name of the winery or producer, followed by the appropriate classification: DO (Spain), RD or IPR (Portugal). This producer has wineries in two DO areas.	**MARQUÉS DE RISCAL** **Rioja DO, Rueda DO**	
	PAÍS VASCO, CASTILLA Y LEÓN	The autonomous region (Spain) or province (Portugal) in which the winery is located.

◀ Almond trees clothe the hillside behind a vineyard in the mountains of Priorato.

SPAIN

Spain is a wine-making country through and through: every region has its vineyards, and every local bar its glass of co-op *tinto*. From the lush, green, hillside pastures of Galicia to the scorching, stony, central plains of La Mancha, from the foothills of the Pyrenees down (almost) to the beaches of the Costa Dorada, you will find vines. Great patches of the wine map may look to be vine-free, but in fact only half of Spain's production qualifies for DO and there are enormous belts of uncharted vineyard.

Nearly 50 per cent of the EC's vineyards lie in Spain, and the EC is offering grants to growers who are willing to pull up their vines – a tempting prospect in bulk plonk areas such as Extremadura, and parts of Castilla-La Mancha and the Levante. Having half the vineyards doesn't mean that Spain makes half the wine: grape yields in this dry, sunny country are only one-third of those of France, and one-fifth of Germany's bumper crops. But there's a lot of wine nevertheless.

We would love to announce that all this wine was wonderful, that Spain had undergone a thorough wine-making revolution, but this would not be true. What's more, that glass of rather dubious red in the bar is just as likely to come from a denominated region as from totally anonymous vines. Several DOs have scarcely any good wines to justify their existence. But Spain does have wonderful wines, of course – some made in ultra-modern wineries bristling with stainless steel, others in very traditionally-run *bodegas*.

In this confusing scenario of old and new, good and bad, one thing remains practically constant – the grapes from which the wines are made. Unlike France, Italy and even Portugal, Spain has very few star grapes. The one white star is Albariño, but since that grows only in the north-west, it is not surprising that most Spanish white wine is unexciting. The Verdejo, practically confined to Rueda, is a bit more characterful than the rest, but not a winner on an international scale. As for the reds, apart from the Riojan rarity Graciano, Tempranillo is the only really top-quality grape. Luckily, it grows in many parts of northern, north-eastern and central Spain (under a variety of pseudonyms). And in a number of regions, growers are being offered strong incentives to replant their vineyards with Tempranillo. But let's get this into perspective: there's still three times as much Monastrell (making tough, alcoholic reds), five times as much Garnacha Tinta (source of jammy, alcoholic reds or sometimes modern, fruity young reds and rosés) and 14 times as much of the incredibly boring white Airén grape! Spain has far greater need than Portugal to resort to international stars Cabernet Sauvignon and Chardonnay. Top-class Spanish wines not based on Tempranillo are generally made – at least in part – from such foreign varieties.

What the Tempranillo and the Cabernet Sauvignon have in common, apart from fine, interesting flavours, is their ability to improve with age. This is very important in Spain, a country that still holds firm to the belief that old red wine is good red wine. Spaniards attach great importance to *gran reserva, reserva* and *crianza* qualifications for wines aged in oak.

One flavour you can expect to find in many bottles of Spanish red is oak, that vanilla-scented, woody, almost sweet taste which comes from maturation in oak barrels. Lovers of Rioja may complain that their favourite wines are less oaky than they used to be, but the current style appeals to a wider public. However, some of the reds from Valdepeñas, in central Spain, offer those old, oaky flavours, and at prices well below Rioja-level.

But all over Spain, the more forward- and outward-looking of Spain's winemakers have discovered the freshly fruity flavours of *young* wine. The most important factor has been the realization that it is vitally important to pick grapes at the right moment of ripeness. Nearly two-thirds of Spain's wine is made in co-operatives, which used to pay their growers by the ripeness of the grapes they brought in – the riper the grapes, the better the money. As millions of holidaymakers know, most of Spain is exceedingly hot in summer, and grapes can easily shoot up to levels of ripeness that make over-alcoholic, flabby wine. And that was exactly what most Spanish co-ops were making until recently, when a new generation of winemakers began to reward growers for picking grapes before they had ripened too far.

So that has been a major step in the right direction for many Spanish wines, but there are still plenty of laggards, often co-ops that can't afford new machinery or refuse to change their wine-making ways. Most of the large wine companies whose names we see on bottle labels are immaculately equipped, as are the growing numbers of small, high-quality estates in areas like Rioja and Ribera del Duero.

And Spain is not all hot, dusty vineyards.

Northern Spain, whether sheltered and watered by the Pyrenees or washed on the western coast by the cold waters of the Atlantic, has a much more temperate climate than the centre, south-east and south. Here, in these cooler regions, it is possible to make fine white wine, while only a little way to the south the River Ebro winds its way through the classic vineyards of Rioja.

This diversity of climate is one of the factors that increases Spain's wine-making potential. Cool and wet enough for the delights of the Albariño in the north-west, hot yet wet enough for the splendour of fine sherries in the south-west, with red wines of every price and quality in between.

1. Rias Biaxas
2. Ribeiro
3. Valdeorras
4. Bierzo
5. Toro
6. Rueda
7. Ribera del Duero
8. Chacolí de Getaria
9. Rioja
10. Navarra

11. Campo de Borja
12. Somontano
13. Calatayud
14. Cariñena
15. Costers del Segre
16. Conca de Barberá
17. Priorato
18. Terra Alta

19. Tarragona
20. Penedés
21. Alella
22. Ampurdán-Costa Brava
23. Méntrida
24. La Mancha
25. Valdepeñas
26. Utiel Requena

27. Valencia
28. Almansa
29. Jumilla
30. Yecla
31. Alicante
32. Condado de Huelva
33. Jerez y Manzanilla
34. Montilla-Moriles
35. Málaga
36. Binisalem

17

AGE
Rioja DO
RIOJA

❦ Tempranillo, Garnacha Tinta, Cariñena (Mazuelo), Graciano

♉ Macabeo (Viura)

It's rare that you can visit a winery, taste the wines, discuss the wine-making, and come away certain that the best is yet to come. But that's how we felt about AGE Bodegas Unidas just outside the little Rioja village of Fuenmayor. Why? Because they've built a new vinification centre right across the road from the original *bodega*, and the young red wine we tasted in February 1990 is bursting with cherry, damson and almond flavour in a way that AGE red has never done before.

The 'united *bodegas*' of the company's name came together in 1967, when Bodegas del Romeral (the oldest of the three, founded in 1881) merged with Bodegas La Veras and Bodegas Entrena. AGE was an acronym of the initials of the three founding families, Azpilicueta, Garcia and Entrena – but only the Garcias still have an interest in the company. Until the wines from the new installations appear on our shelves, it's fair to describe AGE wines, both red and white, as adequate rather than exciting. Their oak-aged white, aspiring to the style of Murrieta white, is decent and worth noting as one of the few remaining oaky white Riojas. One AGE red, Siglo Saco, comes in a dinky hessian bag. In Spain, sackcloth is not necessarily a sign of penance.

AIRÉN

This simple-flavoured white grape covers nearly one-third of Spain's vineyards. That makes it Spain's (and, astonishingly, the world's) most planted grape variety. The Airén wine lake would be even vaster than it is, were it not for the fact that most of the vineyards are on the hot central plains of La Mancha, where yields are tiny. Airén used to be a grape of purely local interest, making dark, dull, soupy whites, and much of the Airén wine sold in Spain still is like that. But increasingly Airén is being picked early and not-too-ripe, and turned (thanks to modern equipment) into light, fresh, faintly aromatic whites, sometimes with a hint of liquorice. These are wines for drinking as young as possible – preferably within their first year – because their fruitiness and gentle aromas quickly fade.

Airén is also a very important grape in Valdepeñas, to the south of La Mancha. Here there's six times as much Airén as red Cencibel (Tempranillo), despite the fact that Valdepeñas is renowned internationally for its *red* wines. Airén wine is very often blended – quite legally – into Valdepeñas reds, with the disadvantage of making them less long-lived. Further south still, in Andalucía, it is known as Lairén, and makes whites for local consumption, as well as finding its way – illegally but in considerable proportions – into the fortified wines of Málaga.

ALBARIÑO

Albariño is the top-quality white grape of Galicia, the green and fertile region in the far north-west (just over the border from Portugal's Vinho Verde country where they spell it 'Alvarinho'). Wine-making here is often very primitive, but when it's *well* made, Albariño wine can have complex fruity flavours of apricot, peach, grapefruit and even grape, and higher acidity than any other white Galician variety. Left to ripen on the vine, it gets very sweet – even in Galicia's cool and rainy climes – so its wines are more alcoholic than the region's other whites. Though Albariño vines are very productive, the grapes are extremely thick-skinned and pippy, thus producing relatively little juice. Because of this, and because of the quality, the grapes fetch high prices – and the wines are among Spain's most expensive whites.

The Galicians are currently lobbying to join the Cava DO, which would add Albariño to the authorized *cava* grapes. If they are successful, it will be fascinating to see what sort of fizz this flavoursome grape will produce. It could make Catalan *cava* producers envious.

ALELLA DO
CATALONIA

🍷🍷 Garnacha Tinta, Tempranillo (Ull de Llebre), Pansá Rosada, Garnacha Peluda

🍷 Xarel-lo (Pansá Blanca), Garnacha Blanca

▼ The verdant hills of Galicia in the far north-west of Spain, home of the Albariño grape. In a country cursed by boring white grapes, the Albariño stands out for its fine acidity and complex fruity flavours.

You might not even catch sight of a vine as you whizz past Alella on the coastal motorway just 16km (10 miles) to the north of Barcelona. This is one of Spain's smallest DOs, making mostly whites, the best of them light and fresh. Over the last two decades, vineyards have rapidly been giving way to villas. When the motorway sliced through Alella's vineyards in the seventies, there were 1400 hectares (3459 acres) of vines. By 1989 there were only 380 hectares (939 acres). As well as destroying the vineyards in its path, the motorway opened up the region to commuters and weekenders from Barcelona and – with building land suddenly fetching 15 times the price of an agricultural plot – farmers were easily persuaded to sell out to property developers. The first plots to go were the prettiest, high up in the rolling hills, and these, sadly, were also the coolest and best vineyard sites. Many other upland vineyards have since been abandoned as uneconomic. The Consejo Regulador finally produced a solution in 1989, adding four more upland villages to the DO region. This has extended the Alella vineyards by around two-thirds.

Alella is white wine country: the inland vineyards grow mainly Pansá Blanca (the Xarel-lo of the Penedés), while the slopes that face east, seawards, grow Garnacha Blanca in the more Mediterranean climate. The few reds and rosés are nothing special. The co-operative produces 60 per cent of the region's wine, with unimpressive results, and most of the rest comes from the excellent firm of Alta Alella, which makes good, aromatic dry and off-dry whites for drinking young. Alta Alella – supplying vines and equipment – has done deals with upland farmers to replant some of the finest vineyards with high-quality vines and some varieties new to the region, such as Parellada, Macabeo, Cabernet Sauvignon and Chardonnay. Alta Alella's sister company, Parxet, turns much of its produce into very pleasant *cava* fizz – among Spain's best.

ALICANTE DO
VALENCIA

🍷 Monastrell, Garnacha Tinta, Bobal

🍷 Merseguera, Moscatel, Verdil

Down in the hot, dry south-east corner of Spain, Alicante makes mostly red wines, traditionally very dark and heavy with alcohol. Recently, with investment in both vineyards and wineries, there have been improvements and some lighter, better quality reds are being made. The whites (dry, medium and sweet) are dull, alcoholic and best avoided, apart from some pleasant Moscatel from the Marina Alta area, a quite separate patch of DO Alicante, up the coast beyond Benidorm. The region's finest wine – and a local curiosity well worth seeking out for tourists venturing away from the beach – is Fundillón, a liqueur Monastrell with a minimum of 16 per cent alcohol, aged in a *solera* for at least eight years. It's one of Spain's best *rancios*, with rich, nutty, toffee flavours. Few of Alicante's vineyards actually reach down to the sea. Most are way inland, in the hills of the Upper Vinalapó. The firm of Salvador Poveda makes a characterful, strong, herby red Viña Vermeta Tinto, and a strong, quite tannic, oaky-herby-plummy red Viña Vermeta Reserva.

ALMANSA DO
CASTILLA-LA MANCHA

🍷 🍷 Garnacha Tintorera, Monastrell, Tempranillo (Cencibel)

🍷 Merseguera

Almansa, lying to the east of La Mancha DO, is a sort of transitional area between the great central plains and the Levante. So it's not surprising that the Valencian grapes grow here, along with a little of La Mancha's Cencibel (Tempranillo). Officially, under the DO regulations, Cencibel isn't allowed, but the Consejo Regulador authorizes its use nevertheless, because it improves the quality of wines intended for ageing. Three-quarters of the wine made here is red, and though the Garnacha Tintorera (also known here as Alicante) is the main grape, the best reds have a higher proportion of Monastrell and/or Cencibel. The best can stand a little ageing. The exceptionally dark red wines from Garnacha Tintorera grape are prized for blending with paler stuff in Tarragona and Valencia. Quality here has historically been slightly better than in La Mancha, but La Mancha has modernized and caught up in the last half of the eighties. Look out for Bodegas Piqueras, a small family firm making light, fruity Castillo de Almansa and, under the same label, a flavourful *gran reserva*.

ÁLVAREZ Y DÍEZ
Rueda DO
CASTILLA Y LEÓN

🍷 Verdejo, Palomino

While most of the *bodegas* of Rueda are turning away from the traditional but outmoded sherry-style wines, Álvarez y Díez, the biggest private company, proudly sticks to tradition. For, although they have stainless steel galore for fermentation, they have more wooden barrels than the rest of the region put together and, besides making the *flor*-affected, sherry-like wines, they still use barrels to age the best of their light wines, too – even now that wood ageing is no longer required for light wines under the Rueda DO. 'As scrupulously clean as a hospital' is how the company's oenologist describes his efficient, modern winery and the eight ancient cellars that burrow in all directions under the streets of Nava del Rey. It *is* clean, and it needs to be, because Álvarez y Díez also pride themselves in being absolutely organic. They must be one of a very few companies in the world who make wine totally without the use of sulphur as a disinfectant and preservative.

Álvarez y Díez produce about half the grapes they need in 70 hectares (173 acres) of vineyard, and they use much more of the high-quality, flavourful Verdejo than most in the region. Their Mantel Pálido and Mantel Dorado are the best of the region's sherry-style wines, but most interesting are the light whites: soft, nutty Mantel Nuevo Rueda and finer, freshly acidic, nutty Mantel Blanco Rueda Superior.

Despite their air of tradition, Álvarez y Díez are a relatively young company founded only in 1978 when they took over the premises of another very long-standing company.

AMÉZOLA DE LA MORA
Rioja DO
RIOJA

🍷 Tempranillo, Cariñena
(Mazuelo), Macabeo (Viura)

Founded in 1986, this is one of a new breed of Rioja estates challenging the tradition of Rioja as a wine blended from all over the demarcated region. Iñigo Amézola de la Mora gets all the grapes that go into his wines from his own vineyards and those belonging to close relations in and around the little hamlet of Torremontalbo, on the road between Cenicero and Haro. Actually, the *bodega* is a resurrection, not a new enterprise, but wine has not been made here for almost 100 years. Iñigo Amézola de la Mora's grandfather was a close friend of the original Marqués de Murrieta and Marqués de Riscal, and his *bodega* was a *crianza bodega* like theirs. But, when the phylloxera plague crossed the Pyrenees at the beginning of this century and wiped out any vine not grafted on to American rootstock, he played safe and replanted his land with barley, not vines.

Iñigo Amézola de la Mora intends to sell no wines younger than four years old, and has just released his 1986 *crianza*. *Reservas* and *gran reservas* will follow in due course. The new wines look set to be classics when all have emerged from the Torremontalbo cellars, combining traditional Rioja oak with a good concentration of rich, plummy fruit and elegant, wild strawberry fragrance.

AMPURDÁN-COSTA BRAVA DO
CATALONIA

🍷 Garnacha Tinta (Lledoner),
Cariñena

🍷 Garnacha Tinta (Lledoner),
Cariñena, Macabeo, Xarel-lo

🍷 Macabeo, Xarel-lo

There's not a lot to recommend in this tiny region, hemmed in by the French Pyrenees to the north and the Mediterranean to the east. This is windswept country, where vines need stout stakes. Smallholders own most of the land, and generally supplement their income from grapes by keeping pigs and sheep, and growing cereals and olives. Home wine-making on such a small scale just isn't viable and co-operatives are very important here, making 95 per cent of the region's wines. Unfortunately, most of their equipment is antiquated, with dull and coarse results. More than half the region's wines are rosés, usually unimpressive and alcoholic. The whites are mostly sold off in bulk to the *cava* firms of Penedés. Reds have traditionally been alcoholic and aged – at least for a short time – but in recent years there's been a fashion for Beaujolais Nouveau look-alikes, *vi novell* or *vi del any*. Sadly, they're rarely up to much. The co-ops also make sweet, fortified Garnachas, fat and alcoholic, as well as rough, sherry-style *rancios*, but both are best left to the natives. Understandably, few of the wines of Ampurdán-Costa Brava are ever exported. But they are cheap enough to find a willing market among the tourists along the region's beaches.

ARROYO
Ribera del Duero DO
CASTILLA Y LEÓN

🍷 🍷 Tempranillo (Tinto del País),
Albillo

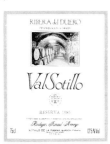

This is exactly the kind of *bodega* that shows why the reds from Ribera del Duero are so fashionable and, unfortunately, shooting up in price. Rich reds and good fresh rosés are made by Ismael Arroyo, a medium-sized family business in Sotillo de la Ribera, where Señor Arroyo shares the vineyard, cellar and sales work with his two sons. Their own six hectares (nearly 15 acres) are planted almost exclusively with Tinto del País, and they also buy in some grapes from neighbours. The *crianza* and *reserva* wines are aged in American oak barrels. These are stored in 400-year-old galleries cut into the rock behind the modern fermentation cellar, which boasts an array of large temperature-controlled stainless steel vats. New presses and more tanks have recently expanded the cellar capacity by one-third. The aged reds are the impressive wines, very much influenced by vintage (the 1985 Val Sotillo Reserva is fat and super-ripe, the 1986 Mesoneros de Castilla Crianza more elegant and balanced), but all wines show the virtues of modern fermentation and careful (not overdone) oak maturation. Every *crianza* wine we have tasted will improve with more bottle age.

ANDALUCÍA

Andalucía, vast spread of eight provinces stretching right across the sunbaked south of Spain, welcomes millions of tourists each year. But relatively few of them ever stray far from the Costa del Sol. Those who *do* discover a land quite different from the rest of the Iberian peninsula. This was the part of Spain longest occupied by the Moors. Whitewashed walls, cool courtyards and roof terraces on the oldest houses testify to eight centuries of Arab dominion, as do the place names, local crafts and even the inevitable flamenco dancing. Solitary farmhouses are a feature of the countryside, set in the eastern provinces among landscapes of olive trees or cereals, irrigated fruit trees or early veg, and in the west among fields of sunflowers, more cereals . . . and vines.

Andalucía overflows with vines, but there are far more in the west than the east. All four of Andalucía's DOs (Jerez, Montilla-Moriles, Málaga and Condado de Huelva) lie to the west of Granada, and the DOs themselves account for over half Andalucía's vineyards. But it seems strange that the famous wines made in such a hot climate should all be fortified – until you taste the *un*fortified wines. It is hard to get excited by any of the bland, flavourless whites, and those are the good ones. The bad are horrific. Thank goodness the Andalucians evolved a way to turn their plonk into nectar to accompany the incessant socializing and lengthy meals. For this is a part of Spain where lunch never starts before three in the afternoon, and you consider yourself lucky if you sit down to dinner by midnight, after delicious hours of *tapas* – copious nibbles of olives, anchovies, fried peppers, salted almonds, squid – and glass after glass of chilled *fino*.

In Jerez the tulip-shaped *copita* would contain *fino*, in Sanlúcar de Barrameda, *manzanilla*, in Córdoba it might be Montilla, and in Málaga, down by the coast, a stiff tot of the 'mountain' wine loved by the Victorians.

Despite the relentless, glaring heat, the sherry region in particular is well suited to vines. The best soil – dazzlingly white *albariza* – contains between 60 and 80 per cent chalk and acts as a sponge, soaking up and storing the ample winter rainfall until the vines crave it in the height of midsummer. Accordingly, yields are high, for the vineyards of Jerez, all trained on wires, are among the most modern in Spain, and the Palomino Fino – the main grape – is always a generous bearer. But the wine not turned into sherry often finds a buyer who will distil and age it to make the rich, dark brandies for which Andalucía is also famous. More than 90 per cent of Spain's brandies come from Andalucia – a good end to a meal begun with the perfect aperitif.

▶ This beautiful landscape, to the east of sherry country, is amazingly one of the rainiest parts of Spain.

GRAPE ENTRIES	Málaga	González Byass
Airén (Lairén)	Montilla-Moriles	Harveys
Moscatel		Hidalgo
Palomino	WINERY ENTRIES	Internacionales
Pedro Ximénez	Barbadillo	Lustau
	Caballero	Osborne
WINE ENTRIES	Díez-Mérito	Valdespino
Condado de Huelva	Domecq	
Jerez	Garvey	

23

BALBÁS
Ribera del Duero DO
CASTILLA Y LEÓN

🍖 🍷 Tempranillo (Tinto del País), Albillo

The Balbás family have taken advantage of the current fashion for Ribera del Duero reds to move from growing and selling grapes to making their grapes into wine, and then selling that. Owning 16 hectares (40 acres) of vines in La Horra, a little town 19km (12 miles) north-west of Aranda de Duero, they pulled out of the local co-op in 1985 to start making their own wine. Juan José Balbás, the young winemaker, does not crush the grapes before fermentation (although he removes the stalks), and this sometimes gives a juicy-fruity, Beaujolais-like flavour. The Balbás wine can be quite herby and tough when young, but opens out to a gentle, silky, elegant balance that caresses the tonsils with savoury, strawberry fruit as it slides gently down.

BARBADILLO
Jerez y Manzanilla DO
ANDALUCÍA

🍷 Palomino Fino, Pedro Ximénez

Antonio Barbadillo is the largest of the sherry companies based in Sanlúcar de Barrameda, seaside home of *manzanilla*. It is privately owned, although 11 per cent of the shares are held by Harveys.

Barbadillo set up a joint venture in 1973 with Harveys to establish a modern wine-making plant at Gibalbín, on an estate of 520 hectares (1285 acres); today nearly 80 per cent of this area is planted and producing grapes. This is where all the wine destined for Barbadillo sherries is now made, before it goes to Sanlúcar for maturation.

There is a huge range of Barbardillo sherries. Among the best are the Manzanilla de Sanlúcar, delicate and saltily tangy, the Manzanilla Pasada Solear, lean and almost herbaceous, and Principe, a *manzanilla amontillada*, rich but soft, fleshy but elegant, with the nutty, toffee character of *amontillado*. The company also makes a dry white table wine, Castillo de San Diego, pleasant enough in a neutral sort of way when sitting in front of a plate of fried fish in one of Sanlúcar's seafront restaurants, but unimpressive when removed to cooler northern climes.

BARÓN DE LEY
Rioja DO
NAVARRA

🍖 Tempranillo, Cabernet Sauvignon

🍖 Garnacha Tinta, Tempranillo

🍷 Macabeo (Viura)

This is one of the new breed of Rioja estates that intends to make all the red wine sold under its label from its own grapes, grown in 90 hectares (222 acres) of vineyards at Mendavia in the Rioja Baja. The 1987 pure Tempranillo wine will be the first to come entirely from Barón de Ley grapes. Over half the *bodega's* 4000 barrels are of French Limousin oak, which the owners believe will give a more refined style of red wine. Barón de Ley white and rosé are made from bought-in grapes. They also grow some Cabernet Sauvignon on an experimental scale, but this is not currently permitted for wines labelled Rioja. The magnificent buildings were a monastery from the sixteenth to the twentieth century.

BERBERANA
Rioja DO
RIOJA

🍖 🍷 Tempranillo, Garnacha Tinta, Cariñena (Mazuelo), Graciano

🍷 Macabeo (Viura), Malvasía

Berberana, one of Rioja's largest *bodegas*, has had a chequered career – especially in the last 20 years or so when it has changed hands five times. Since 1971, however, through all these upheavals, the wines have been made by Gonzálo Ortiz Peña, who has managed to keep a fairly consistent style of elegant rather than weighty Rioja. The *reservas* and *gran reservas* from the seventies are particularly good – if you can find them. The Carta de Plata and Carta de Oro wines – three reds, a rosé and a white – are uninspiring. In common with many other Rioja houses, Berberana does not age its red wines in barrel for as long as it used to, and this, too, has lightened the Berberana style.

Nowadays, Berberana has few vineyards. Its 35 hectares (86 acres) of Tempranillo and 20 hectares (50 acres) of Viura and Malvasia in the Rioja Baja supply only two and six per cent respectively of its needs for red and white wines. Most of its grapes come from the group of Rioja co-operatives who together own just over half of Berberana's shares.

BIERZO DO
CASTILLA Y LEÓN

🍷 🍷 Mencía, Garnacha Tintorera

🍷 Doña Blanca, Godello, Malvasía, Palomino

This small region was granted DO status in December 1989. Between the mountains of Galicia and the plains of Castilla-León, it's a mild and verdant region protected on almost all sides by mountains. It opens to the world only in the valley of the Sil to the south-east. The vines are planted on the river terraces. Traditionally, not much Bierzo wine has been sold in bottle – it was mostly sold as bulk plonk. A number of the region's wineries have also specialized in blending the local wines with wines from elsewhere. They have been making efforts, though, in the past few years, and growers have been encouraged to plant more of the region's highest-quality grape, the Mencía. This now covers more than half of the vineyards, and must make up at least 70 per cent of red DO wines, 50 per cent of rosés. The Mencía has been optimistically identified as the Cabernet Franc, but its wines have a slightly bitter flavour as well as being herbaceous, and it needs a little oak ageing if it is to become anything more than a pale, simple red for early glugging.

BILBAINAS
Rioja DO
RIOJA

🍷 Tempranillo, Garnacha Tinta, Graciano, Cariñena (Mazuelo)

🍷 Macabeo (Viura), Malvasía, Garnacha Blanca

Bodegas Bilbainas is an ultra-traditional wine producer. Any changes that have happened in recent years give the impression of having been wrung out of the management. For instance, the last time we visited, we were told by one of the owners – his voice tinged with regret – that the company had stopped fermenting red wines in oak vats because they had difficulty finding workers who would clear the residue of skins and pips out of the vats after fermentation. Likewise, fashion has forced Bilbainas to abandon their oak-aged whites in favour of modern wines, cool-fermented in stainless steel tanks. However, despite the fact that the company owns over 243 hectares (600 acres) of vineyard, the Bilbainas wines continue to disappoint. The young Viña Ederra wines lack fresh, appealing fruit. Viña Pomal, the company's best-known brand, comes from a vineyard in the Rioja Alavesa, and is principally Garnacha, which does little for the wine's ageing ability. Viña Zaco, with a predominance of Tempranillo, comes from the Rioja Alta, and is hardly better. They also make a *cava*, Royal Carlton, which is pleasantly appley rather than exciting.

BINISALEM
BALEARIC ISLANDS

🍷 🍷 Manto Negro, Callet, Monastrell, Tempranillo

🍷 Prensal, Parellada, Macabeo

Currently a Vino de la Tierra, this is due to be Spain's next DO, though one wonders quite why. It's one of two wine-growing regions of Mallorca – the only Balearic Island with any vines to speak of. Of the three producers on the island making wines of anything approaching quality, two are in Binisalem. Reds are the most important, the best made from the local Manto Negro grape, which covers about half the vineyards. Mallorca's gently undulating central plateau, where the vineyards are sited, is hot country, protected by mountains from the cold north winds, and the grapes can become extremely ripe. Sweet, ripe grapes usually mean baked, coarse, alcoholic wines, but the best, from Jaume Mesquida and Franja Roja, score for their lower levels of alcohol. Anyway, it's all nearly academic. Once the locals have bought their own supplies, there's very little left. And they are likely to get even scarcer as more and more vineyards are turned over to villas and hotels.

BODEGAS Y BEBIDAS

The name recently given to SAVIN, Spain's largest wine company. SAVIN's reputation is firmly linked in the Spanish consumer's mind with cheap table wine, so the new name was introduced to give a more up-market image to a company that owns good wine producers such as Campo Viejo and Marqués del Puerto in Rioja, Vinícola Navarra in Navarra and one of Jumilla's best *bodegas*, Señorio del Condestable.

CABALLERO
Jerez y Manzanilla DO
ANDALUCÍA

♀ Palomino Fino, Pedro Ximénez, Moscatel

Caballero, sixth largest sherry producer, is (unusually nowadays) totally family-owned. It has four *bodegas* in the seaside town of Puerto de Santa María, and also owns the famous castle of Puerto, the Castillo San Marcos, from which Christopher Columbus set forth to discover America. The wines are still made in a fairly traditional way – and are even fermented in big, concrete Ali Baba pots called *tinajas* – but the quality is nevertheless very good. Caballero is ahead of the region in one respect, however. It is one of only two *bodegas* (the other is Barbadillo) who have recently started to put their sherry back for a couple of months into casks – under the yeast-film of *flor* – after filtering it (when most firms bottle it) and before bottling. This keeps the *fino* fresher and tangier. Caballero bought the firms of José de la Cuesta and Burdon in the 1930s, and still sells some sherries under these brand names. All Caballero sherries are Burdon in Britain (González Byass was already selling a brand called Caballero) but Caballero in the US. Puerto Fino (called Fino Pavón in Spain) is a lovely, soft, bread-yeasty and tangy *fino*, Dom Luis Amontillado is a soft, gentle, yeasty *amontillado*, pleasantly light in alcohol at 17.5 per cent, and Burdon's Heavenly Cream Rich Old Oloroso is delicious, sweet, raisiny, nutty wine. The firm thrives principally, however, on producing Spain's best-selling liqueur, orange-flavoured Ponche Caballero.

CABERNET SAUVIGNON

There can hardly be a region of Spain that *isn't* experimenting with this most famous of international red varieties. It's capable in Spain of making dark, richly blackcurrant-flavoured wines, which can be elegant and long-lived when made from grapes grown in the cooler regions, such as the Upper Penedés. It makes a lovely blend, too, with Spain's finest indigenous black grape, the Tempranillo. But in most Spanish regions, the authorities tend to be reluctant to give it their official stamp. Researchers and hopefuls have planted some in Rioja, but the official view is that Cabernet would alter the character of Rioja wines in an unacceptable way. However, Cabernet has made it into the rule-books of Penedés, Navarra, Costers del Segre and Ribera del Duero.

Ribera del Duero, in the central north of the country, was the first Spanish region to grow Cabernet when it was planted on the Vega Sicilia estate at the end of the last century. The authorities there will still only allow it 'in areas where it has traditionally been grown', which in practice means the Vega Sicilia estate. Vega Sicilia's vineyards are one-quarter Cabernet, and they're planting more. The finest Penedés reds are totally – or principally – Cabernet Sauvignon, from extensive vineyards planted by Miguel Torres and Jean León in the 1960s. Torres' Gran Coronas and Mas La Plana and Leóns Cabernet Sauvignon are big, dark, blackcurranty and, in some years, quite elegant and complex wines. There's also a good, lighter Cabernet from the nearby estate of Naverán. With official approval, other Penedés firms have planted Cabernet for blending in smaller proportions (usually 15 to 20 per cent) into reds from local grapes to add some body. Further inland, the Raimat estate, owned by the powerful Codorniu group, had planted many acres of Cabernet in the seventies, and was in a good position to dictate the official grape varieties when the DO regulations were being drawn up in 1988. Some good blends of a little Cabernet with local varieties are now being made in Navarra, where the authorities are unusually open to new ideas, and even offer subsidies to growers who plant Cabernet.

Elsewhere, it's hard to find Cabernet in commercial quantities. An important oddball is the Marqués de Griñón estate on the central plateau to the north-west of La Mancha, outside any DO region, which is making soft, rich, blackcurranty-oaky wines.

CALATAYUD DO
ARAGÓN

🍷 Garnacha Tinta, Cariñena (Mazuelo), Tempranillo, Monastrell

🍷 Macabeo, Malvasía, Moscatel Blanco, Garnacha Blanca

There seems little to justify the recent promotion of Calatayud, in February 1990, to DO status. The Aragón government has been concentrating most of its wine research resources on the region, with the aim particularly of improving the rosés, and some modern, fruitier wines are beginning to emerge from a lake of old-fashioned plonk. But it's hardly the stuff that DOs should be made of. The Garnacha is the principal grape, made into both reds and rosés, and there are some whites. Most of the wine is produced by co-operatives. Calatayud is a big area, extending to 21,000 hectares (51,890 acres), which makes it the second largest wine region in Aragón.

CAMPO DE BORJA DO
ARAGÓN

🍷🍷 Garnacha Tinta, Macabeo

🍷 Macabeo, Moscatel Romano

▼ The little town of Ainzón, where a number of Campo de Borja's *bodegas* are to be found. Traditionally, only red and rosé wines sported a DO, but Campo de Borja's small production of white wines has also been eligible for the DO since 1989.

Take a bottle of headache pills if you venture south of Rioja and Navarra down on to the undulating plains of Campo de Borja. The *minimum* alcohol permitted for the reds and rosés of this fairly small DO is 13 per cent, and it can reach as high as 18 per cent! Happily for the local heads and livers, wineries here are finally catching on to the modern trend towards lower alcohol levels. Some wines are being turned out younger, fruitier, less astringent and somewhat less alcoholic, though 13 per cent is still considered the lightest of light! Wood ageing has always been traditional here, but some wines are now being sold with no wood ageing at all (and are the better and fruitier for it) while others are wood aged for shorter periods, so that they end up less tired and tough. Almost all the wine is made from Garnacha Tinta, with ten per cent white Macabeo permitted. Experiments with Tempranillo and Mazuelo for blending with Garnacha have produced some more appetizing results. White wines have also been included in the DO since the spring of 1989 and these, commendably, can be made with as little as 10.5 per cent alcohol.

A small area of Campo de Borja is allowed to produce *cava*. The one from Bodegas Bordejé is the best, and they also have an unusually good young, Beaujolais-style Tinto Joven. The best, freshest rosés come from the Co-operativa del Campo San Juan Bautista, and some good reds from the Sociedad Co-operativa Agricola de Borja.

CAMPO VIEJO
Rioja DO
RIOJA

🍷 Tempranillo, Cariñena
(Mazuelo), Garnacha Tinta,
Graciano

🍷 Macabeo (Viura)

Campo Viejo, the main company in the Bodegas y Bebidas group
(ex-SAVIN), is huge – easily the largest producer of Rioja. And it looks it,
with an enormous, factory-like *bodega* in the hinterland of Logroño. But
the wines are, mostly, good. The basic Rioja can be fairly forgettable, as
can the *crianza*, but, at *reserva* and *gran reserva* level, it is unusual to
find a disappointing wine.

The company owns nearly 283 hectares (700 acres) of planted
vineyard (in which there are various experimental varieties, such as
Cabernet Sauvignon, Pinot Noir and Chardonnay, as well as traditional
Rioja grapes), and says these vineyards supply one-third of its needs. A
recent Campo Viejo entrant is Albor, one of the best examples of
modern white Rioja, clean, appley and perfumed; the 100 per cent
Tempranillo, Viña Alcorta Reserva is even better, lean and stylish, with
lively, raspberry and wild strawberry fruit. The basic Campo Viejo Gran
Reservas are good, but the Marqués de Villamagna Gran Reservas are
excellent, made only in the very best years, with lovely, aromatic, wild
strawberry fragrance, and elegant fruit.

CARIÑENA

Deeply coloured, astringent wines are made from this grape, high in
alcohol, acidity and body. They are never rich, aromatic or flavourful, but
they keep well, and make useful additions to blends destined for ageing.
Predictably, this is the same grape as the French Carignan and though it
carpets the South of France, it doesn't even rank amongst Spain's top
twenty vine varieties. The story goes that the Cariñena grape originated
in the region of Cariñena, in the northern province of Aragón. It *is* still
grown in Cariñena, but is only third in line there among red grapes
(dominated by Garnacha and Bobal). Most of Spain's Cariñena is grown
in Catalonia, where it almost always forms part of a blend with softer
grapes. Alias the Mazuelo or Mazuela, it used to be an important grape
in Rioja, but has become unpopular with growers as it's far more prone
to disease than the other Riojan varieties. It now accounts for only 1.5
per cent of Riojan vineyards.

CARIÑENA DO
ARAGÓN

🍷 Garnacha Tinta, Cariñena,
Tempranillo and others

🍷 Macabeo (Viura), Moscatel
Romano, Garnacha Blanca

Cariñena is one of the driest parts of Spain. It's not only that the rainfall
is minimal, but a north wind, the *cierzo*, considerably lowers the
atmospheric humidity as well. About half the wine from Cariñena –
Aragón's largest DO – is still sold as bulk plonk, and much of the wine
that gets bottled can only be described as basic and alcoholic. Things
are getting better, however, and one major improvement has recently
been enshrined in the DO regulations: minimum alcohol levels for rosés
and whites have come down to 11 and 10.5 per cent respectively, from
12 per cent, which is still the lower limit for reds. The *maximum* is still a
whopping 18 per cent. It's very hard to keep alcohol levels down in this
bakingly hot climate. The grapes can become extremely sweet and it's
this sugar that gets converted to alcohol. Picking the grapes early,
before they overripen, is the modern solution.

Also under the new regulations, the basic, boring red grape, Bobal,
has been banned for DO wines, and Tempranillo has been officially
authorized. Garnacha Tinta is still the main grape variety, but it is hoped
that Tempranillo will one day account for nearly two-thirds of the
vineyards. The Cariñena *grape* doesn't get much of a look-in. The bland,
usually over-alcoholic whites are made mostly from Macabeo. Almost all
Cariñena wine (around 90 per cent) is made in co-ops. Best-equipped,
with the best results, is the huge Bodegas San Valero, which makes
young, fresh, spicy reds and rosés under the Don Mendo label, and
good, oak-aged Gran Reserva Monte Ducay reds.

CASTELLBLANCH
Cava DO
CATALONIA

🍷 Monastrell, Tempranillo (Ull de Llebre)

🍾 Macabeo, Xarel-lo, Parellada

Castellblanch – with a large, unattractive, modern *bodega* in San Sadurni de Noya, Penedés – is one of the largest 'Champagne-method' sparkling wine companies in the world. Along with Segura Viudas, it is now a subsidiary of another *cava* giant, Freixenet, and makes the *cava* sold under the Conde de Caralt label as well as Castellblanch and a lot of *cava* for clients' own labels. It owns some vineyards, but mostly buys in grapes and wine from elsewhere. The wines, under the brand names Brut Zero (which now, unusually for *cava*, has no sweetening) and Crystal, are clean and simple.

CAVA DO

Winery entries: Castellblanch, Codorníu, Faustino Martínez, Ferret i Mateu, Freixenet, Hill, Juvé y Camps, Marqués de Monistrol, Mont Marçal, Muga, Naverán, Raimat, Segura Viudas

🍷 as below, plus Garnacha Tinta, Monastrell

🍾 Parellada, Macabeo, Xarel-lo, Chardonnay

Cava differs from all the rest of Spain's wine DOs in that it's not confined to one geographical area. The word *cava* is Catalan for 'cellar', and came to be applied to the 'Champagne-method' sparkling wines of Catalonia. Colloquially, these wines used to be known in Spain as *champán* but after losing a few legal tussles with the authorities in the Champagne region of France, the Spanish accepted that they had to find a new name for their 'Champagne-method' fizz. Since all but a tiny proportion of Spain's 'Champagne-method' fizz comes from Catalonia, the Catalan name was adopted for these sparkling wines throughout Spain.

There was a problem, however. The EC wine authorities insisted that any newly created DO should have specific *geographical* qualifications as well as rules relating to how the wine should be made and out of which grapes. So the Cava DO rules, declared in February 1986, specified 159 villages across the northern third of Spain where the grapes were authorized for *cava* production. Most of them are in Catalonia, with a scattering of individual villages in the still wine regions of Rioja, Campo de Borja, Cariñena, Calatayud, Costers del Segre, Ampurdán-Costa Brava and Tarragona. These villages gained *cava*-dom simply because they had a long tradition of making 'Champagne-method' wines – generally using the same grapes as their still wine neighbours. Quality didn't come into it. Indeed, many of the Cava DO villages turn out mediocre wines, while a strong contender for top spot on the quality scale doesn't even qualify: Castilla La Vieja in Rueda simply hadn't been at it for long enough. Several other villages that *would* have qualified failed to send their applications to Madrid by the prescribed date, so they can't call their fizzy wine *cava* either. To describe a 'Champagne-method' wine that doesn't fit on to the official *cava* map, you have to get your tongue around *vino espumoso natural, método tradicional*. Some other regions have been trying to include parts of their territory in the Cava DO, but so far without success.

Unfortunately, very few brands of *cava* have particularly fruity, interesting flavours, DO or not. The grape varieties traditionally used are either dull or bland, and they don't age well, despite the fact that the *cava* regulations insist upon a *minimum* of nine months' ageing. The majority of Spanish fizz, from Catalonia, is made from Macabeo, Parellada and Xarel-lo; Xarel-lo in particular suffers with maturation, taking on the earthy smell and flavour that is so characteristic of *cava*. This earthy, fruitless character becomes even more evident with age, so ironically, the best, fruitiest buys are the youngest and therefore cheapest wines. The few fizzes from Rioja are boring, too, made from Viura, alias Macabeo. Our favourite *cavas* made with the traditional grapes are from the firms of Mont Marçal and Cavas Hill in Penedés, and Parxet in Alella (both regions of Catalonia). But look out especially for *cavas* made from the Chardonnay grape by Codorniu (the best) and Raimat in Costers del Segre, and a few others now springing up with Chardonnay on the label. Spanish Chardonnay fizz can have lovely fruit and flowery-buttery flavours, and a softer character than Champagne.

CATALONIA

Catalonia is almost another country. It has a separate language, Catalan, an immensely cultured capital, Barcelona – and a thriving separatist movement. It also has the reputation of being the hardest-working and most efficient of Spain's autonomous regions. Biggest earner in this wealthy region is the manufacturing industry of Barcelona, but wine, and especially fizzy wine, is also a major source of prosperity. The production of both sparkling wine and much of Catalonia's quality still wine is centred on the DO region of Penedés, between Barcelona and Tarragona. Here, well-equipped wine producers turn out palatable to excellent wines around every corner. And while the rest of Spain, even the rest of Catalonia, was catching its breath after entry to the EC, the Penedés companies were in there, applying for grants while calling in the cranes and bulldozers to extend their cellars and vineyards.

Practically every other DO region in Catalonia has its star property or properties testifying to the potential of the vines. But most are still bedevilled by backwoods co-operatives and lacklustre companies without the equipment and the know-how to make good wine. With eight still wine DOs plus a large area overlapping these that qualifies also for the Cava DO, Catalonia scores more DOs than any other autonomous region, and 90 per cent of Catalan wine is sold with a DO. Three of the wine regions are quite recent: Terra Alta, declared in 1985, Costers del Segre in 1988 and Conca de Barberá in 1989. None of these really deserved the title, though Costers del Segre houses the wonderful estate of Raimat, and Conca de Barberá makes Torres's stunning Milmanda Chardonnay.

Most of the DO regions fan out from the dusty plain of Tarragona, into the gentle slopes of Penedés, the hills of Terra Alta and Conca de Barberá and the steep, glittering mountains of Priorato. Dotted elsewhere are only tiny Alella on the Costa Dorada above Barcelona, verdant Ampurdán-Costa Brava up between the rocky northern coast and the French border, and the small, scattered patches of Costers del Segre right out in the arid west bordering Aragón.

1. Ampurdán-Costa Brava
2. Alella
3. Penedés
4. Tarragona
5. Terra Alta
6. Priorato
7. Conca de Barberá
8. Costers del Segre

0   20 km
0   20 miles

White wines
Red and white wines

◀ Vineyards near San Sadurní de Noya in the Penedés, in the shadow of the craggy peaks of the Sierra de Monserrat, where most of the grapes go to make *cava* sparkling wines.

GRAPE ENTRIES
Cabernet Sauvignon
Cariñena
Chardonnay
Garnacha
Macabeo
Moscatel
Parellada
Tempranillo (Ull de Llebre)
Xarel-lo

WINE ENTRIES
Alella
Ampurdán-Costa Brava
Cava
Conca de Barberá
Costers del Segre
Penedés
Priorato
Tarragona
Terra Alta

WINERY ENTRIES
Castellblanch
Codorniu
Ferret i Mateu
Freixenet
Cavas Hill
Celler Hisenda Miret
Juvé y Camps
Jean León
Marqués de Monistrol
Masia Bach
Mont Marçal
Naverán
Raimat
Segura Viudas
Torres

31

CENALSA
Navarra DO
NAVARRA

🍷 Garnacha Tinta, Tempranillo, Cabernet Sauvignon

🍷 Garnacha Tinta

🍷 Macabeo (Viura)

This company, part-funded by the Navarra government, was set up in 1983 to advise co-ops on wine-making and to blend and bottle their wines for export. Seven years on, almost half the entire wine production of the Navarra co-operatives is cool-fermented (and nearly 90 per cent of all Navarra wine is made in co-ops), very largely thanks to Cenalsa's insistence that this was the path to take. Cenalsa has also encouraged its co-op partners to replace the predominantly Garnacha Tinta vineyards with Tempranillo. The Cenalsa wines have been among the best of modern Navarra, from the clean, fresh Campo Nuevo cheapies to the finer, fruity Agramont range. Verjus and Principe de Viana are the two labels used for the best wines (in the past, the red Verjus has sometimes included a small proportion of Cabernet Sauvignon). The management of the company has recently changed; it is to be hoped the quality of the Cenalsa wines stays as good as it has been.

CHACOLÍ DE GETARIA DO
PAÍS VASCO

🍷 Ondarribi Beltza

🍷 Ondarribi Zuri

It's hardly surprising that almost all the wine of Spain's latest DO (declared mid-1990) gets drunk near where it is made, in the coastal Basque country between San Sebastián and Bilbao. Only 34 hectares (84 acres) of vines are currently in production, and vineyards are tiny – some not even measuring half a hectare.

The wine is Chacolí in Spanish, Txacoli in Basque (sometimes spelt Txakolin, or Xakoli, and the Ondarribi Zuri white grapes that constitute 90 per cent of the plantings have optional spellings too). The vines are traditionally grown here on overhead trellises. This system protects the young shoots from early frosts, gives the grapes and leaves good exposure to the sun, and allows for aeration – an important factor in this damp region, where moulds quickly take hold. The wine is high in acidity, with a strong fruity flavour, a refreshing, natural prickle of gas and lowish alcohol, usually 9.5 to 10 per cent, sometimes as high as 11 (the minimum is 9.5). A little red Chacolí is also made.

Making Chacolí a DO was part of a last-ditch attempt to save the wine from extinction. The Chacolí vineyards declined from over 100 hectares (247 acres) at the beginning of the last century, when the wine was made right along the coast from Bilbao to Bayonne. Various vineyard pests and fungal diseases did away with the vines, especially around the turn of the century. Recently, the local authorities have been making an effort to rationalize the few remaining vineyards, replanting them with younger vines, introducing mechanization wherever possible, and also helping producers to install modern vinification equipment.

CHARDONNAY

In Spain, as elsewhere, the Chardonnay can make fine, buttery or flowery wine, light or rich, oaked or not. It is even less widespread than the Cabernet Sauvignon, however, except on an experimental scale, and it has been officially authorized in very few regions. The only part of Spain that grows it in commercial quantities is Catalonia, where it has the local authorities' blessing in Penedés (though not officially permitted in DO wines) and is one of the DO grapes in Costers del Segre, and is also grown without anyone's blessing in Alella. Torres' Gran Viña Sol from Penedés is a half-and-half blend of Chardonnay with Parellada and Torres' Milmanda Chardonnay is undoubtedly Spain's richest and finest, from vineyards in neighbouring Conca de Barberá. Jean León's Chardonnay, more elegant now than it used to be, is the main unblended Chardonnay of Penedés. Spain's other big Chardonnay producer is the Raimat estate in Costers del Segre, which makes excellent-value still and sparkling Raimat Chardonnays, as well as providing wine for the delicious Codorniu sparkling Chardonnay.

CHIVITE
Navarra DO
NAVARRA

🍷 Tempranillo, Garnacha Tinta, Cariñena (Mazuelo)

🍷 Garnacha Tinta

🍷 Macabeo (Viura)

You couldn't get much more family-run than Julián Chivite, Navarra's largest wine producer. Julián Chivite senior is the boss, and his children, Julián junior (export), Fernando (winemaker), Carlos (finance) and Mercedes (public relations) are all actively involved. Not only is the company large, however, with over half the exports of Navarra's wine, but its wines are reliable as well.

The *bodega* started out as a coaching inn on the main road through Cintruenigo. The Chivite family began to make their own wine to sell to thirsty clients, and gradually the wine edged out the inn-keeping. In 1989, they completely overhauled the outdated winery equipment, installing new grape presses and stainless steel, temperature-controlled fermentation tanks. A new barrel-ageing cellar, bottling line and 5000 new oak barrels completed the renovations. The family recently bought a 300-hectare (740-acre) vineyard at Estella, destined to produce a single-estate wine, Señorio de Arinzano. Sixty hectares (148 acres) of this vineyard are being planted each year. This supplements the existing 105 hectares (260 acres) in Cintruenigo, Corella and Marcilla which are already in production.

The Viña Marcos and Gran Feudo reds, whites and rosés are all clean, fruity and well-made, the Parador Reserva perhaps a little too elderly for some tastes, and the pure Tempranillo 125 Aniversario Gran Vino rich and savoury, a clear reminder of how good this grape can be in Navarra.

CODORNÍU
Cava DO
CATALONIA

🍷 Monastrell, Parellada

🍷 Macabeo, Parellada, Xarel-lo, Chardonnay

This family-owned Penedés giant is the largest 'Champagne-method' sparkling wine company in the world. It occupies a spectacular estate in San Sadurní de Noya, 60km (37 miles) south-west of Barcelona, complete with nineteenth-century art nouveau buildings that have been declared national monuments. For two months in the autumn, Codorníu processes more than a million and a half kilos of grapes a day using sophisticated equipment, and turns the wine into *cava* in the world's largest underground cellars – 30km (19 miles) of man-made caves.

Quality is good. Codorniu Chardonnay is in our view the best *cava* on the market – richly fruity, with honeyed, tropical fruit flavours and a commendably affordable price. The big brand, Codorníu Brut, is also good in its class, clean, fresh and lively. Anna de Codorníu, with 20 per cent Chardonnay, is sometimes disappointing.

Codorníu also owns the Penedés still wine company of Masía Bach, the exciting Raimat estate in Costers del Segre, Rondel, another huge *cava* company, and Agro 2001, who supply most of Spain's best quality, clonally-selected vines to much of the Spanish wine industry.

CONCA DE BARBERÁ DO
CATALONIA

Winery entry Torres

🍷 🍷 Garnacha Tinta, Trepat, Tempranillo (Ull de Llebre)

🍷 Macabeo, Parellada

A DO only since December 1989, this small, promising Catalan region has lovely rolling hills, thick with hazel and almond trees as well as vines. Lying to the west of Penedés, it is the highest region in Catalonia, therefore cooler, and capable in theory of making really fresh, aromatic wines with lower alcohol than the other Catalan regions. Mixed crop small-holdings are the rule here, so that most growers have too few grapes to bother making their own wine, and co-operatives account for most of the production. This is one of the Cava DO regions, but little fizzy wine is actually made within its boundaries. As much as 80 per cent of Conca de Barberá's grapes, juice and wine is sold to the *cava* firms of Penedés. With white fizz-base grapes so much in demand, many growers have turned over their red-grape vineyards to white, and white grapes now account for nearly three-quarters of production. Much of the small proportion of Conca de Barberá wine that doesn't go to make fizz is also sold off for blending (often illicitly) outside the region.

Alcohol levels under the new DO are mercifully low by Spanish standards: 10 to 11 per cent for whites made from Parellada, 10 to 12 per cent for other whites and rosés, and 10.5 to 13 per cent for reds. Whites can be fresh, fruity and lemony, but reds are usually astringent and tannic – because the best juice is run off first to make fresh and flavourful rosés, traditionally the region's strong point. Star of the region is the Torres estate of Milmanda, producing spectacular Chardonnay, with Cabernet Sauvignon and Pinot Noir vines soon to come on line. It is a measure of Conca de Barberá's anonymity that Torres has quietly chosen to label the Milmanda wines as 'Penedés'.

CONDADO DE HUELVA DO
ANDALUCÍA-

♀ Zalema, Moscatel, Palomino Fino, Garrido Fino

In sherry's heyday, Condado – down in the far south-western corner of Spain – used to sell at least half its sherry-like produce to neighbouring Jerez, where it was miraculously transformed into DO sherry. Now the sherry producers have more wine of their own than they can cope with, and much of the vineyard land in Condado has been turned over to strawberries, grain, sugar beet and olives. Condado still makes sherry-style Condado Viejo (*oloroso* type, ranging from dry to sweet, aged for a minimum of two years, with an alcoholic content of between 15 and 23 per cent, usually mediocre but occasionally rich and complex) and Condado Pálido (aged for at least two years under a film of *flor* yeast, like *fino* sherry, but fatter and less fine in style, with 14 to 17 per cent alcohol). But these are really only consumed locally.

Making light white wines in these climatic conditions is no easy job. Condado has a similar climate to that of the sherry country, with an *average* annual temperature of 18°C. Grapes must be picked in August, a whole month earlier than usual, while they are fresher and more acidic. To add to the problems, the majority grape, the Zalema – which makes 75 per cent of the region's wine – quickly browns during picking and crushing unless extreme care is taken. The authorities are promoting Jerez's Palomino as a better alternative, but even with Zalema, some pleasant, fresh, fruity, not-too-alcoholic whites are being made. Pioneers of this new style of wine in the early 1980s were the Sociedad de Vinos del Condado who, using modern equipment, now make a good, fresh, light white. But today's biggest producer of light whites, also good, is the huge Bollullos co-operative which makes 65 per cent of the region's wine.

CONTINO
Rioja DO
RIOJA

♀ Tempranillo, Garnacha Tinta, Cariñena (Mazuelo)

Contino is one of the few wines made in Rioja from the grapes of a single estate, and an outstanding testimony to the fact that, if you want to make the best wine, it pays to select the best site – in this case, a 45-hectare (111-acre), west-sloping vineyard in the heart of the Rioja Alavesa. In 1974, the estate's owners went into partnership with CVNE, and founded Sociedad Vinícola Laserna, named after a tiny hamlet on the dusty track leading to this remote vineyard. The wine is made by the CVNE winemakers in an immaculate *bodega* set inside a beautifully restored farmhouse at the heart of the vineyard. The majority of the wine is made from Tempranillo, with some Graciano and Mazuelo, and all the fermentation is in stainless steel tanks. Contino is always sold as a *reserva*, and aged for two years in oak barrels and two in bottle before release. Any wine from the estate considered not up to Contino standard is sold to CVNE, and used in one of their blends. Contino is one of the best wines in Rioja, with staggeringly rich, blackberry fruit. It will always improve for another five years after release, and sometimes longer. The 1982 is still one of the best Riojas around, and the 1985 looks as though it will be another star.

CORRAL
Rioja DO
RIOJA

🍷 🍷 Tempranillo, Garnacha Tinta, Cariñena (Mazuelo), Graciano

🍷 Macabeo (Viura), Garnacha Blanca, Malvasía

Bodegas Corral, in the Rioja Alta village of Navarrete, is a traditional *bodega*, making fairly austere, lightly oaky red Don Jacobo and Corral wines – plus a little rosé and white. Tempranillo is the main grape, accounting for 70 or 80 per cent of the red blends. Corral owns 40 hectares (99 acres) of Rioja Alta vineyard, but this supplies only one-fifth of its grape needs, and more is bought in from local growers. All the reds spend at least 18 months in American, French or Yugoslav oak barrels, but each year only a small proportion of the barrels are new (and therefore strongly flavoured). The winemaker aims to get a subdued oak flavour, dominated by the flavour of the wine itself. The *bodega* is owned by the grandson of the founder and a group of local friends.

COSTERS DEL SEGRE DO
CATALONIA

Winery entry: Raimat

🍷 Garnacha Tinta, Tempranillo, Cabernet Sauvignon and others

🍷 Macabeo, Parellada, Xarel-lo and others

▼ The marble-pillared entrance to the spectacular new winery on the Raimat estate in Costers del Segre. It was lobbying by Raimat (and powerful parent company Codorníu) that won DO status for this otherwise dull area.

The winemakers of the 'banks of the Segre', at the western limits of Catalonia, can thank the powerful *cava* firm of Codorníu for their elevation to DO status in May 1988. Few of the region's wines are ever worth a second sip, except, that is, for the excellent wines of the Raimat estate, subsidiary of Codorníu. Costers del Segre is not a single geographical entity, but four smallish separate zones, mostly in the dry, slightly undulating province of Lérida. This was traditionally white wine country and, in general, any vineyard land that has not sunk into decline still produces dull whites and the odd tough red. Thankfully, they are rarely seen outside the area. Ten of its 29 municipalities may also produce grapes for DO Cava.

Raimat's vast oasis of vines is fed – amid an almost desert landscape – by canals from the Pyrenees. Many of the vines are top foreign varieties such as Chardonnay, Merlot and Cabernet Sauvignon and the wine-making is as modern and high-tech as the vineyards. The high-quality whites, rosés, reds and sparkling wines, sometimes blends of foreign varieties with local ones, sometimes straight Cabernet, Chardonnay, Pinot Noir or Merlot, bear no relationship whatsoever to the other wines of this one-horse DO.

EL COTO
Rioja DO
RIOJA

🍷 Tempranillo

🍷 Garnacha Tinta

🍷 Macabeo (Viura)

If you notice a similarity between two *bodegas* on a road just outside Oyón, this would not be surprising: El Coto and the new Martínez Bujanda *bodega* were both designed by Jesús Martinez Bujanda. El Coto preceded the other by 14 years. About one-third of the company's grape needs come from their 90 hectares (220 acres) of vineyards around Cenicero. The winery is immaculate.

El Coto has stopped selling basic Rioja as the price made it uncompetitive. The company was in a good position to withdraw from the bottom of the market, as its reputation lies in *crianza* wines. Eighty per cent of sales are to Spanish restaurants. There is no advertising: everything is done by word of mouth. El Coto Crianza is decent, mature Rioja *crianza* with a suggestion of toffee in the taste, and the Coto de Imaz Reserva and Gran Reserva are classic, elegant red Riojas, not the richest in the region but full of wild strawberry and vanilla flavours.

CVNE
Rioja DO
RIOJA

🍷 Tempranillo, Garnacha Tinta, Cariñena (Mazuelo) and others

🍷 Garnacha Tinta

🍷 Macabeo (Viura), Garnacha Blanca, Malvasía

'The biggest of the smaller *bodegas*' is how the Compañia Vinicola del Norte de España (CVNE, pronounced 'coonay', for short) describes itself. 'And one of the best of the lot,' it might justifiably add. Quality here is extremely high, and can only improve with the recent massive installation of new wine-making equipment. It *looks* a big company, with its various buildings spread around the railway station in Haro. Where CVNE *is* among the region's big boys is in its vineyard holdings – 470 hectares (1160 acres), which provide over two-thirds of the red grapes needed and one-third of the white. Red wines are the main business, all based on Tempranillo grapes with minor additions of other varieties. The wines are crushed and fermented in the standard way, not fermented as whole grapes in the old Rioja tradition. Much of the wood ageing is done in elderly wood, which doesn't impart too strong an oak flavour to the wines. As well as the excellent, elegant, plummy Viña Real wines, *crianza*, *reserva* and *gran reserva*, there's a lovely, young, light, plummy CVNE Tinto. A prestige red called Imperial is made in the best years, sometimes *reserva*, sometimes *gran reserva*, aged for at least a year in tank, three in oak, and three in bottle before being sold, brimming with concentrated, savoury and wild strawberry flavours.

CVNE is one of the few Riojan companies to make really appetizing versions of the old-style, wood-aged whites. Monopole (Viura with 20 per cent Malvasía) is fresh with a nice balance of oak from 13 months in barrel. The unoaked Rioja Blanca Viura is also pleasantly fruity.

DÍEZ-MÉRITO
Jerez y Manzanilla DO
ANDALUCÍA

🍷 Palomino Fino, Pedro Ximénez, Moscatel

Diez-Mérito wines are among the biggest sellers in Jerez, yet no wine is made these days in the Diez-Mérito winery. The company was bought in 1985 by Marcos Eguizábal, a Rioja businessman who had made his fortune in the fruit and veg greenhouses of Almería. At the same time, he acquired Bodegas Internacionales and resolved to rationalize the production costs, laying off or retiring half the Diez-Mérito employees, and making all the wines under the same enormous roof. So in 1987 the Diez-Mérito wines moved out of their old-fashioned Ali-Baba jars (*tinajas*) and into new, super-modern, temperature-controlled stainless steel at Bodegas Internacionales – now Jerez's biggest *bodega*. Diez-Mérito does well out of the deal. The best wines of all are selected for the expensive Fino Imperial and the deliciously nutty and saltily concentrated Victoria Regina Oloroso (brands of Diez Hermanos, the original name of Diez-Mérito). The second quality, still excellent, goes to the Don Zoilo range (a brand belonging to Diez-Mérito). That leaves the remainder for the unexciting Duke of Wellington range – the Bodegas Internacionales brand – and for myriad own-label supermarket sherries.

DOMECQ
Jerez y Manzanilla DO
ANDALUCÍA

♀ Palomino Fino, Pedro Ximénez

BOTAINA
JEREZ AMONTILLADO VIEJO
SHERRY

▼ Domecq's El Alcalde vineyard, just to the north-west of Jerez town.

Pedro Domecq, the world's biggest brandy producer and the oldest and largest of the sherry companies, finding itself in the financial doldrums a few years ago, cut back considerably on staff (by further modernizing its equipment) and sold just over one-quarter of its shares to Allied Lyons (the rest remain in the family). Big certainly isn't bad in this case: La Ina, fresh and yeasty-tangy, is one of the best of all *fino* sherries and one of the lightest in alcohol. It is the second best-seller in the world, and accounts for one-third of Domecq's sherry production. Domecq has considerable vineyards of its own (1600 hectares/3954 acres) and also buys in quantities of grapes from local farmers. Double Century and Pedro are the main brands apart from La Ina. Río Viejo, a medium-bodied dry *oloroso* and especially the elegant, dry, austere Botaina Amontillado Viejo are worth a try. But best of all is Domecq's top range: Amontillado 51-1A, a gloriously drinkable dry *amontillado*, with tangy, salty concentration to the fore and toffee and hazelnut in the background; Sibarita Palo Cortado, richer, sweeter, but still with a streak of lean, iodiny concentration; and Venerable Pedro Ximénez, an alcoholic, liquid version of raisin toffee – unctuous and very sweet.

DOMECQ
Rioja DO
PAÍS VASCO

♟ Tempranillo, Cariñena (Mazuelo), Graciano, Macabeo (Viura)

♟ Garnacha Tinta

♀ Macabeo (Viura)

The giant sherry firm has invested heavily in Rioja since the early seventies, when it bought extensive vineyards in the Rioja Alavesa, and built a winery in the village of Elciego – which still isn't working to capacity. With 544 hectares (1344 acres), Domecq is by far the biggest vineyard owner in Rioja. Most is Tempranillo, with some Viura, and an experimental plantation of young Cabernet Sauvignon, in the hope that this will one day be permitted in Rioja DO wines. Unusually for Rioja, the vines are trained Bordeaux-fashion along wires – a far more efficient method officially outlawed (for no good reason) by the DO in favour of little stumpy bushes. The authorities turn a blind eye. Domecq still needs to buy in some grapes from outside growers. Most of the wines are red, 90 per cent Tempranillo from the Rioja Alavesa, the rest Graciano, Mazuelo and Viura. Domecq Domain (also known as Privilegio del Rey Sancho) is a lightish, fruity, reliable wine, considerably better than the simpler Viña Eguia. Whites and rosés are fair.

FAUSTINO MARTÍNEZ
Rioja DO, Cava DO
PAÍS VASCO, RIOJA

🍷 Tempranillo, Garnacha Tinta, Cariñena (Mazuelo), Graciano

🍷 Tempranillo

🍷 Macabeo (Viura)

Excellent *reservas* and *gran reservas* are the specialities of this large family-owned Rioja *bodega*, though all their wines are good. Few wineries can be cleaner than Faustino Martínez, and the technical equipment is impressive. They buy some grapes from growers, but their own 350 hectares (865 acres) of Rioja Alavesa vineyards supply about half the grapes they need, including an unusually high proportion of the excellent but rare Riojan grape, Graciano. There are also experimental plantings of Cabernet Sauvignon and Pinot Noir. The reds start with a delicious, fresh, fruity Vino Joven or Viña Faustina, made nearly in Beaujolais style by fermenting the grapes uncrushed. With the oak-aged wines in their dark, frosted bottles, the accent is on bottle ageing rather than long wood ageing, which leaves them fruitier and more attractive: light, fine, strawberry-scented Faustino V Reserva and deep, rich, spicy Faustino I Gran Reserva rate amongst Rioja's best. The whites are fair, the *cavas* pleasant, simple and honeyed.

Faustino Martínez also own Bodegas Vitorianas, makers of Don Darias and Don Hugo – oaky, Rioja-like table wines.

FERRET I MATEU
Penedés DO, Cava DO
CATALONIA

🍷 Cariñena, Tempranillo (Ull de Llebre), Garnacha Tinta, Cabernet Sauvignon

🍷 Cariñena, Tempranillo (Ull de Llebre)

🍷 Macabeo, Parellada, Xarel-lo, Cariñena

The unusual thing about this small family *bodega* is the extraordinary machine that Josep Ferret has invented (and patented) to crush his grapes. He feeds 500kg at a time of red grapes into the top of the machine's cylinder, seals it, and builds up a high pressure inside; then releases the bottom of the cylinder so that the grapes come shooting out like a cannon ball. Result: transparent wisps of grape skin floating in richly coloured and aromatic juice. Practically all the growers of the village of Santa Margarida i els Monjos and many from a couple of nearby villages supply their grapes to Josep Ferret to supplement the 20 hectares (49 acres) owned by his family. It's a co-operative system – they are paid, with profits, when the wines are sold. Reds, meaty, aromatic and richly cherry-fruity with some tannin, are what we found stunning, but Ferret has also won prizes locally with his light, clean, fruity whites and fresh, rounded rosés, and he has also started to make *cava* in the last few years. Brand names abound: Valle del Foix, Viña Laranda, Viña Soric, Viña Vermella, Vinya Ferret Mateu and Viña Foix.

FREIXENET
Cava DO
CATALONIA

🍷 Macabeo, Parellada, Xarel-lo, Tempranillo (Ull de Llebre)

🍷 Macabeo, Parellada, Xarel-lo

◀ Freixenet's ornate reception and office building perches over nine layers of underground factory-warrens, which are visited by train.

Only Codorníu makes more *cava* than Freixenet, and when you take into account Freixenet's sparkling wine subsidiaries, Castellblanch and Segura Viudas, the Freixenet group is in fact the biggest 'Champagne-method' producer not just in Spain, but in the world. The Freixenet cellars, in San Sadurní de Noya, Penedés, have the air of an underground factory warren. Visitors trundle through long caverns and passages on a little electric train, admiring stack after stack of bottles and countless crates of bottles on rockers. Quality here is sound, but most of the wines suffer from the inherent defects of Catalan *cava* – lack of character and an earthiness because of the grapes used and the lengthy ageing. However, the Brut Nature is fresh and lemony, if slightly earthy, and the Cordon Negro Brut is clean, honeyed and attractive.

Freixenet own three other Spanish *bodegas*, apart from those already mentioned: Conde de Caralt (*cava* and still wines), René Barbier (still wines) and Canals & Nubiola (*cava*).

GARNACHA

The red Garnacha Tinta, the Grenache of France, is Spain's most cultivated red grape variety. It is vigorous and can be very productive, but yields tend to be low as it generally grows in Spain's hotter, drier vineyards. It is especially abundant in Navarra, the hotter, drier parts of Rioja, Penedés, Priorato, Tarragona, Terra Alta, Ampurdán-Costa Brava, Campo de Borja, Somontano, Cariñena, La Mancha and Utiel-Requena, but there's some to be found almost everywhere except the Levante, Galicia and Andalucía. Garnacha grapes become very sweet, and all that sugar turns into head-thumping degrees of alcohol unless the grapes are picked early, as soon as they are ripe. Much of Spain's Garnacha is made into rosé, and both rosés and the gutsy reds can be very plummily flavourful if drunk young, ideally within their first year. Garnacha wines oxidize quickly, becoming dull and brown, and the reds quickly lose their vibrant colour. The best solution is to blend Garnacha with wine of a less fat and blowsy variety, such as Tempranillo. Only the richest and best of Garnachas, notably in Priorato, stand up to much ageing.

The white version, Garnacha Blanca, is also found in most parts of Spain, particularly in the Catalan DOs of Alella, Tarragona and Terra Alta. It makes big, dull, alcoholic wines with little flavour.

Garnacha Peluda ('hairy' or 'shaggy' Garnacha) is a variant of the red Garnacha Tinta, found in a few regions of Spain, especially the Catalan regions of Alella, Priorato and Terra Alta. Garnacha Tintorera is something quite different. Sometimes known as the Alicante, it is the only Spanish grape with red flesh. Almansa is its main home, but there is also some in Alicante and parts of La Mancha.

GARVEY
Jerez y Manzanilla DO
ANDALUCÍA

🍷 Palomino Fino, Pedro Ximénez, Moscatel

San Patricio, Garvey's famous *fino* sherry, went through a quality dip in the early eighties after the company was bought by RUMASA in 1978. They advertised heavily, sales increased ten-fold and quality just couldn't keep up. Things have changed, however, since the German co-op AG took over in 1985, and San Patricio is once again one of the finest *finos*, as well as one of the sherries that has had its alcohol level lowered. Other favourites from this company are the rich, nutty Garvey Palo Cortado, and a wonderfully treacly Pedro Ximénez. Other brands include Tío Guillermo old *amontillado*, Ochavico nutty old *oloroso*, Long Life Oloroso (medium sweet) and Flor de Jerez Cream. Garvey still use their beautiful old *bodegas* in Jerez town (and have recently acquired a *manzanilla bodega* in Sanlúcar de Barrameda) as well as a new winery built on the outskirts of the town in the early seventies. They own 500 hectares (1236 acres) of top-quality vineyards.

GONZÁLEZ BYASS
Jerez y Manzanilla DO
ANDALUCÍA

♀ Palomino Fino, Pedro Ximénez, Moscatel

Tío Pepe, González Byass' *fino*, is the top-selling sherry in the world and accounts for a quarter of all sherry sold at home in Spain. Unusually for such a big brand, it's also one of the very best. González Byass' enormous, modern Las Copas *bodega* among the vineyards on the outskirts of Jerez's urban sprawl contrasts strongly with the maze of whitewashed buildings, and sun-dappled, cobbled alleys of the firm's original *bodegas*, still used to age the wines, just outside the walls of the old town. Las Copas processes 25 million kilos of grapes during the few weeks of the harvest. González Byass own over 2000 hectares (nearly 5000 acres) of prime vineyard themselves, and have long-term contracts with grape-growers from a further 1000 hectares (2471 acres). Unlike many Jerez firms, they never buy grape juice or ready-made wines from outside, preferring to put all raw materials through their own quality-oriented plant. González Byass are also unusual in fermenting a considerable amount of their wine in wooden casks but this is now gradually to be phased out, and all their wine will be fermented in temperature-controlled stainless steel tanks.

Amontillado del Duque is a fine, dry, austere, pungent and nutty wine, one of the world's great wines for a snip of a price. Matusalem is a slightly sweetened old *oloroso*, big, deep and pruny. And Apostoles Oloroso Viejo is medium-dry, nutty and grapy. The next step down, Alfonso Dry Oloroso, is also very good. As well as Tío Pepe, there's a cheaper *fino* sold under the brand name Elegante and, typically sweetened for the British market, La Concha Amontillado, San Domingo Pale Cream and Caballero Amontillado.

The company is still largely owned by the González family, who bought out the Byass side of the firm a few years ago. In 1990, however, 15 per cent was sold to the clothing company Benetton. González Byass also own Bodegas Beronia in Rioja and Castel de Vilernau, producers of Jean Perico *cava* in Penedés.

GRACIANO

Sadly, this high-quality grape of Rioja and Navarra is disappearing because today's growers are not prepared to put up with its scant yields. The Riojan authorities don't even bother to calculate what percentage of the vineyards it represents; it's now almost totally restricted to the oldest vineyards and, even there, individual Graciano vines are interspersed with more popular varieties. The Rioja producers prize it, when they can get it, for the lovely, fragrant, plummy and savoury aroma, subtle, spicy flavour, good balance and excellent ageing properties of its wines. It also has high acidity, which is useful in a blend with the low-acid Tempranillo. Interestingly, Bodegas Faustino Martínez have planted 15 per cent of their extensive vineyards with Graciano and Marqués de Riscal have just planted 25 hectares (62 acres).

Graciano is even rarer in Navarra, where it is also a traditional grape. Though one of the official varieties, it is now only found scattered amid old Garnacha Tinta vineyards.

HARVEYS
Jerez y Manzanilla DO
ANDALUCÍA

♀ Palomino Fino, Palomino de Jerez, Pedro Ximénez

Harveys is the biggest, though certainly not the greatest. This huge Jerez company, owned by Allied Lyons, was founded only in 1970, though sherry had been sold under the Harveys label long before that. The Bristol wine company that became John Harvey & Sons dates from 1796. For 174 years, Harveys did not have their own *bodega* or vineyards in Jerez but bought the wine which went into their sherries from various producers. However, on being taken over by Allied Lyons they bought *bodegas* in Jerez, set up joint vineyard ventures on a massive scale with Barbadillo and Garvey, and built a super-modern vinification plant among the vines. More recently, they bought the firms of de Terry and Palomino y Vergara. Apart from the famous Bristol Cream, brands include a *fino*, Luncheon Dry(ish), and a medium Club Amontillado. The best wines are the 1796 up-market range, *oloroso*-style, full, dry, soft, nutty-savoury Palo Cortado and a slightly sweetened, curranty-nutty Fine Old Amontillado. Fino Tío Mateo (Palomino y Vergara) is also good, light and tangy.

HIDALGO
Jerez y Manzanilla DO
ANDALUCÍA

♀ Palomino Fino, Pedro Ximénez

This small (by Jerez standards), 200-year-old company in the seaside town of Sanlúcar de Barrameda is one of a very few sherry companies that are still family-owned. The three Hidalgo cousins who run it specialize with great success in *manzanilla*, and make all their wines from their own 160 hectares (nearly 400 acres) of vineyards, plus 40 hectares (nearly 100 acres) belonging to other members of the family. Besides Manzanilla La Gitana (the best-selling *manzanilla* in Spain) and a wonderful, fine, concentrated, softly nutty and tangy Manzanilla Pasada, they also make a good range named Mariscal, excellent Fino Especial and Miraflores, Amontillado Napoleón, Pedro Ximénez Viejo, Oloroso Viejo and a lovely, softly concentrated, dry nutty Jerez Cortado.

CAVAS HILL
Cava DO, Penedés DO
CATALONIA

♟ Garnacha Tinta, Cariñena, Tempranillo (Ull de Llebre), Cabernet Sauvignon

♀ Garnacha Tinta, Cariñena

♀ Macabeo, Xarel-lo, Parellada

The Penedés firm of Cavas Hill makes just over a million bottles of wine a year, half sparkling, half still, most of it simple in flavour but very fresh and pleasant. The *bodega* belonged to the English Hill family till the early seventies, and is still privately owned. Fifty hectares (124 acres) of vineyards supply most of their needs; a little is bought in as grapes or wine. The cellars are an interesting mixture of ancient and modern: a hi-tech fermentation *bodega* equipped with vacuum filters and stainless steel galore, then down to the gothic-looking cellars, where all the 'Champagne-method' fizz is still turned, and even disgorged, by hand. Their *cavas* are less earthy than most, and Reserva Oro has good, lemony flavour. Simple, fresh still whites include Blanc Cru and Blanc Brut; Rioja-like reds go by brand names Gran Civet and Gran Toc.

HISENDA MIRET
Penedés DO
CATALONIA

♀ Parellada, Macabeo, Xarel-lo

Celler Hisenda Miret was founded in 1984 by the enthusiastic Ramón Baladá. Unlike most Catalan producers, he doesn't make *cava*. Even more strangely, he bottles wines made from the three Catalan grapes, Parellada, Macabeo and Xarel-lo, *separately*, as varietal wines. His own favourite is the Xarel-lo, which, when young, does have an attractive, creamy, gooseberry concentration, but which ages fast and unpleasant-ly to the perfumed, earthy flavour so typical of aged *cava*. His Parellada was our choice, light, fine and almost herby, though with no great length of flavour. These make a fascinating trio of wines to try if you want to find out what the three white Catalan grapes really taste like.

INTERNACIONALES
Jerez y Manzanilla DO
ANDALUCÍA

♀ Palomino Fino, Palomino de Jerez, Pedro Ximénez, Moscatel

Bodegas Internacionales has Jerez's newest and biggest cellar, a huge complex built by the RUMASA group in 1977 to house six old established sherry firms including Varela and Bertola. After the demise of RUMASA, the firm was sold to Rioja businessman, Marcos Eguizábal, in 1985. At the same time he bought the big firm of Díez-Mérito, and in 1987 completed an impressive new production *bodega* at Bodegas Interna-cionales to make the wines of both companies. The best-quality wines go to Díez-Mérito brands, the remainder to Bodegas Internacionales' own Duke of Wellington brand, supermarket own-label sherries and the brands of the companies who were taken over.

IRACHE
Navarra DO
NAVARRA

🍷 Garnacha Tinta, Tempranillo, Graciano, Cariñena (Mazuelo)

🍷 Garnacha Tinta

🍸 Macabeo (Viura)

We have vivid memories of our first visit to Bodegas Irache. Each room seemed dirtier than the last, and there was a rank smell of vinegar in the air. The disappointing wines came as no surprise. But that was seven years ago, and the place looks much better these days. Moreover, the company has just built an impressive modern *bodega* and planted new vineyards of Cabernet Sauvignon, Merlot and Viura. Irache hopes to increase the 40 hectares (99 acres) of vineyard to 120 hectares (297 acres) in a couple of years. All depends on obtaining permission for the new plantations. The new *bodega* has a bottling line on the first floor and storage for 5000 oak barrels underneath, as well as a lot of new stainless steel tanks. It is a magnificent building, and the Spanish government has insisted on high standards as it lies right beside the old pilgrims' road to Santiago de Compostela and the eleventh-century monastery of Irache. Let us hope, then, that the new vineyards, the new barrels and the new *bodega* will improve the quality of the lacklustre Irache wines. The white and rosé are adequate, but the reds (of which the company is proud) are still musty and rather fruitless.

JEREZ Y MANZANILLA DO
ANDALUCÍA

Winery entries: Barbadillo, Caballero, Díez-Mérito, Domecq, Garvey, González Byass, Harveys, Hidalgo, Internacionales, Lustau, Osborne, Valdespino

🍸 Palomino Fino, Palomino de Jerez, Pedro Ximénez, Moscatel

▶ Sandeman's Carascal vineyard near Jerez, planted on the white *albariza* soil that produces the region's finest, most delicate wines. The big firms such as Sandeman own about one-third of the region's vineyards.

As the ads say, *real* sherry comes from Spain, from the triangle of vineyard country between Jerez de la Frontera, Sanlúcar de Barrameda and Puerto de Santa María, down in Spain's south-west corner, near Cádiz. To give it its full title, this prestigious DO is called Jerez-Xérès-Sherry y Manzanilla de Sanlúcar de Barrameda – but Jerez y Manzanilla DO for short. Other Spanish regions (Rueda, Condado de Huelva and Montilla-Moriles) make similar wines, but nothing ever reaches true sherry's quality peaks.

All the sherry we see on export markets comes from the big *bodegas* in the three towns at the corners of the sherry triangle. They own one-third of the vineyards themselves, and buy in grapes, juice or wine from co-ops and private farmers.

The best quality grapes from the finest *albariza* – chalk soil – vineyards generally go to make *fino* and *manzanilla*, the lightest sherries fortified to between 15.5 and 17 per cent alcohol. Both have a characteristic salty-tangy flavour (even more pronounced in *manzanilla*) which they develop while ageing under *flor* yeast. To the English-speaking world, *amontillado* and *oloroso* tend simply to mean 'medium' and 'sweet', and such wines sold here are generally young, cheap and unexceptional. In fact, both are bone dry as made and drunk in Jerez, as are most of the finer versions sold in Britain. Authentic *amontillados* were once *finos*, but were then re-fortified to between 16 and 18 per cent and aged till they turn tawny-brown and develop a rich, nutty flavour as well as the *fino* tang. *Olorosos* are more heavily fortified at the beginning, ending up at between 18 and 20 per cent, and age – without ever growing *flor*, in contact with the air – into richly fragrant, dark, nutty-pruny wines. *Palo cortado*, also dry, lies somewhere in between authentic *amontillado* and *oloroso* in style. Cream is simply inexpensive *oloroso* sweetened up with concentrated grape juice, and pale cream is sweetened cheap *fino*. Some stunning sweet fortified wines are made from the Pedro Ximénez (PX) and the Moscatel grapes, labelled with the grape name.

All sherry has to be aged in barrel for a minumum of three years, but all the really good ones are aged for much longer. As they age, the wines pass through a '*solera* system', a complicated form of pre-blending which also has the effect of preserving the *flor* yeast on *fino* sherries. Only one-quarter of each barrel in the *solera* is ever drawn off at one time for bottling. The space is filled up with similar but younger wine from another barrel and so on, down a line of four or more.

JUMILLA DO
MURCIA, CASTILLA-LA MANCHA

🍷 🍷 Monastrell, Garnacha
Tintorera, Tempranillo (Cencibel)

🍷 Airén, Merseguera, Pedro
Ximénez

Jumilla's speciality has long been big, dark, old-fashioned alcoholic reds for blending with weedy wines from elsewhere. But things are now looking up a little. They need to, because this style of wine is going (or has gone) out of fashion all over the world, and some co-operatives and private wine companies in Jumilla have recently been in grave financial difficulties because no one wanted their produce. About 80 per cent of Jumilla's wine still goes for blending: to Switzerland, Germany, Austria, Hungary, Galicia up in the Spanish north-west, and even, so they say, to Bordeaux in poor vintages such as 1987. Monastrell, the main grape, can offer little more than dark colour and alcoholic strength. Some of the wines are made even darker by running about half the juice off from one batch of crushed grapes and adding a second batch, so that the wine ferments on a double dose of colour-rich, astringent solids: this local speciality is called *vino de doble pasta*. A little white wine is made, almost always alcoholic and dull, and some rosé.

Some wineries have been improving their facilities, however, in the last few years, installing cooling equipment and insulated tanks. But many are still using antiquated equipment and methods. The Murcian local government – keen to encourage an improvement in wine-making and an upturn in sales – recently completed a magnificent new experimental *bodega* which was financed jointly by the DO governing body and the local department of agriculture. The vineyards are divided about half-and-half between the autonomous regions of Murcia and Castilla-La Mancha, but most of the *bodegas* are in Murcia.

Best producers: Bodegas Bleda with the Castillo brand; Ascensio Carcelén with brands Accorde, Con Sello and Sol y Luna; Bodegas Juvinsa with Pedro Gil; Señorío del Condestable with Señorío de Robles; the San Isidro co-operative with its young Casa Alta Vino Nuevo; Mähler Besse with Taja, and Vitivino with Altos de Pio (the last two companies are French-owned).

JUVÉ Y CAMPS
Cava DO, Penedés DO
CATALONIA

🍷 Cabernet Sauvignon, Pinot Noir

🍷 Monastrell

🍷 Macabeo, Parellada, Xarel-lo and others

Juvé y Camps are 'leaders in high class *cava*, selling only to top restaurants, good wine stores and delicatessens'. At the prices they charge, it's not surprising that their sales are so exclusive, though admittedly, quality is very good in this most traditional family-owned Penedés company. Having bought a fourth vineyard estate a few years ago, bringing their total to more than 400 hectares (nearly 1000 acres), Juvé y Camps are now self-sufficient in grapes. They use only free-run (unpressed) juice for all their wines, both sparkling and (made in much smaller quantities) still white; and, with quality in mind, they ferment in small, temperature-controlled stainless steel tanks. All the *remuage* is done by hand. Apart from the traditional Penedés trio of Parellada, Macabeo and Xarel-lo, there are Chardonnay, Cabernet Sauvignon and Pinot Noir vines in their vineyards, with which they intend to launch a range of single-variety still wines. The current still wine, Ermita d'Espiels Blanc Flor, made from the three local white grapes, is pleasant, clean and fresh, but the sparkling wines are much better. Reserva de la Familia Extra Brut is our favourite in the range, soft, honeyed and chocolaty. There is also a prestige brand, Gran Juvé, lighter and less richly flavoured, and a sparkling rosé.

LAGUNILLA
Rioja DO
RIOJA

🍷 Tempranillo

🍷 Garnacha Tinta, Tempranillo, Macabeo (Viura)

🍷 Macabeo (Viura)

The industrial-looking white buildings of Bodegas Lagunilla, in a wide, flat valley between the Rioja villages of Fuenmayor and Cenicero, have belonged since the late sixties to the huge IDV group. The wines are sound but unexciting. Lagunilla own no vineyards, and rely for their supplies on co-operatives and private growers, buying everything as ready-made wine, then ageing and bottling it themselves. Most of the wines are red, made almost exclusively from Tempranillo, and are generally firm, quite dark and agreeably tannic. Best-seller is the young Lagunilla Tinto, but there are also wood-aged reds – the *reserva* brand-named Viña Herminia and a *gran reserva*. The rosé and white are both young and simple.

LAN
Rioja DO
RIOJA

🍷 Tempranillo, Garnacha Tinta, Cariñena (Mazuelo)

🍷 Garnacha Tinta

🍷 Macabeo (Viura)

This well-equipped, efficient *bodega*, next door to Lagunilla in the Ebro valley between Cenicero and Fuenmayor, was founded in 1970 and has changed hands several times since. It is now owned by a number of industrial and private shareholders. Its own 70 hectares (173 acres) of vineyards supply one-eighth of grape needs, and the rest is bought in mostly at grape stage. The whites and rosés are fairly ordinary, but the reds are good, with slightly jammy, raisiny and vanilla-oaky flavours. The *reserva* and *gran reserva* reds go by the name of Lander or Viña Lanciano, and *gran reservas* can be elegant and wild-strawberryish in flavour. The aim is to restrict production to *reservas* and *gran reservas* some time during the nineties. A white *reserva* is to be launched in 1990. Lan also sells its wines under two different brand names, Lancorta and Señorío de Ulia.

JEAN LEÓN
Penedés DO
CATALONIA

🍷 Cabernet Sauvignon, Cabernet Franc, Merlot

🍷 Chardonnay

The story of Jean León is one of a penniless Spanish boy making good in California. He went as an immigrant, served in the US army in Korea, was demobbed into California, and found work first as a taxi-driver, then a waiter in a restaurant owned by Frank Sinatra and Joe di Maggio. In 1956 he bought his own bar in Beverley Hills and, two years later, opened a restaurant. His interest in wine came from the restaurant, and he decided to buy a vineyard. He tried unsuccessfully in California, France and Italy before returning, in 1963, to his native Spain. Finding nothing he wanted in Rioja, Jean León came to Penedés and bought 182 hectares (450 acres). Through French friends he obtained cuttings of Cabernet Sauvignon, Cabernet Franc and Chardonnay, and planted them in 1964. Since then, he has been making Chardonnay and Cabernet Sauvignon wines that have a good claim to be Spain's best from these varieties.

The Chardonnay, made in a distinctly Californian style (Jean León still lives in California), is oaky, with rich, biscuity, pineappley fruit underneath. More Chardonnay has been planted on the estate, as demand for the wine far exceeds supply. Up till 1980, the Cabernet Sauvignon was made from 95 per cent Cabernet Sauvignon, and was left, during and after fermentation, to macerate on the skins for ten days. The result was a big, tannic red wine that sometimes needed as much as ten years to become drinkable. Since then, the maceration period has been shortened to between three and five days, and the wine has 13 per cent Cabernet Franc and two per cent Merlot. This gives a softer wine, easier to drink in its youth – although the 1983, the most recent vintage released, is much richer and more full-bodied.

LOS LLANOS
Valdepeñas DO
CASTILLA-LA MANCHA

🍷 Tempranillo (Cencibel), Airén

🍷 Airén

◀ Lorry-loads of grapes waiting in the queue outside the reception centre of Bodegas Los Llanos in Valdepeñas. The firm can process nearly a million kilos of grapes each day.

Some of the best-value mature red wines in Spain come out of this large, sparklingly clean and well-equipped Valdepeñas *bodega*. Los Llanos' huge barrel-maturation cellar is unparalleled in Valdepeñas, where most reds are drunk young and without any wood ageing. Reds are the best buy here, but whites (Don Opas, Señorío de Los Llanos and Armonioso) are also good and fresh, though very simple in flavour. The cheapest red, Don Opas, contains 40 per cent Viura and is a bit feeble, but the remarkably inexpensive Señorío de Los Llanos *reservas* and *gran reservas*, made exclusively from Cencibel, can be excellent, strawberry-herby or curranty-fruity wines. Los Llanos own 205 hectares (506 acres) of vineyards, but buy in ten times as many grapes from local growers. The *bodega* was founded as a family concern over a hundred years ago, but has belonged since 1971 to a Madrid wine company, Cosecheros Abastecedores, who have been responsible for its massive growth and extensive modernization.

LÓPEZ DE HEREDIA
Rioja DO
RIOJA

🍷 Tempranillo, Garnacha Tinta, Cariñena (Mazuelo), Graciano

🍷 Garnacha Tinta, Macabeo (Viura)

🍷 Macabeo (Viura), Malvasía

▶ Vineyards on the banks of the Rio Ebro, north of Haro in the Rioja Alta.

Walking into the offices and *bodegas* of López de Heredia near the railway station at Haro takes you back approximately a century. But this endearingly old-fashioned *bodega* makes wines that are fine and delicious by any standards, ancient or modern. No stainless steel here: wines ferment and pass their early months in large wooden fermentation vats, they are clarified in the age-old way with egg whites, and never see a filter. Even the water used to keep the *bodega* immaculately clean is pumped up from underground by an old windmill. All the grapes López de Heredia use come from the Rioja Alta, half of them from their own vineyards. Reds, which represent three-quarters of their production, are a blend of 50 per cent Tempranillo, 30 per cent Garnacha and 10 per cent each of Graciano and Mazuelo. All the reds age for a considerable time in wood, but the casks here are mostly so old that they have no more flavour to give, so the vanilla-oaky character in these wines is not overstated: from the youngest red, Viña Cubillo, soft, fine and lightly oaky, to elegant, strawberry-fruity, oaky Viña Tondonia Tinto, quality is very high. Whites are excellent too and will mature for many years: this is one of the few *bodegas* still making old-style, oaked white Rioja. All the whites are made, unusually nowadays, half-and-half from Viura and Malvasía, and all are wood aged. Best is the delicious, spicily oaky, honey-and-vanilla flavoured Viña Tondonia Blanco. López de Heredia have a special dispensation from the Riojan authorities not to use the official ageing designations of *crianza*, *reserva* and *gran reserva*. They are sold with a simple vintage.

LUSTAU
Jerez y Manzanilla DO
ANDALUCÍA

🍷 Palomino Fino, Pedro Ximénez

With imposing cellars buried in Jerez's fourteenth-century Moorish walls as well as a new *bodega* out in the vineyards, Emilio Lustau fills as many sherry bottles under supermarket own-labels as it sends out under its own name. General quality here is sound to good, but rises to some delightful peaks. Lustau's wonderful *almacenista* sherries are unique. If you lived in Jerez and appreciated good things, you would probably make a regular pilgrimage to your favourite *almacenista*, jugs or empty bottles in hand. There remain about 50 of these smallish sherry-maturing businesses, more often than not run by wealthy individuals with a career elsewhere — doctors, lawyers, cattle breeders. Lustau hit upon the idea of bottling *almacenista* wines from single casks, and selling them as small-scale specialities, under its own name in conjunction with that of the *almacenista*. These can be really exceptional, complex sherries. The up-market range under the Lustau label also includes some excellent wines, such as the rich, bone-dry, salty-nutty Principe Pio Very Rare Oloroso and rich, nutty Dry Oloroso Solera Reserva Don Nuño. There is also a good range of Landed Aged sherries, shipped to Britain in cask and bottled after further maturation (though the process appears to make no perceptible difference to the smell or taste of the wines).

Lustau owns few vineyards, buying its raw materials as grapes, juice and ready-made wine, much of it from one of the local co-operatives.

MACABEO

The most common white grape variety of northern Spain, the Macabeo makes light, fresh, fairly fruity wine that has a slight floral perfume when young — but loses its freshness within a year or so to become dull and flat. Alias the Viura, it is very important in Rioja, where it accounts for well over 90 per cent of all white grapes. More often than not, white Rioja is now made totally from Viura, picked early, fermented cool and bottled fast to give a simple wine for drinking young. Traditionally, the Riojan Viura was blended with Malvasía and then aged in oak —

sometimes with a little extra acidity added – to make, at best, really rich, fat, complex and oaky wines but, at worst, the dark, heavy, tired brews that gave white Rioja a bad name. Only a very few producers still make the oaked style of wine. Finest by far and very oaky is Marqués de Murrieta, but CVNE make a good one with a moderate amount of oak ageing. Viura occasionally finds its way into the *red* wines of Rioja, especially in the Rioja Alavesa. It is also known as Vlura in Navarra and Rueda. Elsewhere it generally goes by the name of Macabeo: in Somontano, Campo de Borja, Cariñena, Penedés, Terra Alta, Conca de Barberá and just as far south as Tarragona. Along with Xarel-lo and Parellada, Macabeo is one of the trio of grapes that make most of Spain's *cava* fizz in Catalonia.

MAGAÑA
Navarra DO
NAVARRA

🍷 Merlot, Cabernet Sauvignon, Cabernet Franc and others

The Magaña brothers used to be nurserymen, growing vines as well as other plants. They sold young vines to many of the best producers in Rioja, Ribera del Duero and even Jerez before deciding that they too would try their hands at wine-making. So they sold the nursery and started Bodegas Magaña in 1973, with the intention of making top-quality red wine. With plantings of Merlot, Cabernet Sauvignon, Cabernet Franc, Malbec and Syrah, they have pioneered the use of French varieties in Navarra. They were, for instance, the first to make a Spanish wine from pure Merlot. Their 90 hectares (222 acres) of vineyard all lie within easy reach of the little *bodega* in Barillas, a small town south of Tudela in the Ribera Baja – the driest area of the Navarra DO. Juan Magaña, who now runs the *bodega*, hopes to have over 150 hectares (370 acres) planted within three years, and intends to build a fermentation cellar in the vineyards, to avoid the problem of grapes heating up and spoiling between vineyard and winery. At the moment, during the harvest, picking starts at dawn and stops at 11 am; after that Juan Magaña feels the grapes suffer under the midday sun.

Magaña wines are made only from their own grapes which, because of the dry climate, yield little juice – but of high quality. After fermentation, they are aged for up to six years before bottling: a few months in new oak barrels followed by perhaps a year in tanks, then back into the barrels for a further spell, into the tanks again, and so on. The intention is to make wines in which the new oak influence is not too obvious, but the result is often that the excellent, rich fruit of the young wine has faded by the time the wine is released for sale. Both the pure Merlot and the Magaña blend are very fine wines, but we feel they should be drunk as soon as possible after release – or earlier if Señor Magaña changes his ageing policy.

MÁLAGA DO
ANDALUCÍA

🍷 Pedro Ximénez (Pedro Ximén), Moscatel de Málaga

Most bottles of Málaga contain a curious blend of wines, juices and alcohol, which can be stunningly complex, or, more often, cloyingly sweet and boring. The basic wines are made in varying degrees of sweetness out of Pedro Ximén grapes – often with the illegal addition of Lairén (Airén) – or from Moscatel de Málaga. These are then blended with a variety of sweetening, flavouring and colouring liquids: partially-fermented raisin juice, fortified grape juice, and grape juice that has been boiled down until it's thick, dark and gooey. Alcohol ranges from 15 to 23 per cent. The label gives an indication of sweetness and colour: official colours in Spanish are *blanco, dorado, rojo-dorado, oscuro* and *negro*, though these are often translated to 'golden', 'brown' and so on for export markets. *Lagrima* should mean that only the first and finest juice was used, squeezed out of the grapes simply under their own weight. This sort of heavy, sweet, alcoholic brew is hardly what the world

is clamouring for just now, and sales are on the wane. Production has been dwindling throughout this century. Málaga used to make 30 million litres a year at the turn of this century; and, back in the 1700s, Málaga – known as 'mountain' wine – was more popular in Britain than sherry. Now the annual total is six million litres, less than some single wineries in other parts of Spain. The Pedro Ximén vineyards have naturally been dwindling, too, giving way to other crops, or to higher-yielding Lairén for turning into basic white wine. Despite the drop in production, there is actually a shortage of Pedro Ximén, hence the illegal inclusion of Lairén in the Málaga blends, as well as hefty dollops of Pedro Ximénez from Montilla-Moriles just to the north. All Málagas have to spend at least two years ageing in single barrels or a *solera* system and this must by law be done in the city of Málaga, which is cooler than the inland vineyards where the wines are actually fermented.

Easily the best of the Málaga producers is Scholtz Hermanos, whose best wines are excellent, and offer a glimpse of why 'mountain' wine was so popular. Their Málaga Semi-Dulce is rich and concentrated, with a long, black treacle flavour; the Málaga Dulce Negro has an intense taste of date and treacle, very sweet and quite complex; the Lagrima Delicioso is treacle-toffee and raisin on the nose, with a delicious nut and raisin aftertaste; and the Solera 1885 is gloriously raisiny, long and nutty, an excellent example from this waning DO.

MALUMBRES
Navarra DO
NAVARRA

🍷 Garnacha Tinta, Tempranillo, Cariñena (Mazuelo)

🍷 Garnacha Tinta

🍷 Macabeo (Viura), Garnacha Blanca

Part of the reason for the flourishing fortunes of Bodegas Vicente Malumbres lies in Huddersfield. The Malumbres family makes most of its money from a business that sells teazles to the textile industries in Huddersfield, Iceland, Germany and Eastern Europe and, with the teazle profits, has been able to expand its vineyard ownership. The wine business was started in 1940, and the company now has over 100 hectares (247 acres) of vineyard, as well as three cellars in Corella. Nearly all the red and rosé wine comes from the firm's own vineyards, but most of the white wine is bought in from growers and co-ops as they have few white grapes in their own vineyards. The new fermentation *bodega* is crammed with temperature-controlled stainless steel vats, sophisticated filters, and up-to-the-minute nitrogen injection equipment to protect the wines from contact with the air. However, some of the fermentation is done by the traditional semi-carbonic maceration method, in which red grapes are fermented without being crushed, to give a fragrantly fruity wine similar in style to Beaujolais. This red wine, either by itself or blended with normally-fermented wine, is the best thing the company produces: brand names to watch out for are Viña Ontinar, Don Carvi and, in the future, Heredad Floral.

MALVASÍA

The Malvasia is one of Spain's few really *flavourful* white grapes. It makes rich, full-bodied wines with a lovely musky-apricot aroma and flavour, and just enough acidity. The trouble is, there's hardly any left: it accounts now for only about one per cent of the white vineyards of Spain. Producers throughout Spain have gradually uprooted it simply because it produces less than other white varieties. The grapes, juice and wine need careful handling, because they oxidize (brown and spoil) quite easily. Malvasia wines can also age well, however, and are often delicious both young and mature. The best producers of white Rioja used to use up to 50 per cent Malvasia, but there, too, the grape has fallen into disfavour, and the majority of white wines are now pure Viura. Its other principal habitats are Valencia, the Canary Isles and in undemarcated vineyards in the province of Zamora.

LA MANCHA

Castilla-La Mancha is flat. So flat that far away on the horizon beyond the windmills, the castles and the vast expanses of olives, cereals, saffron and vines, you half expect to catch a glimpse of the sea. But this is in fact the land-locked heartland of Spain, a great tilted tableland some 500 metres (1640 feet) or more above sea level, in which Madrid beats out the cultural pulse of the nation. It is the land of Miguel de Cervantes (creator of Don Quixote), who died in poverty the same day as Shakespeare, and of the prized black steel swords of Toledo, inlaid with copper, silver and gold.

Climatically, the central plain is inhospitable country, veering wildly between extremes. Summers are relentlessly hot and dry, with temperatures sometimes over 40°C. Winters are very cold. Rain comes in spring or autumn – if at all – and is generally accompanied by violent storms, but amounts are minimal. Indeed, the name La Mancha originally derives from al-Manshah, the Arabic for 'dry land'.

The local solution to the lack of water is to plant the vines in a very widely spaced grid pattern, then to prune them in such a way that their straggly arms trail on the ground and provide a canopy to protect the grapes from the burning sun. Yields of grapes per hectare are inevitably small, but then small yields – often much smaller than this – are the rule in most parts of Spain. At the last count, Castilla-La Mancha was said to have 48.6 per cent of the nation's vineyards, and to make over half of all Spanish wine, the majority of it white.

This is one of the Spanish regions where efforts are now being made (with EC subsidies as an incentive) to persuade growers to uproot their vines and plant other crops. There is plenty of scope to do away with vines without eroding the actual DOs. Little over one-tenth of the region's wines have DO status. And even among the DO wines themselves, many are very poor. Despite vast expenditure in the 1980s by the regional government and by individual wineries, still less than one-quarter of the region's white wine is new-style – pale, fresh and fruity. The remainder is yellow-orange, heavy and tired, and much of this lesser DO wine goes for distillation along with the non-DO wine.

Glut there may be, but ironically there is a serious shortage of red grapes in the region's two principal DO areas, La Mancha and Valdepeñas. In La Mancha, nine white vines are planted for every one red. The situation is slightly better in Valdepeñas, with a ratio of six to one. By tradition, large quantities of white grapes are added to all but the tip-top red wines of La Mancha and Valdepeñas; the result is feeble stuff, pale and thin, that turns up its toes if left to mature. The authorities and the big wine companies are trying to persuade growers to replant with Tempranillo (locally known as Cencibel), which is the most important quality red grape in Castilla-La Mancha, but progress is slow. In 1989, the Consejo Regulador of Valdepeñas was caught literally red-handed – trying to buy in three million kilos of red grapes from outside the region.

▼ On the monotonous central plateau, high spots such as this one at Consuegra with its twelfth-century castle and liberal scattering of windmills are extremely rare. Most of the hillier country lies in the far north and the far south of the Castilla-La Mancha region.

LA MANCHA DO
CASTILLA-LA MANCHA

🍷 🍷 Tempranillo (Cencibel), Garnacha Tinta, Moravia and white varieties

🍷 Airén, Macabeo, Pardilla, Verdoncho

La Mancha DO – the biggest quality wine region in Europe –makes two distinct types of white wine nowadays, both of which are pretty cheap. There's the domestic version: alcoholic, oxidized and rough, sold by the litre or barrel, and used to swill down food in the more basic bars and restaurants in central Spain. And there's the export version. Open a standard-sized bottle of La Mancha in Britain, the USA or even in Spain, and provided it's the most recent vintage, it stands a good chance of being pale, fresh, light, fruity and vaguely aromatic.

These great central plains are among the Spanish regions that have made most progress in wine-making in recent years. During the late 1980s, the local authorities poured much-needed finance into improvements in both private wineries and the co-ops (which make 60 per cent of La Mancha's wines), and have also helped to promote the lighter, fresher results. However, still only 25 per cent of all the DO wine is made in the modern style. La Mancha whites can never be great because the raw material is almost exclusively the characterless Airén grape. But these are cheap wines, and the best give good value for money, even after recent price rises. Ninety per cent of La Mancha's wines are white. The rest are made mostly from Cencibel (Tempranillo).

Some of the best modern producers are: the huge, ultra-modern Vinícola de Castilla with well-made whites and juicy-fruity reds under the Castillo de Alhambra and Señorío de Guadianeja labels (their best reds contain some Cabernet Sauvignon); Rodriguez y Berger, producers of the Don Cortes brand, also with a good Viña Santa Elena; Julian Santos Aguado with fresh whites and light, soft, fragrant reds called Don Fadrique; Férmin Ayuso Roig with their soft, appley Vina Q Blanco and meaty, savoury Estola Reserva; Torres Fíloso with young, fruity Arboles de Castillejo and more mature Torres Filoso reds; and the co-operatives of Nuestro Padre Jesús del Perdón with its excellent Lazarillo brand, and Nuestra Señora de Manjavacas.

MARQUÉS DE CÁCERES UNIÓN VITIVINÍCOLA
Rioja DO
RIOJA

🍷 Tempranillo, Cariñena (Mazuelo), Graciano

🍷 Tempranillo, Garnacha Tinta

🍷 Macabeo (Viura)

Back in the 1970s, Marqués de Cáceres was the first Rioja *bodega* to produce light, fresh, fruity whites that had never seen the inside of an oak barrel – a white Rioja style that has now become almost universal. It is ironic that they have just begun to barrel-ferment Viura on an experimental basis: could this be white Rioja's next direction? Going on a sneak preview of the new white, we rather doubt it.

The *bodega* was established in the early seventies by Henrique Forner, a Spaniard who had been brought up in Bordeaux. He came prospecting in Rioja and settled, on quality grounds, on the village of Cenicero in the heart of the Rioja Alta. When buying vineyards proved too difficult, he set up agreements with local growers.

Until the late eighties, the reds were made in the growers' cellars or in local co-operatives under the close supervision of the *bodega*. Now over 90 per cent of reds are made in-house, in recently-installed, up-to-the-minute equipment. But from the start, thanks to French methods, Marqués de Cáceres reds have been made in the fruity, not-over-oaky style – now more popular with other Rioja *bodegas* too. This has meant they have never been recognizably 'Rioja' in style, more jammy than delicately wild-strawberry-oaky.

The white wines are all made in the *bodega* by the most modern methods and are very good, fresh, herby and grassy-fruity, more reminiscent of wines made from Sauvignon Blanc grapes than of other white Riojas. Rosés are fresh and good, too.

Marqués de Cáceres sell over seven million bottles of wine a year, and intend to stick to that figure. They recently added *gran reserva* reds to their established *crianza* and *reserva* wines.

MARQUÉS DE GRIÑÓN
Non-DO, Rueda DO
CASTILLA-LA MANCHA

🍷 Cabernet Sauvignon, Merlot, Cabernet Franc, Petite Syrah

🍷 Verdejo, Marsanne

▲ Prestigious wooden cases for central Spain's rebellious red.

These characterful wines are brain-children of a real Marquis of Griñón, Carlos Falcó, who returned to his family estate in the mid-sixties – after studying agriculture at universities in Belgium and California – with a compelling interest in wine. The 1400-hectare (3500-acre) Casadevacas estate lies on the edges of the Tagus River valley, 50km west of Toledo. Then as now, it grew seed oats and barley, sunflowers, and tomatoes for canning, while a quarter of the land was, and still is, used as a wild boar reserve. Instead of the faceless Airén – traditional to Spain's parched central plains – Falcó planted Cabernet Sauvignon and a small proportion of Merlot, having smuggled in the vine cuttings from Bordeaux in a consignment of apple trees. Trained quite high off the ground along wires, his vineyards look very different from any others in central Spain, and they are almost unique in being irrigated – a necessity if Cabernet is to grow in these conditions, but against Spanish law. For several years, Falcó periodically paid fines (and revelled in the publicity), but finally the regional government authorized irrigation since the vineyards are now officially considered 'experimental'. Some Cabernet Franc, Californian Petite Syrah and the high-quality northern Rhône grape, Marsanne, are also being planted during 1990 and 1991.

Though the red wines have always been crushed and fermented on the estate, until 1990 they were sent for wood ageing to Bodegas de Crianza Castilla La Vieja in Rueda, some way to the north. From the 1989 vintage onwards, however, the reds are being aged in a new Moorish-style winery on the Casadevacas estate. The Marqués de Griñón red can be utterly delicious, with richly minty Cabernet character and quite firm tannin, but vintages of the mid-eighties taste rather 'baked', overripe and slightly coarse, though pleasant. Whichever, these are not wines for long ageing, best drunk within five years.

The white wine will continue to be made in Rueda, however, again at Castilla La Vieja and from Rueda grapes. The only white currently on the market is a Rueda Superior, crisp, fresh, fruity and grassy, with good body – from 100 per cent Verdejo grapes. A white *reserva*, fermented and aged in new oak, was made for the first time in 1989.

The Marqués has been at been at work in other areas of Spain, too. In 1989, he began to produce a barrel-aged Tempranillo wine from the demarcated Ribera del Duero region. This Marqués de Griñón Durius is due for launch in 1992. Production started in 1990 of a barrel-fermented Garnacha Blanca in the high-quality DO region of Somontano.

MARQUÉS DE MONISTROL
Cava DO, Penedés DO
CATALONIA

🍷 Tempranillo, Garnacha Tinta, Cabernet Sauvignon

🍷 Monastrell (Cava), Garnacha Tinta (Penedés)

🍷 Xarel-lo, Macabeo, Parellada

This is a beautiful *bodega*, built around a medieval monastery and set, among its own vines, in a wooded valley with hills to the north and a river to the south. The *bodega* itself has been owned since 1980 by Martini & Rossi, but the surrounding vineyard – at 520 hectares (1102 acres) apparently the biggest single vineyard in Catalonia – is still owned by the eponymous Marqués and leased to the *bodega*. All the wine comes from these vineyards: up to 1.5 million bottles of still wine each year, and 2.5 million bottles of *cava*. Marqués de Monistrol describes itself as 'the biggest of the small or the smallest of the big' *cava* companies. Among the *cavas*, we prefer the youngest, Brut Selección, which is fruity, simple and attractive and lacks the earthy flavour of its elders and theoretical betters – Brut Reserva, Gran Tradición and others. The still whites are better than the reds: good, simple and fruity Blanc de Blancs and the fuller Blanc en Noirs (made in the red wine style by crushing the grapes and fermenting the juice in with the skins) which has really concentrated appley fruit, though a shade bitter round the edges. The red Viña Artal is quite good, made entirely from Tempranillo in recent vintages.

MARQUÉS DE MURRIETA
Rioja DO
RIOJA

🍷 Tempranillo, Garnacha Tinta, Cariñena (Mazuelo), Graciano

🍷 Garnacha Tinta, Tempranillo, Cariñena (Mazuelo), Macabeo (Viura)

🍷 Macabeo (Viura), Malvasía, Garnacha Blanca

▲ The little village of Paganos near Laguardia in the Rioja Alta, backed by the crags of the Sierra de Cantabria. The Rioja region is flanked to both north and south by stunningly beautiful mountain ranges.

Marqués de Murrieta was making superlative, traditional, rich but elegant, oaky wines *before* it was bought in 1983 by Vicente Cebrian, Count of Creixell – whose plan for the *bodega* is that it should become the leading producer of red wine not only in Rioja, but in the whole of Spain! Whether Murrieta will topple Vega Sicilia from its pedestal of adulation is dubious, but certainly the wines are as good as ever they have been. Sadly, however, they are shooting up in price.

Cebrian has so far invested around £5m in renovations and improvements to the *bodega* buildings, equipment and surrounding estate. He has installed a museum and excellent facilities for visitors. The vineyards, outside the village of Ygay, have already been extended to 162 hectares (400 acres), planted 90 per cent with Tempranillo, and will eventually cover 210 hectares (520 acres). And Marqués de Murrieta is already a single-estate wine. Ygay is a fine spot for vineyards, right at the conjunction of the three Rioja regions.

No wine spends less than two years in oak at Marqués de Murrieta, and *gran reservas* may well stay 30 to 40 years in barrel! But most of these are old barrels, coated inside with natural crystals, through which no wood flavour and little air actually gets at the wine. Out of a total of 11,500, the *bodega* buys around 500 new or nearly-new barrels each year – mostly made of American oak; but some come second-hand from top Bordeaux *châteaux* Yquem, Lafite and Pavie.

The *bodega* has until now sold its wines as Etiqueta Blanca (a *crianza* with three years' oak ageing), a 'young' *reserva* perhaps ten years older than that, an even older *reserva* which might be another ten years older, and a *reserva especial*, Castillo Ygay, made from the best wines in the finest years. From the 1985 vintage onwards, however, there will be just three wine styles per colour: Marqués de Murrieta *reserva* and *gran reserva* (approximately five and ten years old respectively), and Castillo Ygay, the special *gran reserva* made only from the best years' wines, and only released after decades of ageing in barrel (the current vintage, at the time of writing, is 1968).

MARQUÉS DE RISCAL
Rioja DO, Rueda DO
PAÍS VASCO, CASTILLA Y LEÓN

🍷 Tempranillo, Graciano, Cariñena (Mazuelo) and others

🍷 Garnacha Tinta, Macabeo (Viura)

🍷 Macabeo (Viura), Verdejo, Sauvignon Blanc

Things have been changing in this duo of family-owned *bodegas* in Rioja and Rueda since the younger generation, including the current Marqués de Riscal, took over the reins in 1986. On the red wine front, however, quality has certainly not risen yet, and there is often talk of a fungus in the ancient barrels that is giving the wines an unattractively musty flavour. However, this may change, because the Rioja *bodega*, where they make their red wine, is investing heavily in new oak. They now intend to change their barrels every five to seven years, and to go for a more modern, younger and fruitier style in export countries such as Britain, but are likely to keep their 'older-fashioned' style in Spain where Marqués de Riscal is the best-selling red Rioja by far.

This is the only Rioja *bodega* with an official dispensation to use Cabernet Sauvignon and Merlot in its wines. (Riscal was the first *bodega* to import Cabernet into Spain in 1864.) Most of the original Cabernet was in fact ripped up in the sixties, but 40 hectares were replanted in the eighties, and the new wine from these vineyards, called Barón de Chirón – a 1986, 80 per cent Cabernet, 20 per cent Tempranillo, aged in new oak – is due to go on sale in 1991. Ultimately half of the *bodega*'s 200 hectares (nearly 500 acres) of vineyard will be planted with Cabernet Sauvignon. About 15 per cent of these French grapes used to go into the *reservas*, but these will now be made mainly from Tempranillo, the major grape planted in the rest of the company's vineyards. An important part of the new Riscal blend is to be the excellent Rioja grape Graciano: while this grape is declining elsewhere, Riscal have recently planted 25 hectares (62 acres) with it.

Marqués de Riscal has until now been a rather light style of Rioja, lacking concentration, though it has a striking wild strawberry flavour as well as the curious mushroomy character, liked by some (the Spaniards), hated by others (almost everyone else). There is also a little rosé (fresh, light and attractive) but no white in Rioja.

White Marqués de Riscal in fact comes from Rueda, some way off to the south-west, source of some of Spain's better whites. Riscal built a *bodega* there called Vinos Blancos de Castilla in the early seventies, and have recently extended their vineyard. Their simple, fresh Rueda is made from 80 per cent Verdejo, 20 per cent Viura; the Sauvignon Rueda is grassy, rounded and fruity; and the Rueda Reserva Limousin, made 100 per cent from the characterful local Verdejo grape, is soft, oaky, lemony-fruity and well balanced.

MARTÍNEZ BUJANDA
Rioja DO
PAÍS VASCO

🍷 Tempranillo, Cariñena (Mazuelo), Cabernet Sauvignon

🍷 Garnacha Tinta

🍷 Macabeo (Viura), Malvasía

Martínez Bujanda, founded in 1890, is a hi-tech company that never stops trying to do better – even though their wines are already some of the best modern Riojas around. Latest trials are with their white wines, to see whether they prefer them fermented and aged in American or French oak (or neither). And for some years they have been growing and making wine from Cabernet Sauvignon, as an experimental variety, with the permission of the Consejo Regulador, Rioja's ruling body.

All the grapes they use for their wine come from their own 250 hectares (618 acres) of vineyards, which are divided between the three Rioja regions – Alavesa, Alta and Baja. The Tempranillo, from their vineyards in the Alavesa, is made by the carbonic maceration method into deliciously soft, fruity, cherry-flavoured red wine. This is sold under the Valdemar label, as are the white and the rosé, both excellent examples of fresh, modern, fruity wines. *Crianza*, *reserva* and *gran reserva* red wines are sold as Conde de Valdemar, and, with the exception of a rather harshly oaky 1980, have always been full of all the best flavours of Rioja, wild strawberry, plum and vanilla when young, developing into prune, cream and mint with age.

MASÍA BACH
Penedés DO
CATALONIA

🍷 Tempranillo, Garnacha Tinta, Cabernet Sauvignon

🍷 Tempranillo, Garnacha Tinta, Cariñena and others

🍷 Macabeo, Xarel-lo, Parellada, Chenin Blanc

'Masía' means 'farmhouse', but to call this huge, early twentieth-century mansion a farmhouse would be misleading, to say the least. And it doesn't take much imagination to visualize wild, Great Gatsby-style weekend parties here in the late 1920s! Today, the house, near Sant Esteve Sesrovires in the Upper Penedés, is sadly under-used. The empty rooms echo to a visitor's footsteps, while a fountain tinkles pathetically into the indoor pool of the entrance hall. The action now takes place in the winery, and the results rest in cellars tunnelled into the hill. Masía Bach used to belong to the brothers Bach – both cotton traders – until it was bought by the Raventos family in 1975, and now belongs to the Codorníu group. All but 60 hectares (148 acres) of the 350-hectare (865-acre) estate were sold, and those vineyards that remain are used by another Codorníu company, AGRO 2001, which is one of the foremost suppliers of rootstock and vines, clonally selected and disease-resistant, to growers throughout Spain. Grapes for Masía Bach's wines come from about 300 local growers, and are pressed, fermented and aged at the estate. Fermentation is temperature-controlled, and the red wines are all aged for between two and three years in large oak vats, then small American oak barrels. Masia Bach has been one of the few Penedés companies to use Cabernet Sauvignon in all its red wines (which are good) and is on the verge of releasing a pure Cabernet Sauvignon, not yet available in the UK. One curiosity on the Masía Bach list is the Extrísimo white (not the Extrísimo Seco), one of Spain's few sweet white table wines with pretensions to quality. It is made from barrel-matured white, mixed with a little *mistela* (unfermented grape juice and brandy). If you like the taste of elderly *cava*, sweetened up and without the bubbles, you'll like Extrísimo. We don't.

MAURO
Non-DO
CASTILLA Y LEÓN

🍷 Tempranillo (Tinto del País)

Since the 1989 vintage, Bodegas Mauro have inhabited a lovely, restored seventeenth-century house in the village of Tudela de Duero, just outside the limits of the Ribera del Duero DO, and a little way to the west of the famous Vega Sicilia estate. These rich, fruity, oaky wines began as the small-scale passion of architect Luciano Suárez and two partners, who first rented and borrowed space in other people's wineries in 1978 to make 500 cases of wine. Their new winery is well equipped, with stainless steel for fermentation and an array of new or nearly-new oak barrels for ageing – 60 per cent of them top-quality, subtly-flavoured Nevers oak from France. They buy Tinto del País (Tempranillo) grapes from the Duero area. Consultant on the wine-making has been Mariano García, winemaker of Vega Sicilia. They are now making as much as they ever intend, around 4500 cases a year.

MÉNTRIDA DO
CASTILLA-LA MANCHA

🍷🍷 Garnacha Tinta, Tinto Madrid, Tempranillo (Cencibel)

Take an hour's car ride north-east from Méntrida into the heart of Madrid and ask around until you find someone who has tasted Méntrida wine – you could be there for weeks. Very little Méntrida wine ever sees the inside of a bottle. Most of these dull, solid, tannic reds and heavy rosés are sold in bulk for blending, or as anonymous house-wine plonk in the bars of Madrid. The rest is drunk in Méntrida itself, or ends up in the distillery. This is one of those DOs that should never have been. Reds and rosés made largely from Garnacha can officially range from 13 to 18 per cent alcohol, and the even tougher, darker *tinto doble pasta* wines from 14 to 18 per cent. There have been experiments recently with picking earlier before the grapes are overripe, with more modern fermentation methods, and using more Cencibel and Bobal for reds (plantations of Cencibel are increasing), but Méntrida still has a long way to go before it justifies its DO.

MONTECILLO
Rioja DO
RIOJA

🍷 Tempranillo, Garnacha Tinta, Cariñena (Mazuelo)

🍷 Tempranillo, Garnacha Tinta

🍷 Macabeo (Viura)

The lawn outside the modern Montecillo *bodega* in Fuenmayor is strewn with what look like dumpy bee hives. In fact these are ventilation grilles for the large cellar beneath. The efficient complex was built with no expense spared after the sherry firm of Osborne bought the *bodega* in 1973. Montecillo own no vineyards, but their stringent selection of others' grapes shows in the excellent quality of their wines. In really bad vintages, they have been known to buy no grapes and make no wine at all. Eighty-five per cent of Montecillo's production is red and the wines owe their rich, fruity style to long bottle ageing for fine wines, rather than excessive periods in wood. Montecillo wines *are* oaky, however, in a balanced, subtle degree. The youngest reds, Viña Cumbrero Tinto, have rich, savoury, strawberry-raspberry fruit, and the *gran reservas*, Viña Monty – quite tannic when first sold – have wonderful, rich, savoury wild strawberry flavour. Montecillo Especial is made from the pick of the red grapes in the best years. The white Viña Cumbrero Blanco is excellent, too, with a grassy-gooseberry flavour.

MONTILLA-MORILES DO
ANDALUCÍA

🍷 Pedro Ximénez, Airén (Lairén), Moscatel and others

Montilla, sold in Spain as *fino, amontillado* and *oloroso*, resembles sherry in style. It is made in the same way as sherry, though from Pedro Ximénez grapes rather than Palomino, and needs less grape spirit to fortify it because the grapes get riper and sweeter and produce more alcohol of their own. It also has to age in a *solera* system, but for a shorter period. Montillas can be good, but never reach sherry's peaks of quality, generally tasting rather baked, raisiny and uncomplex.

The wines exported to the UK – as a cheap alternative to cheap sherry – are lighter in alcohol and go by the names Dry, Medium and Sweet (or Cream). They are sweetened with varying amounts of concentrated grape juice, and are a very pale imitation of sherry indeed.

Like other producers of fortified or naturally high-alcohol wines, the Montilla-makers have recently found it difficult to sell their wares. Half the wine made in Montilla now ends up in the distillery or is sold off as bulk plonk. And many of the vineyards have been turned over in recent years to olives and cereals. A less defeatist way of coping with the excess grapes has been the invention of a new style of Montilla – light (10 to 12 per cent alcohol) and fresh. But these are simple wines, quick to lose their freshness and not really worth buying.

Moriles is a little village in the region, reputed to make lighter, more elegant wines than Montilla itself, but in practice these wines are rarely seen outside the immediate area, except blended with Montilla wines.

Most Montillas are pretty forgettable, but the Gracia Hermanos wines have a nutty concentration much more reminiscent of good, aged sherry. Another wine to look out for is the Carbonell Moriles Solera Fina, with a clean, tangy *flor* character, and a honeyed, buttery side as well.

MONT MARÇAL
Penedés DO, Cava DO
CATALONIA

🍷 Cabernet Sauvignon, Cariñena, Garnacha Tinta, Sumoll

🍷 Cariñena, Monastrell, Garnacha Tinta

🍷 Parellada, Macabeo, Xarel-lo, Chardonnay

Set among its own 70 hectares (173 acres) of vineyards, this Penedés *bodega* makes both still (66 per cent) and sparkling wines of good quality at reasonable prices. As well as traditional Penedés grapes, they grow Chardonnay and Cabernet Sauvignon partly for blending with the local varieties, partly for varietal wines. The soft, honeyed Chardonnay *cava* has only just been exported. The standard *cavas* made from local varieties are clean and pleasant, the Vintage Brut quite honeyed. The dry whites – Blanco, Opus 4, Vi Novell and Nova Generacio (the first two containing a little Chardonnay) – are clean and fresh, though Opus 4 is slightly earthy. The reds are better: a pleasant, slightly over-oaked, spicy, blackcurranty Cabernet Sauvignon, and a good, rich, vanilla-oaky Tinto Reserva with blackcurrant overtones.

MOSCATEL

▶ Moscatel vineyards east of Málaga. Moscatel grapes get extremely ripe, yet, unlike other super-ripe grapes, they manage to retain their aromas.

The Muscat family is a big one, and within it quality varies enormously. Unfortunately, Spain houses the least exciting of the lot, the Muscat of Alexandria, which is generally known in Spain as the Moscatel de Málaga. This grape is more often grown as a table grape, but it also makes aromatic, raisiny wines throughout many of the southern regions of Europe as well as in hotter parts of the New World. Other Muscats can make dry or sweet, deliciously grapy wines, but there's generally a coarseness to wines made from Moscatel de Málaga. Like other members of the Muscat family, Moscatel grapes become very ripe under a hot sun, and most of the wines they make are heavy and sweet, golden to dark brown. Málaga and Valencia are its principal habitats in Spain, but there's also some in Catalonia, the Canaries, Jerez and elsewhere. Miguel Torres grows a finer version, Moscatel de Grano Menudo (the Alsace Muscat à Petits Grains) in the upper reaches of the Penedés to blend with Gewürztraminer in Viña Esmeralda.

MUGA
Rioja DO, Cava DO
RIOJA

🍷 Tempranillo, Garnacha Tinta, Cariñena (Mazuelo) and others

🍷 Macabeo (Viura), Garnacha Tinta, Tempranillo

🍷 Macabeo (Viura)

If you visit Isaac Muga's *bodega* by prior appointment, you will no doubt arrive to find him busily beating egg whites. It's not that he's obsessed with meringues, simply that Muga wines stick to tradition and are still clarified with beaten egg whites, about six per cask. Isaac Muga, in a rather shy way, enjoys putting on the egg-white show for visitors! Red wine production at Muga can have changed little since the *bodega's* foundation in 1932. The reds are still fermented in huge wooden vats, then filtered off through bundles of vine prunings for ageing in oak casks. The results of these artisanal methods are very good. Muga Crianza has soft, rich but elegant strawberry fruit, the Reserva, Prado Enea, is rich and intense with strawberry-minty flavours.

Whites and rosés were, until recently, best avoided, but in the late eighties, new, modern pressing equipment was installed and the *bodega* began to buy grapes more selectively. Though still fermented in big wooden vats, the whites are now delicious, extraordinarily perfumed and grassy-flavoured. The rosés are pleasantly fresh and fragrant, too. Whites and rosés together account for only ten per cent of the *bodega's* production. They also make a sparkling wine with the Cava DO, called Mugamart in Spain, and, more appealingly, Conde de Haro for export.

The *bodega* was started initially to process the grapes from the family's own vineyards, and although these 35 hectares (86 acres) now cover only 40 per cent of production, Muga remains a fairly small enterprise. The family still owns 90 per cent, the remaining shares belonging to Spain's largest insurance company. They have been reducing the Tempranillo in their vineyards in order to plant more of the interesting but unpopular Mazuelo grape. All the grapes that are bought in come from the Rioja Alta.

NAVAJAS
Rioja DO
RIOJA

🍷 Tempranillo, Macabeo (Viura), Garnacha Tinta, Cariñena (Mazuelo)

🍷 Garnacha Tinta, Macabeo (Viura)

🍷 Macabeo (Viura)

'It's easy to find – right behind the police station in Navarrete', the British agent told us before we visited Bodegas Navajas. And so it was. Not the kind of *bodega* that has its name writ huge on vast walls, because Bodegas Navajas isn't that kind of company. In fact, it consists of Navajas father and son, both Antonio, and a large, plain warehouse. They employ other workers only at harvest time and for bottling.

The wines used to be sold largely to other, bigger *bodegas*, but now Navajas export to Germany, Denmark, Holland and the USA as well as the UK, and only sell off parcels of wine to 'friends', and that rarely. They have a very good relationship with Murua, the principal barrel-producers in Rioja, and Murua often use Navajas wines to experiment with new types of barrel. This link means Navajas are certain of getting their 100

new barrels a year at a time when there is a great demand for new barrels in Rioja. First into the new barrels is the white wine, followed by *rosado* and red.

Navajas are particularly proud of their whites and this pride is not misplaced. The young wine is lean, clean and lemony, the Crianza, at four and a half years old, still needed more time and was very dominated by new oak; and there was an amazing 1962 Blanco Reserva, not kept that long on purpose, but discovered in a corner of the old cellar. The wine had a rich, vanilla character, and overtones of grilled almond and cream as well a high, lemony acidity. Reds are good, with a lively, cherry fruit in youth mellowing to spicy richness with barrel age. They, too, are wines that should be kept.

NAVARRA DO
NAVARRA

Winery entries: Cenalsa, Chivite, Irache, Magaña, Malumbres, Ochoa, Señorío de Sarría, Vinícola Navarra

♥ ♥ Garnacha Tinta, Tempranillo, Cariñena (Mazuelo) and others

♀ Macabeo (Viura), Garnacha Blanca, Malvasía and others

Navarra is our tip for the future, a shining example to the rest of wine-making Spain. Through an ambitious programme of research and education, largely funded by the regional government, the Navarra authorities and producers have raised the quality of their wine to rival that from neighbouring Rioja and Penedés.

Such a revival only echoes history, for long ago Navarra wine was as renowned as its kings were powerful. At the beginning of the eleventh century the kingdom of Navarra included Bordeaux and Rioja as well, thus uniting three very prestigious wine regions. But, in the late 1800s, the phylloxera plague hit Navarra just as badly as Bordeaux and Rioja, and most of the first half of the twentieth century was spent building up the vineyards to their former size, most growers banding together to form co-operatives. During the 1970s, however, Navarra's wine-making fortunes declined, but have revived during the last decade.

COSECHA 1988
PRINCIPE DE VIANA
NAVARRA

The research station at Olite has done very useful work on grape varieties, yeasts and wine-making techniques, while the Navarra government offers a subsidy (or generous waiving of interest on bank loans) on projects to improve the quality of Navarra wines.

Although Garnacha has been the principal red grape grown in Navarra in recent decades, almost all replanting of red wine vineyards is now with Tempranillo. Yet Garnacha still predominates – but not all is made into red wine. Some of Navarra's best wines are *rosados*, made from Garnacha and usually cool-fermented.

Other newcomers to Navarra vineyards are the Cabernet Sauvignon, Merlot and Chardonnay. The latter must be harvested promptly, as it can make very fat, alcoholic wines if the grapes overripen.

▼ Young vines near Cintruenigo in Navarra. Nine-tenths of Navarra's vineyards still grow red Garnacha, but growers are no longer allowed to replant it. They get subsidies for planting Tempranillo or Cabernet.

All these grapes can produce excellent results in Navarra, as is shown by the wines made at the Olite research station and, increasingly, in *bodegas* throughout the region. Fresh, pure whites and rosés for drinking in their youth; young, Garnacha-based reds with lively, plummy fruit; and serious reds, stiffened with Tempranillo and Cabernet Sauvignon, that are capable of maturing into something even better.

NAVERÁN
Penedés DO, Cava DO
CATALONIA

🍷 Merlot, Cabernet Sauvignon, Tempranillo (Ull de Llebre)

🍷 Chardonnay

At the village of Sant Martin Sadevesa in the rolling hills of the Upper Penedés – and right next door to the famous Cabernet Sauvignon and Chardonnay vineyards of Jean León – Cavas Naverán's 110 hectares (272 acres) have also for the past 12 years grown Cabernet Sauvignon and a little Merlot, Cabernet Franc and Chardonnay. There's also some of the local Ull de Llebre (Tempranillo), and an expanse of the three white Penedés varieties for the *cavas*, which constitute this family firm's main business. These are rather expensive, being single estate wines, sold under the names Naverán or Señora. The *bodega* imports Limousin oak barrels from France for the still wines. The pleasant, oaky, herbaceous Cabernet Sauvignon wine contains five per cent Cabernet Franc. Sant Martin Naverán Tinto, made from 45 per cent Merlot, 40 per cent Cabernet and the rest Tempranillo, is also good, with honeyed, raisiny fruit. The first Chardonnay was picked in 1989.

OCHOA
Navarra DO
NAVARRA

🍷 Tempranillo, Cabernet Sauvignon, Garnacha Tinta

🍷 Garnacha Tinta

🍾 Macabeo (Viura), Ugni Blanc

When you know that Javier Ochoa's principal job is running the experimental station at Olite, it is hardly suprising that his own family concern, Bodegas Ochoa, is the perfect demonstration of the vastly improving face of Navarra wine – with all the fermentation done in stainless steel, maceration of grape skins before fermentation for both whites and rosés, controlled temperature fermentation, and sophisticated filters to ensure there are no problems when the wine is bottled. Add to this the high proportion of Tempranillo and Cabernet Sauvignon in the red wines, and the new barrels, and the results are first-class.

The white is ultra-modern, fresh, clean and lemony-minty, and the rosé soft, attractive and dominated by almondy, buttery flavour. Even the basic young red now has 80 per cent Tempranillo, which gives it a fragrant, wild strawberry fruit with a hint of cherry at the end. There are wines made from pure Tempranillo and pure Cabernet Sauvignon, both with over a year's ageing in oak barrels, both excellent, the Tempranillo savoury and herby, the Cabernet Sauvignon, blackcurranty, herbaceous, ripe and gluggable. We preferred these younger reds to the older Tinto Reserva (rich and deep, made from 80 per cent Tempranillo and 20 Cabernet Sauvignon), because of the lively concentration of fruit in the younger wines. The Ochoa wines are already excellent, and will almost certainly get better.

OLARRA
Rioja DO
RIOJA

🍷 Tempranillo, Garnacha Tinta, Cariñena (Mazuelo), Graciano

🍷 Garnacha Tinta, Macabeo (Viura)

🍾 Macabeo (Viura), Malvasía, Garnacha Blanca

The most impressive thing about Olarra is the architectural style of the *bodega* itself – for the wines, though consistently very well made, are rarely exciting or complex. Sadly, few people other than industrial workers, lorry drivers and determined visitors ever set eyes on this extraordinary building, set as it is in the heart of an industrial estate east of Logroño. Completed in 1973, the main building forms a huge Y-shape, and filling in the space between two of the arms are 111 hexagonal pointed roofs, fitting together like the cells of a beehive and providing ventilation for the ageing cellar beneath. Olarra owns no vineyards, but has long-term contracts with a considerable number of growers, taking in all its raw materials as grapes; these are then fermented at very low temperatures in the highly automated winery. Nearly three-quarters of the wines are red, and range from a not-very-characterful Añares Tinto Crianza to decent *reservas* with some wild strawberry and vanilla perfume and quite good but not especially concentrated *gran reservas*. The simple Reciente white, totally Viura, is pleasant when young, but the honeyed, musky-lemony and slightly oaky Añares white is better, containing Malvasía and Garnacha Blanca as well as Viura. The rosé is simple and pleasant. Otoñal and Catedral are sub-brands.

OSBORNE
Jerez y Manzanilla DO
ANDALUCÍA

🍾 Palomino Fino, Pedro Ximénez

Though the family-owned Osborne group is the biggest drinks company in Spain, the original sherry side of the business accounts for only a fraction of sales. As the largest brandy producer in the sherry region, it sells more than 40 million bottles a year, mainly under the brand names Magno and Veterano. (This compares with 7.5 million bottles of sherry.) It also produces a whole range of other spirits such as gin and vodka, and owns three distilleries in La Mancha, the excellent Rioja company of Montecillo and a third-share in a large producer of *jamón de Jabugo* (wonderful, moist, flavourful Andalucian raw ham). It absorbed the sherry company of Duff Gordon many years ago.

Osborne has the potential to make *finos* of very high quality, based as it is in the seaside town of Puerto de Santa María (in 40 delightful, whitewashed *bodegas* in the old town centre). *Flor* grows thicker here than in Jerez, so that resultant sherries can be finer and tangier.

Osborne's raw materials are good, too: two-thirds of the grapes come from its own 400 hectares (988 acres) of top quality *albariza* vineyard, and the rest are bought in from the same area. Fino Quinta has been phenomenally successful since Osborne switched its long-running TV advertisement (of bulls running in the countryside) from Veterano brandy to Fino Quinta. It is light and honeyed, relatively young (envious locals say its rapid ascent to the second most popular *fino* in Spain has meant Osborne is short of stock), but pleasant. Amontillado Coquinero and Bailén Oloroso are stylish and concentrated.

PALACIO
Rioja DO
PAÍS VASCO

🍷 🍷 Tempranillo

🍷 Macabeo (Viura)

This Rioja *bodega*, almost 100 years old, has belonged to a Frenchman, Jean Germain, since 1986. Though based in Paris, Germain spends three days a week in Rioja; the rest of the time, he is mostly on the road selling, and now has export customers in Switzerland, France, Britain, the USA, Canada, Denmark, Japan and Hong Kong.

Most of the grapes for the Palacio wines are bought in, and come from the Rioja Alavesa, with some from the Rioja Alta. The greatest change Jean Germain has introduced is 3000 new French Limousin oak barrels, bought not because he is French, but to make the wines taste different. That, plus advice from Michel Rolland, a well-known Pomerol oenologist, have given some of the company's younger wines a distinctly French character.

Germain is putting most effort into marketing his Cosme Palacio brand. The white Cosme Palacio spends almost a year in Limousin oak, and emerges biscuity and rather Burgundian – good wine, but not at all typical of white Rioja. The red Cosme Palacio is sold as a *crianza* in Spain, but Germain doesn't bother with such Spanish wine terms for export markets: he feels they are too complicated. Moreover, this gives him the freedom to bottle the wine when he feels it is ready, rather than wait until it qualifies for a *crianza* label. The export Cosme Palacio red is plummy and soft, with good, savoury oak flavour, whereas the traditional Glorioso Crianza and Reserva wines are jammier, though still full of rich, plum-puddingy fruit. The Glorioso Gran Reserva, however, is an excellent wine, rich and plummy with a fine, wild strawberry overtone.

PALOMINO

Even with the very best technology, the Palomino grape makes very boring table wine – maybe fresh and fruity when young, but flavour is not its strong point. Take it a step further, however, turn it into sherry, and it can become one of the world's great wines, simply packed with flavour. There is one version of Palomino that is even more boring than the other. The coarse Palomino Basto, alias Palomino de Jerez, used to be the major grape of the sherry region, but has been ousted by the much higher-quality Palomino Fino. Formerly, this grew only around the seaside town of Sanlúcar de Barrameda, home of *manzanilla*, but today well over 90 per cent of the vines planted in Jerez are Palomino Fino, and most of the vines are high-quality, high-yielding, clonally-selected plants (Jerez began clonal selection decades before other regions of Spain). A quarter of Spain's extensive Palomino vineyards lie outside the sherry region in other parts of the country, including Galicia and the Duero Valley, where the grape is often called Jerez or Listán. Palomino Fino is gradually replacing the local Zalema in Jerez's neighbouring DO, Condado de Huelva. The Palomino's low acidity is no problem for the production of sherry-style wines, but it shows in the table wines. Much Palomino is still made into heavy, yellow, traditional table wine, but there is an increasing tendency nowadays to pick it young and ferment it cool. It is still never exciting but can be pale, clear, fresh and fairly fruity.

PARELLADA

Parellada – the most aromatic of the three major white grapes in Penedés – is exclusive to Catalonia. Apart from Penedés, it is very important in Tarragona DO, but also grows in the province of Lérida (including the new Costers del Segre DO) and in Conca de Barberá DO. It makes light, fresh, fruity wines with a floral aroma, good, fresh acidity, and, unlike most Spanish whites, fairly low in alcohol, usually somewhere between 9 and 11 per cent. These wines are not for long keeping – they are at their best in the spring after the harvest, and usually begin to taste dull by the following year. To preserve the grape's aromas, Parellada tends to be grown in the coolest spots, often up in the hills; and it is late to ripen – always the last of the whites to be picked.

In the last few years, Torres has taken to macerating the skins for a number of hours in the juice before pressing, in order to extract more of these aromas and flavours. Torres' Viña Sol is the best of the single-variety Parellada wines; its Gran Viña Sol and Fransola are Parellada blended with Chardonnay and Sauvignon Blanc respectively. The single-variety Parellada of Celler Hisenda Miret (Baladá) is also excellent. The grape occasionally goes by the name of Montonec. Parellada is also the most characterful constituent of the Catalan *cava* sparkling wines.

PATERNINA
Rioja DO
RIOJA

🍷 Tempranillo, Garnacha Tinta, Cariñena (Mazuelo)

🍷 Garnacha Tinta, Tempranillo, Macabeo (Viura)

🍷 Macabeo (Viura), Garnacha Blanca, Calagraño

Though the wines of Paternina are decent and pleasant, it's rare to find in them any real character or elegance. Their best-seller by far is Banda Azul with the blue-striped label, which accounts for about 60 per cent of sales. Like the other reds, this is made largely from Tempranillo and tastes only lightly oaky: most of the oak barrels here are elderly, with no more flavour to give. The older wines go by the name of Viña Vial. Paternina make no red wine themselves, buying it in ready-made for treatment and ageing, but they buy in juice to make whites and rosés. The *bodega* was founded at the end of the nineteenth century, and the old cellar in Ollauri is still used for ageing Viña Vial. However, most of the action is now in modern factory-like buildings, including one impressively enormous ageing cellar, on a 12-hectare (30-acre) site in Haro. The firm had various owners before RUMASA took it over in the early seventies. Like the rest of the RUMASA empire, it was then appropriated by the Spanish government. It is now owned by Marcos Eguizábal.

PEDROSA
Ribera del Duero DO
CASTILLA Y LEÓN

🍷🍷 Tempranillo (Tinto Fino), Cabernet Sauvignon, Merlot

Viña Pedrosa reds are delicious, elegant wines made by the small family *bodega* of Perez Pasqua Hermanos – the sort of family wine-making business you find all over France, but so rarely in Spain or Portugal. The immaculate winery, up in the little village of Pedrosa de Duero, was expanded considerably in 1989 and now has modern stainless steel tanks for fermentation, the latest in filtration and bottling equipment, and ranks of new oak barrels for ageing. Most of the grapes (Tinto Fino, supplemented by a little Cabernet Sauvignon and Merlot) come from the family vineyards – 24 hectares (60 acres) of mature vines to the north of the Duero River, in one of the highest and coolest parts of the Ribera del Duero region. After their recent success, however, they have also begun to buy in some grapes from local growers.

The business was founded in 1980 when the family decided to pull out of the local co-operative and go it alone. It is still run by three brothers and two of their sons. Viña Pedrosa is the brand name. There is a lovely, burstingly fruity Tinto Joven (young, un-oak-aged red). The *crianzas* and *reservas* have wonderful raspberry fragrance, nice oak flavour, and enough tannin to age well. About one-fifth of the production is rosé, but this is only sold on the domestic market.

PEDRO XIMÉNEZ

The stronghold of the PX – as it's generally known – is Spain's hottest vineyard country, Montilla-Moriles, in the heart of Andalucia. Given enough sun (and only the hottest parts of Spain can provide enough) it produces incredibly sweet grapes, which are sometimes dried practically into raisins before use. As much as 95 per cent of the Montilla-Moriles vineyard is planted with PX, and it ripens here to perfection. While Jerez makes its sherries out of the Palomino grape, using PX only for sweetening and darkening its blends, Montilla makes its sherry-style wines totally from PX – even the *flor*-affected, *fino* style. Ripening PX in Jerez is a more difficult matter. Traditionally, the picked grapes were dried out in the sunshine on mats, or more recently under plastic cloches. However, little PX is now grown in Jerez, and there has always been a quiet influx from the vineyards of Montilla. Pedro Ximén, as it's known locally, is also the major grape of Málaga, where it makes dull to stunning, dry to treacly-sweet wines of high alcoholic degree. These regions, with Valencia, are the PX's main habitats, but it is found all over Spain – quite extensively in Extremadura (by the Portuguese border) and the Canaries. In fact in Spain as a whole, there's more PX than Palomino. Not all of it is made into fortified or highly alcoholic wines. Traditionally, it has also been turned into yellowing, coarse, very alcoholic table wines, though in recent years, some of Montilla's excess crop has been made into a light, fresh but bland style of table wine.

PEÑALBA LÓPEZ
Ribera del Duero DO
CASTILLA Y LEÓN

♥ Tempranillo (Tinto Fino), Garnacha Tinta, Cabernet Sauvignon

♥ Tempranillo (Tinto Fino), Garnacha Tinta

We have not been particularly impressed so far with the wines of this Ribera del Duero *bodega*, but better things are probably in store since there has been a major investment in modern equipment, new cellars, and new vines. The first wine made in the new installations, a 1985 red *crianza*, is very pleasant, raspberry-ish and light. Later vintages, made for longer keeping, have not yet been released.

The Peñalba López family bought Bodegas Torremilanos and its then run-down vineyards in 1973, really just as a country house, with no intention of carrying on the wine business. The wine bug soon bit them, however, and they are now keen to establish it as a high-quality operation. All the grapes come from their own 100 hectares (247 acres) of vineyards, half of which have been very recently planted.

PENEDÉS DO
CATALONIA

Winery entries: Ferret i Mateu, Hill, Hisenda Miret, Juvé y Camps, León, Marqués de Monistrol, Masía Bach, Mont Marçal, Naverán, Torres

♥ ♥ Garnacha Tinta, Cariñena, Tempranillo (Ull de Llebre) and others

♥ Parellada, Macabeo, Xarel-lo, Chardonnay

It is partly the enterprising mentality of the Penedés folk, and partly the wealth and technical expertise generated by the booming *cava* industry, that have kept wine-making standards in the Penedés region way ahead of the rest of Catalonia, and ahead of most of Spain. Although many of the grapes for making *cava* come from elsewhere, the vast majority of the *cava* companies are based in Penedés, and many of them make still wines as well. The *bodegas* that specialize in still wines include the famous Miguel Torres, who makes some of Spain's finest wines. Co-operatives are strong here as in the rest of Spain, but so are the companies, who own one-fifth of the vineyards.

White wines predominate, and 90 per cent of these are made principally from the three local grapes, Xarel-lo, Macabeo and (best for quality) Parellada. They can be fresh, lightly aromatic and pleasantly lemony-fruity, but are never great wines. Chardonnay has been permitted in Penedés DO wines since 1986, and is now being used more widely to improve local blends. Reds are mostly thin, sometimes oaky, and it is a poorly kept secret that many are beefed up with heftier Rioja reds, while Penedés whites return the favour in Rioja. The finest of the Penedés reds are made partially or entirely from the Cabernet Sauvignon grape, by Torres and Jean León.

Vine-growing conditions differ greatly from the hot coast to the cooler uplands. The coastal vineyards grow only dessert Muscat and Garnacha Tinta, but it is less torrid just a little way inland and suitable for Cariñena, Monastrell and Ull de Llebre (Tempranillo). Then comes a range of hills, behind which a cooler climate favours the three native whites, plus Chardonnay, Cabernet Sauvignon and Pinot Noir. The most aromatic grapes, however, come from the higher altitudes, 40km (25 miles) inland – traditionally the best spots for Parellada, but now also growing Gewürztraminer, Moscatel de Grano Menudo, Riesling, Chenin Blanc and Pinot Noir. (Most of these foreign varieties, not yet accepted by the DO, are in the vineyards of the enterprising Miguel Torres.)

PESQUERA
Ribera del Duero DO
CASTILLA Y LEÓN

🍷 Tempranillo (Tinto del País), Albillo, Garnacha Tinta, Cabernet Sauvignon

▼ Young Tempranillo vines that will one day supplement the much sought-after reds of Viña Pesquera.

In the mid-eighties, few people outside Ribera del Duero had ever heard of the Viña Pesquera wines of Alejandro Fernández. Enter an American merchant and some influential American wine writers, one of whom compared Viña Pesquera to one of Bordeaux's finest reds, Château Pétrus. Now these richly coloured, firm, fragrant plummy-tobaccoey reds are among the most famous and most expensive wines in Spain.

You wouldn't guess from the lifestyle of the Fernández family that they had suddenly come into a considerable fortune, but they *have* just bought 100 hectares (250 acres) of potential vineyard land in the neighbouring village of Roa, and have plans to build a new *bodega* there. At the moment, their vines cover 65 hectares (160 acres) of very well-positioned land in the village of Pesquera, where – until 1972 – Alejandro Fernández ran the village smithy as well as a business inventing and marketing his own agricultural machinery. With the proceeds, he gradually built up his vineyard holding, and built his own winery – even making his own vats.

Oak ageing is an important part of the production of these wines. The cellar is piled high with 3000 American and French oak barrels, many of them renewed each year. The wines are nearly 100 per cent Tinto del País (Tempranillo), with a dash of Garnacha and white Albillo. They are sold as *reserva* in the very best years, otherwise as *crianza*.

PRIORATO DO
CATALONIA

🍷🍷 Garnacha Tinta, Garnacha Peluda, Cariñena

🍷 Garnacha Blanca, Macabeo, Pedro Ximénez, Cariñena Tinta

Situated in the south of Catalonia, this is one of the loveliest and wildest regions of Spain, with scrubby, craggy mountains and narrow, winding roads leading up through remote villages to the ruins of the twelfth-century Monastery of Scala Dei. As if it were not already hot and dry enough (average annual temperature is 15°C), any remaining moisture is regularly whipped off by dry north-east winds. The vines grow on old terraces, or simply cling to the slopes, where the dark, shiny, slate-like surface reflects heat and prevents evaporation. In places, farmers have to hang from ropes to tend their vines, and after all the effort, each vine is likely to produce only half a kilo of grapes – a fraction of yields in most other areas. Sadly, like other remote, mountainous regions of Spain, Priorato has been losing its population to the cities, though the local government has recently been subsidizing vine and olive growers heavily to encourage them to stay.

Traditionally Garnacha Tinta and Garnacha Peluda predominated, but Cariñena now accounts for a third to a half of most blends. Though daytime summer temperatures can shoot up to 40°C, nights drop to a cool 10° to 12°, which helps preserve the grapes' aromas and flavours. Put together with the tiny yields, this makes Priorato capable of producing extremely concentrated, dark, intense wines. They are also inevitably alcoholic: the *minimum* legal strength for table wines is 13.5 per cent, and many reach an inebriating 18 per cent. Most of the wines are 'young' reds, sold at between three and four years old, but Priorato also makes some excellent *rancios* and *generosos* – dry to sweet, penetratingly flavourful, nutty, raisiny wines that are wood aged for a minimum of five years, and end up sometimes with as much as 20 per cent alcohol. White wines are very scarce, but those that do exist make apéritifs, often the same strength as sherry.

Most of the wines are made in the fairly basic village co-operatives, and tend to be alcoholic, tannic and astringent. There are also two small, high-quality producers of table wines, Cellers Scala Dei and Masía Barril, plus another fledgling estate. And the Tarragona firm of de Muller specializes in the wood-aged *rancios* and *generosos* with some delicious results, buying in wines from the co-operatives.

RAIMAT
Costers del Segre DO, Cava DO
CATALONIA

🍷 Cabernet Sauvignon, Tempranillo, Merlot, Pinot Noir

🍷 Tempranillo, Chardonnay, Garnacha Tinta, Macabeo

🍷 Chardonnay, Parellada, Macabeo, Xarel-lo

Several of Spain's most affordable top quality wines, both sparkling and still, come from this remarkable estate in the near-desert country of Lérida province. It belongs to the Raventós family of the giant Codorníu group, who bought it in a run-down condition in 1914. Vines were growing here since the 1200s, but the land became barren during the rural decline of the nineteenth century. The Raventós re-styled the estate, to the extent of moving hills, thoroughly cleansing all the soil, and building a village for the agricultural workers, complete with school, sports facilities and railway station. In the meantime, the Catalonia and Aragón Canal was built, providing the estate with water for irrigation. Neither the vines that now grow on over one-third of Raimat's 3000 hectares (7413 acres) nor the surrounding fruit trees and cereals could survive without irrigation – and somehow the company has managed to circumvent both national and EC regulations that ban the irrigation of vines.

These are no ordinary Spanish vineyards. On advice from the California universities of Davis and Fresno, the vines are trained along wire trellises and much more densely planted than the traditional vineyards of Spain. Four hundred hectares (988 acres) are planted with Cabernet Sauvignon, 300 hectares (741 acres) with Chardonnay, the rest with Tempranillo, Merlot and the three Catalan whites, Parellada, Macabeo and Xarel-lo. There is also some Pinot Noir.

Raimat and its Codorníu parent were the force behind the recent granting of a DO to several patches of land in Lérida, now collectively known as Costers del Segre. None of the region's other wines were really up to much. Raimat's wines are consistently very good, however: there's an excellent sparkling Raimat Chardonnay as well as a fruity, rounded and honeyed still Chardonnay; fruity, richly-flavoured and subtly-oaked Raimat Cabernet Sauvignon and Raimat Tempranillo; also a blend of Cabernet Sauvignon and Merlot under the brand name Abadía. Most recent additions are a barrel-fermented Chardonnay – rich, toasty with a creamy pineapple fruit, an authentically savoury, fruity Pinot Noir, and an oaky Merlot.

REMÉLLURI
Rioja DO
PAÍS VASCO

🍷 Tempranillo, Macabeo (Viura)

La Granja Nuestra Señora de Remélluri, to give it its full name, was the first of the modern wave of Rioja *châteaux*. The estate, which had 15 hectares (37 acres) of vines, was bought by Jaime Rodriguez in the mid-1960s as a summer retreat. When he found the property had a long history of wine-making, however, he started buying up potential vineyard land from his neighbours. Now there are 52 hectares (128 acres) planted, and the wine-making facilities were modernized in 1984 with the installation of stainless steel vats for fermentation. The Remélluri wine has improved since then, though Jaime Rodriguez's son, Telmo – who recently studied oenology at the Bordeaux University and has just taken over as winemaker – is convinced he can improve quality still further. Certainly the 1989 Tempranillo (the first vintage Telmo has handled), tasted from the vat the following spring, had glorious plum and almond fruit. One tradition at Remélluri is that the wine is never sold until about three years after it has been made, having spent a couple of years maturing in small oak barrels and another in bottle. Even so, Remélluri is not a wine to rush to drink, as the flavour from the excellent chalk and clay hillside vineyards takes time to develop its full potential. The Rodriguez family feel strongly that the future of Rioja lies in finding the best vineyards, and making single estate wines from them. To that end, they have started two other estates, Torre Oña in Laguardia and Torre Andrea in Samaniego, with an American partner, Christina Vasquez. They, and Remélluri, are worth watching.

RIAS BAIXAS DO
GALICIA

🍷 Caiño Tinto, Sousón, Mencía and others

🍷 Albariño, Loureira Blanca, Treixadura and others

The reputation of the Galician wine region of Rias Baixas, demarcated in July 1988, rests on its star performer, the white Albariño grape. The local reds are not really worth bothering about. The Albariño is undoubtedly Spain's most distinguished white grape, a world-ranking player, capable of making white wines that dazzle the drinker with their display of fruit flavours, peach, apricot and grapefruit, all underpinned by creamy-soft richness. In the past, 'Albariño' on the label has been little guarantee, as, before the policing machinery of the DO was in place, much inferior wine was passed off as the real thing. Spaniards will pay serious money for Albariño wines, and the temptation was too great for dishonest producers to pass up. With the advent of the DO, this has changed, and 'Albariño' on the label means Albariño in the bottle.

However, not all white wines from the region are made from this low-yielding, high-quality grape. Rias Baixas is split into three sub-regions, the Valle del Salnés (an area on Galicia's west coast just north of Vigo and Pontevedra), El Rosal (the last tip of Spanish west coast before the River Miño, and Portugal) and Condado del Tea (still along the banks of the Miño, but further inland). Of these, it is the Salnés area that has the reputation for Albariño wines – it was popularly known as 'the region of the Albariño' before the DO was passed. Under the DO rules,

Salnés white wines must contain at least 75 per cent Albariño, El Rosal wines 70 per cent of either Albariño or Treixadura, and Condado del Tea wines 70 per cent of either Albariño or Loureira (unless another permitted variety is specified on the label). Albariño wines (perhaps because of the frauds in the past) have to be made of pure Albariño and contain at least 11.3 per cent alcohol.

Rias Baixas – where the damp maritime climate dictates that vines are trained up on pergolas or tall supports to protect them from rot – has thousands of small producers. Individual vineyards are tiny by comparison with other Spanish regions – the Rioja *bodega*, La Rioja Alta, owns the largest single vineyard in the entire region, 25 hectares (62 acres), from which come the grapes for its Lagar de Cervera Albariño. But there are some immaculately equipped medium-sized and small *bodegas* that turn out white wines quite unlike any others Spain can produce. Rioja, Ribera del Duero and Rias Baixas are the three Spanish wine regions where buyers are snapping up any *bodegas* or vineyards on the market. The wines will never be cheap, but the best examples are among Spain's most deliciously fragrant whites.

RIBEIRO DO
GALICIA

🍷 Caiño, Garnacha Tintorera, Ferrón and others

🍷 Treixadura, Palomino, Torrontés and others

'All over the world, people are asking for young wines. Traditionally, the wines of Spain are mature wines – except for the wines of Galicia. The other areas have to make an effort. For us, it's natural. The time for Galician wines has come.' Those were the words of a lawyer who had painstakingly recreated an old farmhouse – originally as a 'house in the country' for his wife – out of old timbers, local stone and other traditional materials. And, of course, he had planted a vineyard and made himself a winery. The location was near the village of Gomariz, about 30km west of Orense – in the heart of the Ribeiro wine region – an enchanting country of hills and little valleys, with a higher average altitude than the Rias Baixas to the west.

Unusually, the Ribeiro wine-making revolution – of which the lawyer's *bodega* is a typical example – was started by the local co-operative, fully supported by an excellent, local government-funded experimental

bodega. Stainless steel has become commonplace in new bodegas throughout the region, wine-making techniques have improved immensely, and, most importantly, there has been a return to the good, native grapes of the region, Loureira, Treixadura, Torrontés, Godello and, to a lesser extent, Albariño. Palomino, a neutral import from the south of Spain, is still the most widely grown grape in Ribeiro, but even that is being made into better wine, thanks to the improvements.

As well as urging growers to change from Palomino, the local Consejo Regulador is trying to persuade them to concentrate on growing grapes for white wines, as red Ribeiro wines (made mainly from Caiño) are of no great quality, though they have a certain local following.

The modern Co-operativa Vitivinícola del Ribeiro, together with another large local company, the Cosecheros de Vino del Ribeiro, make about two-thirds of all the wines produced in Ribeiro. The co-op's top wine, Bradomin, is made from only the best grapes, predominantly Treixadura. A new company, Lapetena, was started in 1988 to make high-quality sparkling wine, in the hope that one day the cava DO may be extended to include Galicia.

RIBERA DEL DUERO DO
CASTILLA Y LEÓN

Winery entries: Arroyo, Balbás, Pedrosa, Peñalba López, Pesquera, Ribera Duero, Vega Sicilia

🍷 🍷 Tempranillo (Tinto Fino), Garnacha Tinta, Cabernet Sauvignon and others

Ribera del Duero reds, at best richly aromatic, well balanced and very fine, have become something of a cult in the last few years, both in Spain and in the USA. And like all cult items, they have become extremely expensive. Vega Sicilia, Ribera del Duero's oldest and still its most prestigious estate, had been renowned since the last century for its powerful, complex, lengthily wood-aged wines, made partly from the French grapes Cabernet Sauvignon, Merlot and Malbec, and partly from the local Tinto Fino (Tempranillo). But the wine world rather considered this to be a one-off. When the region got its DO in 1982, it still only really boasted one star. Practically all the rest of the region's wines were made in the co-operatives, and though at best rich and attractive, they were very inconsistent. It took an American to discover the bodega of former co-op member Alejandro Fernández – followed by a wealth of publicity for his delicious Viña Pesquera wines – for the outside world to recognize the potential of the region. Next the limelight fell upon a few other small-scale Ribera del Duero bodegas: Hermanos Perez Pasquas with their Viña Pedrosa, Victor Balbás, and Bodegas Mauro, just outside the DO limits. Now everyone is scrambling to buy vineyards in Ribera del Duero. A government-financed research station has recently been set up to keep expansion and progress on the right lines.

Ribera del Duero means 'the banks of the Duero' (better known as the Douro, the port river, over the border in Portugal). The gentle, often pine-covered hills and undulating country around the valley lie 700–800 metres (2300–2625 feet) above sea level, near the limits for grape-growing, and this goes a long way to explain the intense flavours and aromas of the wines. Despite the hot, ripening sun during the day, the summer night temperatures drop very low, and the grapes' aromatic elements do not get burnt up during the vines' night-time respiration, as they would in hotter places. There is adequate rainfall in spring and autumn, and useful mists from the river to pull the vines through the dry summers. Poor, chalky soils and low yields also make for fine, concentrated flavours. Most of the grapes here are Tinto Fino (Tempranillo), but other bodegas have followed Vega Sicilia's example and planted Cabernet and Merlot, though officially these are limited to municipalities which in 1982 already had 'traditional plantations of these varieties'. Legal or not, they make an excellent blend with Tempranillo.

Ribera del Duero makes mostly reds and some rosés. White wines are not included in the DO.

◀ A small, terraced vineyard near Cortegada in Ribeiro. Grape-growers here have been replanting with the region's good, native grapes – Loureira, Treixadura, Torrontés, Godello and Albariño – which had been ousted by the dull Palomino.

BODEGA RIBERA DUERO
Ribera del Duero DO
CASTILLA Y LEÓN

🍷 Tempranillo (Tinto Fino)

🍷 Tempranillo (Tinto Fino), Garnacha Tinta, Valenciano and others

Housed in cellars under the castle hill of Peñafiel, this is the region's best known co-operative *bodega*, and the only one at present producing anything like quality. Its rich, red Protos wines have been sold in Britain at quite high prices for many years, and now prices are soaring along with all the other wines of the region. Protos has become quite a cult wine at home in Spain, too. Unlike most co-operatives, who tend to dispose of much of their wine in bulk, this one bottles everything it makes, and with the Spanish market clamouring for its far-from-perfect product, there is sadly little incentive for members to spend their easily-earned profits on improvements. The trouble has always been that the wines are inconsistent, and many suffer from a curious, mouldy-musty flavour and aroma that undoubtedly come from the ill-ventilated cave-cellars cut into the rock. Open one bottle and it could be rich and aromatic, but the next could be dankly musty, and fit only to pour down the sink. The potential is obviously there, and even 25-year-old Protos can have wonderful flavours. You can just never be quite sure what you are going to get – and at high prices that's not good enough. There is hope. In 1986 the co-op employed its first qualified winemaker and started to pay rather more attention to hygiene and cellar management. And with the region bristling with new technology and new ideas, some of it can hardly fail to rub off.

RIOJA DO
RIOJA, NAVARRA, PAÍS VASCO, CASTILLA Y LEÓN

Winery entries: AGE, Amézola de la Mora, Barón de Ley, Berberana, Bilbainas, Campo Viejo, Contino, Corral, El Coto, CVNE, Domecq, Faustino Martínez, Lagunilla, Lan, López de Heredia, Marqués de Cáceres, Marqués de Murrieta, Marqués de Riscal, Martínez Bujanda, Montecillo, Muga, Navajas, Olarra, Palacio, Paternina, Remélluri, Rioja Alta, Riojanas, Virgen del Valle

🍷🍷 Tempranillo, Garnacha Tinta, Cariñena (Mazuelo), Graciano

🍷 Macabeo (Viura), Garnacha Blanca, Malvasía de Rioja

Twenty years ago, when Rioja first became popular outside Spain, people learned to expect oaky-flavoured reds – smelling and tasting of vanilla: partly because, then, in the seventies there were a lot of new oak barrels in use, and partly because flavour merchants were doing a roaring trade in bottles of dark, gooey oak essence! All that changed in the eighties, as the regulations tightened and the ranks of new barrels, oaky taste long gone, became flavourless containers. Red Riojas today are less vanilla-oaky, more positively fruity, and only 40 per cent of Riojas are oak aged. But some of the best *bodegas* are turning to expensive new oak again, following a worldwide change in fashion – and they can afford it, because Rioja prices have soared in recent years. There is a shortage of grapes at the moment in Rioja, with sales booming and new *bodegas* galore. The Riojans would like to plant an extra 4000 hectares (nearly 10,000 acres) but the EC will permit them only 850 hectares (2100 acres). Grape prices will therefore remain high.

Traditional white Riojas were also oak aged, but this style became unpopular during the eighties, and only a few *bodegas* now make oak-aged whites, which can be rich and lemony-toffee flavoured. The grape blend used to be of Viura, Malvasía de Rioja and Garnacha Blanca, but the new style is simple young Viura, fruity but unexciting.

Though more than three-quarters of the grapes are produced by small-scale growers, most are crushed and fermented in co-operatives or by the big Rioja firms. These big firms bottle and sell practically all Rioja, which are therefore large-scale blends – often a mix of grape varieties from all over the region. The two major grapes for red Rioja are Tempranillo, with an elegant, plummy character that develops well with age in barrel and bottle into wild strawberry and savoury flavours, and Garnacha Tinta, whose fat, jammy-fruit flavours fade fast. Some Riojas are made entirely of Tempranillo, but most are a blend. Of the minor grapes, Graciano and Mazuelo, Graciano has recently been coming back into favour because, though difficult to grow, its flavour is excellent.

In 1988, the wine companies spent over 12,000 million pesetas on improvements, more than the total value of exports that year. With such investment, Rioja could be set to recapture the quality that made its name famous in the 1970s. But it will never be a cheap wine again.

LA RIOJA ALTA
Rioja DO
RIOJA

🍷 Tempranillo, Garnacha Tinta, Graciano and others

🥂 Macabeo (Viura), Malvasía de Rioja

La Rioja Alta is still mainly owned by three of the five original families that founded the business in 1890, plus a number of other shareholders. 'We can't compete on quantity, so we've had to compete on quality' was the way the export director summed up the attitude of this excellent *bodega* when we last visited. Although La Rioja Alta only makes a tiny one per cent of Rioja wine, it sells almost one-fifth of *all* the *reserva* and *gran reserva* wine made in the region. In the past few years, it has made massive investments, building a new cellar with huge, stainless steel vats for blending wines, a new laboratory and vastly extended space for maturing wine. There will be room for 12,000 more barrels – wood ageing is one of the major hallmarks of this traditionally-minded *bodega*. Indeed, La Rioja Alta is to stop producing *crianza* wines and concentrate on *reserva* and *gran reserva*. Viña Alberdi, till now a *crianza*, is to become a *reserva* from the 1986 vintage onwards, with longer wood ageing. Viña Alberdi and the *reserva* Viña Arana contain about 70 per cent Tempranillo and are both rather light, elegant wines. The other *reserva*, Viña Ardanza, is a fuller, richer wine, with about 60 per cent Tempranillo and a higher proportion of Garnacha Tinta. *Gran reservas*, labelled with the numbers 904 and 890, are produced only in the finest years, and, for Reserva 890, the wine has to be truly exceptional. About one-third of the wine is made from the *bodega's* own grapes, grown in some of the best parts of the Rioja Alta region. Of the rest, half is bought in as grapes, half as young wine. Almost all the production is of red wine. The only white wine is the very good Viña Ardanza Reserva Blanco, not as aggressively oaky as Marqués de Murrieta's white, though along similar lines – but, so far, it is made only in tiny quantities. To be able to offer enough good white wine to its clients, La Rioja Alta recently bought the Galician *bodega*, Fernández Cervera Hermanos, which makes a fine Albariño, Lagar de Cervera.

RIOJANAS
Rioja DO
RIOJA

🍷 Tempranillo, Cariñena (Mazuelo), Graciano, Cabernet Sauvignon

🍷 Tempranillo, Garnacha Tinta

🥂 Macabeo (Viura), Malvasía de Rioja

The Artacho family, owners of Bodegas Riojanas for decades, recently sold half their shares to the Banco de Santander in order to finance massive improvements to the *bodega*. These should be completed during 1991, and will, claim Riojanas, make them 'the most modern winery in Rioja'. The old wooden vats are to be conserved as museum pieces, while the concrete vats, used for carbonic maceration, will eventually go. (Riojanas are fairly unusual amongst commercial *bodegas* in still making a considerable proportion of their wines by the traditional, carbonic maceration method, fermenting the grapes whole and uncrushed for a more strikingly fruity effect.) Some of Riojanas' wines were already fermented in stainless steel, and this will now be the norm. They are also buying 15,000 new wooden barrels to age their wine, to add to the 15,000 already in the cellars.

About one-third of their grapes come from 200 hectares (494 acres) of vineyards that either belong to them or are controlled by them on a semi-permanent basis. Of the rest, one-fifth is bought in as grapes, four-fifths as wine, practically all from growers and co-operatives in the Rioja Alta and Alavesa.

Reds are the *bodega's* main business, and the best are the *reservas* and the *gran reservas*, which are consistently fine even before the improvements take effect. Both come under two brand names, Viña Albina, soft, plummy, elegant and principally Tempranillo, and Monte Real, a bigger, darker, more tannic wine with complex wild strawberry and cedar flavours, which contains some Garnacha, but is also predominantly Tempranillo. The younger reds, the basic Canchales and Puerta Vieja Crianza, are both made entirely from Tempranillo. Monte Real Blanco Crianza, peachy and oaky, is one of Rioja's best whites.

RIOJA

Just because you see a sign by the roadside welcoming you to Rioja, there's no reason to believe that you've arrived in the Rioja DO, even if the car window does give you an uninterrupted vista of vines. La Rioja, the autonomous region, has quite different boundaries from Rioja, the Denominación de Origen. Not all the vines that grow in the autonomous region are entitled to the name Rioja. And the Rioja DO stretches way out into neighbouring Navarra, where vines yield priority to asparagus, artichokes and spicy red peppers, all flourishing in the fertile soil, while a few patches of DO reach up into the hills of the Basque country (País Vasco) and west into Castilla-León.

There is a certain logic to the Rioja DO region taken as a whole. Named after the Oja, a tributary of the River Ebro, the region is centred on the Ebro valley and, for much of its length, is bounded to the north and south by chains of mountains. (Take a half-hour drive south of Logroño, through cornfields and vineyards, and you'll suddenly find yourself amid rough-hewn mountains of spectacular beauty, dotted with half-deserted villages.)

But when you get down to the three official sub-regions of Rioja – Rioja Alta, Rioja Alavesa and Rioja Baja – it soon becomes evident that the characteristics of the three regions are less clear-cut than sometimes suggested. The Rioja Baja (mostly in Navarra), accounting for 39 per cent of the Rioja DO, is indeed as hot and dry as books say, and its silt or clay soil does produce fatter, more alcoholic wines – generally from the Garnacha Tinta, which survives better than the Tempranillo in these conditions. But the borders between the Rioja Alavesa (which accounts for just 18 per cent of the total Rioja vineyard) and the Rioja Alta were drawn simply along the edges of the Basque province of Alava, a region with golden sandstone villages sited at strategic points on the lower slopes of the Sierra de Cantabria.

The most aromatic Tempranillo reds come from yellow calcareous clay which occurs all over the Rioja Alavesa and extends well into the Alta region; leaner, more long-lived Tempranillo wines come from these best parts of the Alta. Much more of the Alta soil is very similar to the silt and clay of the Baja and consequently grows Garnacha. But, unlike the Baja, both the Alta and the Alavesa have climates in which the hot, Mediterranean weather is moderated by cooler breezes from the Atlantic.

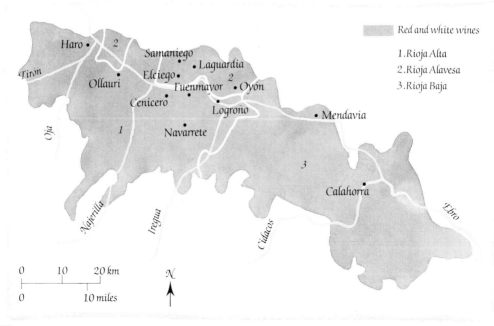

Red and white wines

1. Rioja Alta
2. Rioja Alavesa
3. Rioja Baja

GRAPE ENTRIES	CVNE
Cariñena	Domecq
Garnacha	Faustino Martínez
Graciano	Lagunilla
Macabeo (Viura)	Lan
Malvasía	López de Heredia
Tempranillo	Marqués de Cáceres
	Marqués de Murrieta
WINE ENTRY	Marqués de Riscal
Rioja	Martínez Bujanda
	Montecillo
WINERY ENTRIES	Muga
AGE	Navajas
Amézola de la Mora	Olarra
Barón de Ley	Palacio
Berberana	Paternina
Bilbainas	Remélluri
Campo Viejo	Rioja Alta
Contino	Riojanas
Corral	Virgen del Valle
El Coto	

▲ Autumn colours tint the vineyards of the Rioja Alta region under the gathering rainclouds – a welcome sight after the dry summer.

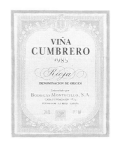

RUEDA DO
CASTILLA Y LEÓN

Winery entries: Álvarez y Diez, Marqués de Griñon, Marqués de Riscal

♀ Verdejo, Palomino, Macabeo (Viura), Sauvignon Blanc

Rueda itself is a smallish town hidden in a fold of gently undulating plateau not too far from the north-east tip of Portugal. As you drive past field after field of oats and barley you see first the steeple, then the earthenware tiles and finally the redbrick houses. You might miss the vines altogether, because although this is an area nearly the size of Rioja, it is more important for other crops, and the few thousand hectares of vines are mostly tucked away around the river Duero.

Rueda is capable of making some of Spain's best whites for two reasons. Firstly, the predominant grape variety, the Verdejo, has more character and flavour than most Spanish white grapes, making fresh, fruity, nutty wines with lots of body. And secondly, the Verdejo's potential is maximized here because of the altitude – between 700 and 800 metres (2300 to 2625 feet) above sea level – and consequent big temperature drops on summer nights, which enable the grapes to retain their aromas. Although Rueda was once famous for its fortified, sherry-style wines, the light, fresh whites are now far more important. Simple Rueda must be made from at least 25 per cent Verdejo (the rest being made up usually of Viura), while Rueda Superior must have a minimum of 60 per cent Verdejo, though the best have 100 per cent; Sauvignon Blanc is also an approved grape for Superior wines.

The fortified wines, which now scarcely leave the area, come in two styles: Pálido Rueda, *fino* sherry style; and Dorado Rueda like a Jerez *amontillado*. Reds and rosés are not included in the Rueda DO.

Our favourite Rueda is full, fresh, aromatic Marqués de Griñon made from the best Verdejo grapes at Bodegas Castilla La Vieja, who also make excellent wine under their own label, both fizzy and still. Marqués de Riscal is also good for simple Rueda and very good Reserva Limousin (aged in new oak) and Sauvignon Rueda Superior. Other good producers are Bodegas Ángel Rodriguez with the brand name Martinsancho, Bodegas Cerro Sol with Doña Beatriz, Vinos Sanz, and Álvarez y Diez.

SEGURA VIUDAS
Cava DO
CATALONIA

♂ Garnacha Tinta, Monastrell

♀ Parellada, Xarel-lo, Macabeo

Now a member of the huge Freixenet group, Segura Viudas still make their sparkling wine in their own premises, and indeed now also make the fizz for Conde de Caralt, another Freixenet name. The Segura Viudas wines all go simply under the Segura Viudas name, apart from the top-of-range Reserva Heredad, an expensive, lengthily-aged wine in a glitzy, hand-blown bottle. The youngest wine, Brut Reserva, is amongst the freshest-tasting Catalonian *cavas*, generally lacking the earthy flavour that, for us, mars most. Rosado Seco, Brut Vintage and Reserva Heredad Brut all have that typical *cava* earthiness.

SEÑORÍO DE SARRÍA
(BODEGA DE SARRÍA)
Navarra DO
NAVARRA

♂ Tempranillo, Garnacha Tinta, Cariñena (Mazuelo), Graciano

♂ Garnacha Tinta, Tempranillo, Macabeo (Viura)

♀ Macabeo (Viura), Malvasía

'Could do better' is this year's report on 'Bodega de Sarría', as it is now known. In fact the *bodega* has a good chance of turning over a new leaf, because the equivalent of £2 million has recently been spent on extensions and technical renovations in the winery. Finance is hardly in short supply for the winery of this beautiful estate, which has belonged since the early eighties to the Caja de Ahorros de Navarra, the local savings bank. A new stainless steel fermentation plant has been built to produce modern, fresh whites and rosés. Reds are currently pleasant but not exciting – soft, toffee-flavoured and curranty; some have just a hint of Cabernet Sauvignon in the flavour, some are slightly coarse. There *is* some Cabernet – five per cent of the estate's 150 hectares (371 acres) of vineyard is planted with Cabernet Sauvignon. Most of the remaining vines are Tempranillo, with some Mazuelo and Graciano, a very little Garnacha Tinta and about ten per cent white grapes – a mix of Malvasia and Viura: the right raw material to make top-class wine.

FELIX SOLÍS
Valdepeñas DO
CASTILLA-LA MANCHA

🍷 🍷 Tempranillo (Cencibel),
Airén, Cabernet Sauvignon

🍷 Airén, Chardonnay, Riesling,
Macabeo

Felix Solis is by far the biggest wine company in Valdepeñas and, according to the brothers who own it, the largest in the whole of Castilla-La Mancha. After upping capacity considerably in the last few years, they are now equipped to process 30 million kilos of grapes each autumn and to hold 40 million litres of wine. Despite the volume, however, Solís make – at the top of their range – some of the very best wines of Valdepeñas and some of the best-value wine in Spain.

In this predominantly white wine area, Solís have planted their own 700 hectares (1730 acres) of vineyards with red Cencibel (Tempranillo), plus the inevitable experimental plantations of Cabernet Sauvignon and a few foreign white-grape vines. By Valdepeñas tradition, a hefty dollop of white wine usually goes into the red wine blends, but Solis say they use no white in their top red, Viña Albali, which can be either *reserva* or *gran reserva*. These wines are aged in oak (some of it bought new every year) in cellars in the centre of Valdepeñas town. The *reservas* tend to be more impressive than the *gran reservas*, with a lovely oaky nose and good, meaty fruit, of a quality you don't expect from the central regions of Spain. Until recently, whites have not been their strong point, but the latest whites are also delicious, particularly the Viña Albali Early Harvest Blanco, super-fruity and aromatic, again way above average for the region. The bulk of the firm's business is in two other, cheaper brands, Soldepeñas and Los Molinos, which are to be found in restaurants all over Spain and are of decent basic quality.

SOMONTANO DO
ARAGÓN

🍷 🍷 Moristel, Tempranillo,
Garnacha Tinta, Parreleta

🍷 Macabeo, Garnacha Blanca,
Alcañón

Somontano means 'under the mountain', and that is just where this enchantingly pretty region is, isolated from other DO areas up in the foothills of the central Pyrenees. Youthful Pyrenean rivers and very adequate rainfall keep Somontano fresh and green right through the summer, the green broken here and there by the grey of poplars and olives; its altitude keeps the temperature bearable, while the mountains protect it from cold winter winds. So far, its wines – light, fresh, fragrant and flavourful – are little known outside Aragón, but there they are becoming extremely fashionable, and Somontano could well be the next star to burst upon the Spanish (and international) gastronomic scene. There have recently been experimental plantations of Cabernet Sauvignon, Chardonnay, Riesling and other international varieties – some of them already very successful. Most common amongst the traditional red grapes is the Moristel, exclusive to the region and quite characterful. Three-quarters of the wines are red and rosé.

The region became a DO in 1985. By far the biggest producer is the huge Co-operativa Comarcal Somontano de Sobrarbe in Barbastro, which makes nearly 90 per cent of all the region's wines. Their young Selección Montsierras Rosado and Tinto are good, and new-oak-aged Señorío de Lazan Reserva is excellent, with rich, concentrated raspberry fruit from mainly Tempranillo grapes with some Moristel. Until recently, five smaller-scale producers made up the rest. However, the delicious and inexpensive wines of a newcomer first came onto the market in 1990. COVISA (Compañia Vitivinícola del Somontano SA) was set up in the mid-eighties, funded by the Aragón regional government and its two main banks. They have built a modern winery and planted millions of vines in 500 hectares (1236 acres) of vineyards around the region. All the grapes they use come from their own vineyards. Viñas del Vero is the brand name. So far there's a soft, honeyed *blanco* made principally from Chenin Blanc, an attractively lemony-appley Chardonnay and even a Gewürztraminer. The *rosado* is attractive, fresh, creamy and dry and the young *tinto* is light, soft and plummy, with a hint of almond and a refreshing, damsony after-taste. This is a producer to watch.

TARRAGONA DO
CATALONIA

🍷 🍷 Garnacha Tinta, Cariñena, Tempranillo (Ull de Llebre)

🍷 Macabeo, Xarel-lo, Parellada, Garnacha Blanca

▲ Scrubby vineyards south of Flix in Terra Alta. Their crop goes to make sacramental wines for use in church services – a curious speciality of this wild, remote region. De Muller is the world's main supplier. They even sell to the Vatican! Neighbouring Tarragona also produces some communion wine.

Down the Catalan coast from Penedés, Tarragona is principally white wine country. It's co-op country, too, and much of the wine is sold off in bulk for blending elsewhere, especially to the *cava* companies of Penedés. Many of the whites, made in crude conditions, are heavy and alcoholic, but picked early, under the management of Tarragona's best firms such as Pedro Rovira and de Muller, Tarragona white grapes can turn into fairly aromatic, fruity and not *too* alcoholic wines. A quarter of Tarragona's wines are red, many of them made in the sub-region of Falset, where only red grapes are permitted for DO wines. This is the high, inland part of the region, up towards the spectacular mountains of Priorato, and the wines are very similar to those of Priorato, dark, astringent, heavy in alcohol (though generally lighter than Priorato's bruisers). Some reds are also made in the other, main sub-region, Tarragona Campo, with its more Mediterranean climate on the flat land near the coast and the gentler hills inland.

Tempranillo is permitted here, as well as the coarser Garnacha Tinta and Cariñena, and the better wineries can make more balanced, fruitier, lower-alcohol wines. Tarragona has two other DO styles: *rancio*, a wine of 14 per cent or more, aged for at least four years in wooden barrels and glass jars and really only of local interest; and Tarragona Clásico, which can be wonderful, rich and complex wines, aged for a minimum of 12 years in wood. These have a minimum alcohol of 13.5 per cent, but often more.

TEMPRANILLO

Spain's best native red grape is grown widely over the northern and central parts of the country. Tempranillo is an official 'principal variety' of the DOs of Rioja, Penedés, Ribera del Duero, Navarra, Valdepeñas, La Mancha, Utiel-Requena, Somontano and Toro. It goes by different names, however, in different regions: Tempranillo in Rioja and Navarra, but Tinto Fino or Tinto del País in Ribera del Duero, Tinto de Toro in Toro, Cencibel in La Mancha and Valdepeñas, and Ull de Llebre or Ojo de Liebre (hare's eye) in Catalonia. These are basically the same grape, sometimes with slight variations in local strains. The Tempranillo performs at its best in the cooler regions: Ribera del Duero, the Rioja Alavesa and Alta, and the higher parts of Penedés. Here, it can make elegant wines with good colour and balancing acidity, and combination of wild strawberry and spicy, tobaccoey flavours. It can be made into lovely young, fruity wines, and works well with the whole-grape method of fermentation typical of traditional Rioja *bodegas*, which gives especially fruity, aromatic results.

Tempranillo grapes are very low in the enzymes that help to cause oxidation (browning and spoiling of juice or wine) so the grapes are easy to handle at harvest time. The wines also keep well, and are very suitable for ageing in oak barrels: oak and Tempranillo flavours blend well, too. Such is its reputation for quality that it is now being planted in new areas, as well as being extended in areas where it is already grown. Cariñena, the Rioja Baja, Somontano, Navarra, Utiel-Requena and Almansa are all regions where Tempranillo plantations are spreading.

TERRA ALTA DO
CATALONIA

🍷 🥂 Cariñena, Garnacha Tinta, Garnacha Peluda

🥂 Garnacha Blanca, Macabeo

This separate DO within the province of Tarragona is really a continuation up into the hills of the Tarragona DO. It is wild, remote country, buffeted by strong winds and baked by hot sun in the summer, freezing in the winter, and with one of Spain's lowest rainfalls. Apart from vines, trained into small, stumpy bushes so as not to waste too much precious moisture on foliage, almonds and olives are about the only option open to farmers. Yields of grapes are tiny. The co-operatives handle almost all the wine-making, in fairly primitive equipment. Three-quarters of the wines are white, made mostly from the Garnacha Blanca, traditionally very alcoholic, now generally somewhere between 12 and 15 per cent and far from fine. Reds account for most of the rest, and there are also *rancios* and *generosos*. The region's best wines are made by the Tarragona companies of de Muller and Pedro Rovira.

TORO DO
CASTILLA Y LEÓN

🍷 Tempranillo (Tinto de Toro), Garnacha Tinta

🥂 Verdejo, Malvasía

Toro, not far from the city of Zamora and beyond that the northern Portuguese border, became a DO in 1987. For years, Toro has had one wine-making star, originally known as Bodegas Porto, now Bodegas Fariña. Fariña's reds are big and fairly alcoholic, but very well made, fruity and oaky – and reasonably cheap. General standards in Toro have been on the up, however, helped by the enthusiasm and co-operative spirit of the region's producers. A number of quality improvements were imposed by the new DO regulations which included a drop in minimum alcohol levels. The flat Toro country is deceptively high above sea level, at between 620 and 750 metres (2034 and 2460 feet), but lower, hotter and drier than the Ribera del Duero. Yields are very small indeed. The reds tend to be darker, more tannic, more alcoholic, lower in acidity and distinctly less fine (also vastly cheaper). Reds must be made at least three-quarters from the Tinto de Toro grape (alias Tempranillo), the rest being Garnacha Tinta, though the best wines are made entirely from Tinto de Toro. Whites are way behind reds in quality, and have not been helped by large plantations of Palomino – now banned for DO wines.

TORRES
Penedés DO
CATALONIA

🍷 Garnacha Tinta, Cariñena, Cabernet Sauvignon, Merlot, Pinot Noir, Tempranillo and others

🍷 Garnacha Tinta, Cariñena

🍷 Parellada, Gewürztraminer, Sauvignon Blanc, Riesling, Chardonnay and others

Spain's supreme winemaker must be Miguel Torres Junior. In recent years he has masterminded vineyards in California and Chile, but his main achievement remains the transformation of the extensive family vineyards and winery in his native Penedés. Since his return from wine-making studies in France in 1961, he has worked magic on the family wines. Bodegas Torres is now Spain's largest independently owned wine company. And the range of Torres wines is known and enthusiastically drunk around the world. The company owns 600 hectares (1500 acres) of vines, mostly in the cooler upper reaches of Penedés. Apart from substantial plantations of the local Parellada and Tempranillo, the vines are French varieties, planted close together on wires in a quite un-Spanish way. About half their grapes (mostly the local Catalan varieties) are bought from local growers, for whom they put on seminars and provide technical assistance.

White brands include the flavourful Viña Sol (Parellada), lively, pineappley, slightly oaky Gran Viña Sol (Parellada and Chardonnay), spicy Viña Esmeralda (Muscat d'Alsace and Gewürztraminer), floral, fragrant Waltraud (Riesling), and rich, grassy, oaky Fransola (Parellada and Sauvignon Blanc). Fransola was formerly called Gran Viña Sol Green Label and is one of a number of wines Torres have recently re-named or launched stressing their single vineyard origin – a great selling point in markets outside Spain. A recent departure from Penedés wines has been the lovely, rich and complex barrel-fermented Chardonnay from the company's Milmanda vineyard in neighbouring Conca de Barberá.

Red wines include two full-bodied wines from local grapes, Tres Torres and Gran Sangredetoro (both Garnacha and Cariñena), Coronas (Tempranillo), soft, oaky, blackcurranty Gran Coronas (Cabernet and Tempranillo) and Viña Magdala (Pinot Noir and Tempranillo), perhaps the least successful of Torres's innovative combinations. Another of the renamed single-vineyard wines, Mas La Plana (formerly Gran Coronas Black Label), Torres has made solely from Cabernet Sauvignon since the 1978 vintage. In its youth, Mas La Plana is ripe and blackcurranty, backed up with good but not overdone oak ageing and it ages very well. Las Torres is a sweetly ripe, honeyed Merlot, with a touch of spicy oak, made from grapes harvested in four Torres-owned vineyards, and Mas Borras, a single vineyard Pinot Noir, is the latest to join the Torres family of single grape wines.

UTIEL REQUENA DO
VALENCIA

🍷 🍷 Bobal, Tempranillo, Garnacha Tinta

🍷 Macabeo, Merseguera, Planta Nova

Utiel-Requena – remote, high-altitude country an hour's drive west of Valencia city – is the source of some of Spain's best rosé. It is made principally from the Bobal grape, and with modern methods is now often light, fresh and fragrant. Much of the wine, however, is sold (illegally) by neighbouring companies as Valencia DO rosé. They *could* label it Utiel-Requena, but to do so they would have to bottle it in one of the ten small towns of the DO region, which would mean going to the expense of building bottling plants only 20km or so from their current plants in the Valencia DO region. The authorities in both regions turn a blind eye.

The producers of Utiel-Requena have been making great efforts to improve quality, especially since they were granted DO status in 1987. Apart from the sometimes excellent rosés, there are also good reds with a strong, herby character in which there is now an ever greater proportion of Tempranillo as new plantations come into production. Like other DOs within the autonomous region of Valencia, Utiel-Requena also makes strong, dark red *tinto doble pasta*, made with a double dose of colour and tannin-rich skins. There are also 'Champagne-method' sparkling wines (granted the Cava DO in March 1989) and still whites, which can be fresh, but never characterful since the grapes are bland.

VALDEORRAS DO
GALICIA

🍷 Garnacha Tintorera (Alicante), Mencía, Grau Negro and others

🍷 Palomino, Godello, Doña Blanca

Valdeorras is a poor third in the Galician DOs, although the largest in vineyard area, with 2500 hectares (6178 acres) currently in production. The land is poor and mountainous, and the inhabitants have little alternative to vine-growing, just about the only form of agriculture that offers any sort of return. And that return is poor, scarcely enough to prevent a drift away from the region by young men and women anxious to find more rewarding ways of making a living. The problem is compounded by the fact that 70 per cent of vines planted are of the vastly inferior Palomino and Alicante varieties, which can never be expected to produce wine of any quality. There are moves to replant the grapes native to the area, mainly the white Godello and the red Mencia, but the process is slower than elsewhere in Galicia as replanting costs money, and there's not a lot of money to spare in Valdeorras.

Production is dominated by two co-operatives, in Barco de Valdeorras and La Rua, both of which have upgraded their wine-making equipment recently, and are able to make good wines – as long as they can get good .grapes from their members. There are a few other privately-owned *bodegas*, well-equipped and making good wines from Godello, but their wines are not seen outside Spain, and seldom outside Galicia. Overall, the picture in Valdeorras is more encouraging than it was three years ago, but the Valdeorras wines still have a long way to go before they become interesting to an international market.

VALDEPEÑAS DO
CASTILLA-LA MANCHA

Winery entries: Los Llanos, Solís

🍷 🍷 Tempranillo (Cencibel), Airén

🍷 Airén

Though some of Spain's best red wine bargains come from this hot, dry, undulating country in the south of the great central plains, much of the region's output is still very poor. Valdepeñas has been slower to wake up to modern wine-making than its gigantic neighbour, La Mancha.

One of the main problems with Valdepeñas red wines is the large proportion of white grapes that goes into the blends. Valdepeñas used to be a red wine region until the vines were devastated by the phylloxera louse at the beginning of this century. When it was eventually replanted, white Airén grapes predominated, and the dull Airén now accounts for nearly 85 per cent of the vineyards. The rest is Cencibel (alias Tempranillo), and the authorities are trying to encourage growers to choose this characterful red grape when replanting, but growers here are a stubborn lot, not easily persuaded by market trends. Red Valdepeñas wines are in great demand, and the wineries simply can't get enough grapes. This led to a scandal during the 1989 vintage. The Consejo Regulador, the region's ruling body, illegally authorized the purchase of three million kilos of red grapes from outside the region, for use in Valdepeñas DO reds and *claretes*. The president got the sack, the deal was cancelled – and Valdepeñas remains short of reds.

The most common style of Valdepeñas, very popular in Spain, is *clarete*, a pale red made with a legal minimum of 20 per cent Cencibel, otherwise with white grapes. These wines can easily shoot up to a headache-inducing 15 per cent of alcohol (though the best are now kept at around 12.5 per cent) but colour and flavour-wise, this is feeble stuff, as is much of the red, because most reds also contain hefty dollops of Airén. Apart from lacking flavour and obviously doing nothing for the colour, tannin and body of red wines, Airén ages badly, tasting dull and tired within a couple of years, long before many of these wines find their way into a glass. The best reds contain nothing but Cencibel. *Bodega* names to look out for are Los Llanos and Felix Solis (under brand name Viña Albali), who make some good oak-aged *reservas* and *gran reservas* for very reasonable prices. Luis Megía is also quite good for younger wines. Some rosés and whites are now made by modern methods, and are simple, fresh and fruity, rather like the whites of La Mancha.

VALDESPINO
Jerez y Manzanilla DO
ANDALUCÍA

♀ Palomino Fino, Pedro Ximénez

This old-fashioned, family-owned sherry company makes wines of very fine quality in limited quantities. Its Inocente *bodega*, in an old monastery with paved patio and beautiful gardens, is one of the oldest in Jerez. Most unusually nowadays, Valdespino still ferments most of its wines in wooden casks (rather than stainless steel) and blends from a myriad of individual wines. Valdespino's best-known wine is the lovely, classic Fino Inocente, made from grapes from its Inocente vineyard. In total, the company owns 275 hectares (680 acres) of vines and also buys in grapes. Other wines include Tío Diego, a good, subtle *amontillado* (in such demand in Spain that it often runs out), a richly flavourful, *amontillado*-style Palo Cortado Cardenal, dark, dry, powerful Amontillado Coliseo, dry, nutty-tangy Don Tomás Amontillado, complex, malty, raisiny Don Gonzalo Old Dry Oloroso and, for the sweet-toothed, a dense, demerara-and-raisin flavoured Pedro Ximénez Solera Superior. They also make brandy and excellent sherry vinegar.

VALENCIA DO
VALENCIA

♟ ♀ Monastrell, Forcayat, Garnacha Tinta, Garnacha Tintorera

♀ Merseguera, Malvasiá, Planta Fina and others

This fairly recent DO (declared in 1987), the northernmost of the cluster of DOs down in the south-east, is one of Spain's big exporters. Much of the wine is made in co-operatives, but it is the five big private companies that do most of the foreign trade. It is interesting that of the five – Vinival, Schenk, Vincente Gandía, Valsangiacomo and Egli – four have Swiss shareholders: the disciplined Swiss appreciate the enterprising attitude of the Valencianos!

Valencian wines are reasonably cheap, even after recent price rises, and can be good value if well made. They can never be great wines, because the raw materials are boring grape varieties. Most of the wines are white, and mostly made from the unimpressive Merseguera grape, with some reds and rosés made largely from Garnacha Tinta and Garnacha Tintorera, and from the Monastrell in the south of the region. None of these is a great grape, but *bodegas* here are among the most modern in Spain, and technology can at least ensure good pig-leather purses, if not silk ones. Wines sold on export markets will be labelled

simply as Valencia DO, but visitors to the region or nearby beaches will find wines from four sub-regions. Alto Turia, up in the hilly north of the region with only ten per cent of the Valencia DO vineyards, makes the best whites – dry wines from the Merseguera, but fruity and well balanced by acidity. Valentino in the centre and north, is the biggest area, with 60 per cent of the vineyards; its whites, reds and rosés can all vary from dry to sweet. Eight of the Valentino municipalities have recently been declared (along with one other municipality) part of the new sub-region Moscatel de Valencia, specializing in lusciously sweet, grapy combinations of Moscatel juice and wine alcohol. The fourth region, Clariano in the south with 30 per cent of the vineyards, makes dry whites, reds and rosés.

Sensibly, minimum legal alcohol levels were recently reduced, so almost all Valencia wines can now be as low as 11 per cent of alcohol, Alto Turia wines even down to ten.

VEGA SICILIA
Ribera del Duero DO
CASTILLA Y LEÓN

Tempranillo (Tinto Fino), Cabernet Sauvignon, Merlot, Malbec

Even the King of Spain is on strict allocation for the legendary reds of Vega Sicilia, Spain's most expensive wine. The estate has been famed since the last century for its rich, fragrant, complex and long-lasting wines, and the world still clamours for more – only one-fifth of the limited production is exported. Prices of Vega Sicilia wines were always extremely high, vying with the prices paid for top Bordeaux, but they have risen dramatically in recent years, cashing in like everyone else in the region on the sudden popularity of Ribera del Duero wines generally. Vega Sicilia's owners are not wholly delighted by their neighbours' success, however: they are currently lobbying for a separate DO all for themselves, and to that end have stopped buying in a small proportion of their grapes from surrounding growers, limiting themselves to grapes grown on their own estate.

The estate as a whole, a mixed farm, extends over 1000 hectares (2471 acres), but at present only 120 hectares (297 acres) is allocated to grapes. Vega Sicilia is unique in Ribera del Duero in the extensive use it makes of the Bordeaux grape varieties. Cabernet Sauvignon makes up about 25 per cent of most blends, Malbec and Merlot another 15 per cent, and the local Tinto Fino (Tempranillo) the remaining 60 per cent. They intend to increase Cabernet to around 40 per cent.

Apart from the extraordinary richness of the grapes themselves, one of the main hallmarks of Vega Sicilia wines has been unusually long (even for Spain) wood ageing. Depending on the vintage (and vintages vary considerably in Ribera del Duero) the top red, Vega Sicilia Único, would spend up to ten years in large wooden vats and oak barrels – new and old, American and French. That was fine for traditional Spanish tastes, but foreigners often suggested that these wines, still richly alive and complex after treatment that would kill most other great wines, would be even greater given more time in bottle and less in wood. At last, the *bodega's* policy is changing. They won't say by how much they will reduce the ageing periods, but their declared intention is to switch more of the ageing time out of oak and into bottle, releasing the top wines for sale perhaps on average ten years after the vintage. They will also be using a higher proportion of new (and therefore flavour giving) oak barrels, and buying more of the finer French rather than American oak variety.

Apart from Único, made from the best grapes from the oldest vineyards, Vega Sicilia also makes two lesser but also excellent wines under the name Valbuena, one released after three years, the other after five. Even these, with their rich fruit and complex vanilla and wild strawberry flavours, equate with really fine Riojas.

◄ The house at Vega Sicilia lies a little way beyond the cellars, which have recenty been extensively renovated behind their old facades.

VERDEJO

The Verdejo is one of Spain's few characterful white grapes, capable of making crisp, fruity white wines that are full in body without being too high in alcohol, and slightly nutty in flavour. Modern winemakers measure the body of a wine by analysing its 'dry extract' – the solid remains left after the wine has been boiled dry in the laboratory – and the Verdejo is unusual for a white wine in having a very high dry extract, higher even than that of many red Riojas. Sadly, there is not much Verdejo planted – only just over 7000 hectares (17,300 acres) in the whole of Spain. Its main habitat is Rueda, over towards the north-eastern tip of the Portuguese border. The best Rueda contains nothing but Verdejo, and there must be a minimum 60 per cent Verdejo in the top-category wines, Rueda Superior. It is also used in Rueda to make the traditional sherry-style wines, aged in wooden barrels under *flor*. The rest of Spain's Verdejo grows in surrounding areas, such as Toro and Ribera del Duero.

VINÍCOLA NAVARRA
Navarra DO
NAVARRA

☥ Garnacha Tinta, Tempranillo, Cariñena (Mazuelo), Graciano

☥ Garnacha Tinta

☥ Macabeo (Viura), Malvasía de Rioja

Vinícola Navarra is one of the most improved producers in the Navarra region. Over £2 million spent since 1983 has re-equipped them with new, temperature-controlled wine-making facilities, ultra-modern filters and bottling line, and 2000 new oak barrels to age their top quality red wines. The company, started in 1864 by a Frenchman fleeing the ravages of phylloxera, is now owned by the giant Bodegas y Bebidas group (formerly SAVIN). They have wineries at Sansol (very close to Rioja), where they ferment their red wines, and at Campañas (in the heart of Navarra), where they make whites and rosés.

The only vineyard they own at present – 10 hectares (25 acres) – is planted with Cabernet Sauvignon, not yet in production. They make 45 per cent of their wine from bought-in grapes. The rest is bought in as wine from co-operatives, then aged and blended.

Las Campañas white and rosé are fresh, appealing modern wines, and there are small quantities of an even better rosé, Castillo de Javier. When it comes to reds, the main factor is the availability of Tempranillo and Cabernet Sauvignon grapes to replace the Garnacha with which most of Navarra is still planted. But the *bodega* is confident that, with yearly investments in more new oak barrels, and more Tempranillo being planted, there will be 'dramatic improvements' within five years. For the time being, we prefer the Las Campañas Tinto Crianza, with creamy, curranty fruit and a nice hint of new oak, to the older (and more expensive) Castillo de Tiebas Tinto Reserva.

VIRGEN DEL VALLE
Rioja DO
PAÍS VASCO

☥ Tempranillo

One of the most popular styles of red in the north of Spain comes from the Rioja Alavesa – Tempranillo wine made by carbonic, or whole berry, maceration. The main principle is that the grapes are fermented without being crushed, and fermentation actually happens *inside* each grape, resulting in a particularly fruity, soft style of wine, similar to Beaujolais.

This is the kind of wine Javier Fauste knew he wanted to make when he bought the old co-op at Samaniego which had stopped making wine 13 years previously. It took him a year and a half to rebuild, and his first vintage was the 1988. Wine made by carbonic maceration is not meant to age but should be sold in time for Christmas and drunk before next year's harvest. Virgen del Valle wine is aromatic, with a rich, savoury, plummy flavour, probably the best of this style we have tasted in Rioja.

About 25 per cent of the wine made is destined to become *crianza* or *reserva*, and this is made in the usual way for reds, with the grapes crushed before fermentation, then aged in small oak barrels. This, too, is richly fruity and should turn into excellent wine.

XAREL-LO

This low-quality grape is the curse of *cava*, though few *cava* producers would admit it. Most Catalan *cava* (and that means practically all Spanish *cava*) is made from a blend of Xarel-lo with the somewhat higher quality Macabeo and the much higher quality Parellada. While none of these three grapes is capable of retaining its fruitiness and freshness throughout the lengthy ageing periods to which much *cava* is subjected, Xarel-lo takes on a particularly unfortunate earthy flavour within a couple of years – and it is precisely this earthiness that we personally dislike so much in the majority of *cavas*. When young and scrupulously made, Xarel-lo wine can show an attractive gooseberries and cream character, but it can easily become over-alcoholic and coarse, or just bland. Some of the best producers in Penedés wisely choose to leave it out of their blends. Xarel-lo is a Catalan exclusivity, but it grows there in such profusion that it ranks as Spain's sixth most-planted white grape variety. It accounts for nearly one-third of white plantings in Penedés, is also very common in Tarragona, and is the principal white grape of Alella, where it goes by the name of Pansá Blanca. In all these places, it makes still wines as well as sparkling, and in Penedés and Tarragona gets blended with Parellada and Macabeo as for the sparkling wines.

YECLA DO
MURCIA

🍷 🍷 Monastrell, Garnacha Tinta

🍷 Merseguera, Verdil

Sandwiched in the midst of the DO regions of Valencia, in the north of the autonomous region of Murcia, Yecla makes mostly roughish, high-alcohol reds, indistinguishable from the traditional wines of its neighbour Jumilla. But while Jumilla is well on its way into the twentieth century and beginning to find more customers for its wines, Yecla, apart from the odd clued-up producer, such as Bodegas Castaño, is lagging way behind, and its exports have all but dried up. The world simply doesn't want this sort of wine any more. Most of Yecla's wine is sold off ignominiously in bulk (a lot of it destined for distillation), to Eastern Europe, North and South America, Africa, other EC countries and even to Australia and Japan. The region's main producer, mega-co-op La Purísima, whose tentacles have been so all-embracing that other smaller wineries in the region have found it difficult to buy grapes outside their own vineyards, is in a financial mess. Recently, though, some good red Monastrell – picked earlier than usual and fermented at low temperatures, but still high in alcohol – has started to appear, and also some young, fresh but alcoholic rosé. Yecla is beginning to listen to suggestions from the nearby Jumilla research station.

If you go to the region, you'll find seven styles of wine available, though only the simple Yecla *tinto*, *rosado* and *blanco* find their way abroad. On the spot, you can also buy a pale red, Yecla *clarete*, and three more alcoholic brews, Yecla *doble pasta* (made as in Jumilla), and two wines from a sub-region, Yecla Campo Arriba *tinto* and *clarete*, which can have up to 16 per cent of alcohol and must have a *minimum* of 14 per cent

It's not surprising that Yecla's wines resemble those of Jumilla – the grapes, climate and soil are all practically the same (Yecla is just a fraction less hot and dry). The only other difference worth mentioning is that Yecla has a slightly higher proportion of white grapes, Merseguera and Verdil. Most decisive for the character of the wines is the climate: extremely hot, dry summers, freezing winters, and scant, stormy rainfall in the spring and autumn. The soil is poor, chalky and stony, producing tiny yields, and risible incomes for the growers. Yecla is a very small region, the only one of Spain's DOs to consist of only one municipality, the town of Yecla. If logic rather than politics ruled the Spanish DO system, Yecla would simply have been part of the Jumilla DO.

PORTUGAL

It's frustrating writing about Portuguese wines. Here you have a country brimming with natural advantages for winemakers: flavourful native grapes, a range of climates to suit almost any kind of wine, and well-established traditions of grape-growing to provide the basis for a modern wine era second to none. The place is sizzling with potential. Yet every time you sum up the situation, the actuality is that Portugal is one of the most conservative wine countries in Europe. Tradition bogs down the pace of progress, there is a chronic shortage of money to buy more advanced technology in the co-operatives (which account for about 70 per cent of output), and the international varieties (Cabernet Sauvignon, Chardonnay and even Riesling) have begun their insidious march into the Portuguese wine scene.

But perhaps that paints an unnecessarily gloomy picture. There are plus points, too. Much of the wine *not* made in the co-ops comes from modern, very well-organized wine merchants. At last Portugal has begun the process of denominating more of its traditional wine regions, so long hidden under the cloaks of brand names or merchants' *garrafeiras* and *reservas*. And some of the more clued-up co-ops have taken advantage of EC grants to modernize their wine-making facilities.

Yet still there is the feeling that the Portuguese themselves like their wines the way they have always been, that the bright, modern flavours introduced by winemakers trained in far-away wine cultures such as California and Australia are unwelcome – not *traditional*, and therefore not good.

Now, what the Portuguese choose to think about what they drink is their own affair, you might say. But when it is enshrined in official legislation forbidding winemakers to do otherwise, that is another matter. And there's quite a lot of that in Portugal.

For one thing, the Portuguese make a great thing about the difference between young (*verde*) and old (*maduro*) wines. Until the Minho region cornered the exclusivity on Vinho Verde as a name, this just referred to *young* wine of the immediately preceding vintage. *Maduro* wine was wine that had been aged for longer, sometimes a *lot* longer. And that was what the Portuguese really preferred. *Vinho verde* was too flippant and easy – OK to wash down a plate of *bacalhão* and boiled potatoes, but not serious enough to require comment and concentration.

So the rules required certain minimum ageing periods in some regions, resulting in wines that tasted of very little and without any trace of youthful fruit. Wines that were delicious young were sacrificed on the altar of barrel- and bottle-age, to appease Portuguese taste – a taste that had been developed through centuries of not knowing *how* to make wines. Reds were fermented skins and all, and usually turned out too tannic; whites were often exhausted before they reached the bottle, let alone a shelf. Such whites were beyond redemption, while the only solution for reds was to age them until some of the astringency dropped out in the form of sediment.

But now this is slowly beginning to change. Go-ahead winemakers may not get much thanks from the die-hard domestic market, but the wines they are making are becoming more and more appreciated overseas. And the result is that some rules are being relaxed in Lisbon. The first areas to change for the better have been Dão and Colares (whose co-operative no longer has a monopoly on the region's wine-making), and there have been signs of cracks in the iron curtain of restrictions elsewhere.

Allied to the recognition of all the new IPR areas, this could spell a new era of prosperity and advancement for Portuguese wines. If the sheer variety of Portugal's landscape and grapes is allowed space to shine, the prospect is exhilarating. The north-west offers *vinho verde*, coming from lush, humid pastures where vineyards alternate with kiwi fruit plantations. The obvious star grapes are Alvarinho and Loureiro, both capable of making wines of dazzling aroma and flavour, as far removed from ordinary, commercial *vinho verde* as it would be possible to imagine.

Further to the east, the terraced vineyards of the Douro region are the source of one of the world's great fortified wines, port, as well as producing an ever-increasing number of fine table wines (mainly reds). Though the Douro is very dry, altitudes are high enough to have encouraged several sparkling wine producers to invest in the region, including famous names from both Champagne and California. The steep slopes of the Douro contrast sharply with the flat, coastal region of Bairrada, its soil part-sand, part-clay, studded with vineyards of gnarled Baga vines. But the rich red table wines of both regions owe their quality to the flavourful native vines, principally Touriga Nacional, Touriga Francesa and Tinta Roriz in the Douro, and Baga in Bairrada.

Touriga Nacional is the link between the Douro and Dão, the rolling granite hill-country to the east of Bairrada, and potentially one of Portugal's finest wine areas when production methods have been updated. Between here and Lisbon lie the majority of the new wine regions, in the large areas known as the Ribatejo and Oeste. The clue to the vast amounts of wine produced in these two areas lies in their mild climates. Torres, Alenquer and Arruda, the most important regions in the Oeste, have the benefit of cool Atlantic breezes to moderate Portugal's sizzling summer heat, while the climate in the Cartaxo, Santarém and Almeirim regions in the Ribatejo is softened by the River Tagus itself.

The regions round Lisbon are flagging somewhat – Colares, Bucelas and Carcavelos are all static if not shrinking in size. But the dynamic growth in the Setúbal peninsula and vast prairies of the Alentejo more than compensates for this, and these could turn out to be the spearhead regions of Portugal's advance into international wine markets. In the Setúbal peninsula, all the running is being made by two of Portugal's finest wine producers, whereas in the Alentejo, progress seems to be the result of the region's inherent potential to make fine wine.

All Portugal needs is the confidence to step forward wholeheartedly into twentieth-century wine-making, brandishing its splendid grapes and making the most of its beautiful and varied terrain. The people of Portugal are some of the most friendly and generous in Europe. It is time their wines caught up with them.

RD wine regions
IPR wine regions
Provincial boundary
1. Vinho Verde
2. Port and Douro
3. Dão
4. Bairrada
5. Bucelas
6. Colares
7. Carcavelos
8. Setúbal
9. Lagos
10. Portimão ⎫ Algarve
11. Lagoa
12. Tavora ⎭
13. Madeira

Madeira 850 kilometers (530 miles)

ALENQUER IPR
ESTREMADURA

Winery entry: Quinta de Abrigada

🍷 Camarate, Periquita (Mortagua), Preto Martinho, Tinta Miuda

🍷 Arinto, Fernão Pires, Jampal, Vital

If the whole project gets off the ground, the influence Lisbon's third airport will have on the little town of Ota is sadly predictable. Ota, one of only 13 villages in the recently demarcated area of Alenquer, will turn from growing vines to building warehouses. New roads will proliferate, light industry will flourish and hotels will mushroom.

We hope the airport-to-be's runways do not extend too far, because, on the evidence of wines from four properties, Alenquer has the potential to become one of Portugal's new stars. Part sheltered by mountains, it lies west of the Tagus river, north-east of Lisbon.

Some of the locals are particularly proud of their white wines (mainly composed of Fernão Pires and Vital), attributing their quality to winters and summers that are much cooler than in neighbouring Torres Vedras. But there are good reds as well (principally based on Periquita), from Quinta de Abrigada, Quinta de Pancas (where the owner has some Cabernet Sauvignon and Chardonnay in addition to local varieties), Quinta dos Plátanos and Quinta do Porto Franco. The first three of these bottle and export their wines, and are worth watching out for.

ALENTEJO

Winery entries: Esporão, Fonseca Successores (JS Rosado Fernandes), Pires

🍷 Periquita, Trincadeira, Tinta Roriz (Aragonez), Moreto

🍷 Roupeiro, Manteudo, Perrum, Rabo de Ovelha

In Spain or Portugal, it would be difficult to survey an area roughly the size of Belgium without finding a few wine regions. And so it proves in the Alentejo, a vast province to the east and south of Lisbon that occupies most of the southern half of the country. Five regions, in fact, were raised to IPR status in 1989 (Portalegre, Borba, Redondo, Reguengos and Vidigueira), and they are not the only contenders in this vast area. Moura, 25km (16 miles) to the south-east of Vidigueira, is where João Pires have made their latest vineyard purchases, while Évora boasts the immaculate Eugenio de Almeida estate and its Cartuxa wines, named after the Carthusian monks who live on the property.

Co-operatives dominate wine-making in the Alentejo, even more than elsewhere in Portugal, and for years have been turning out acceptable to good wine. As well as the co-ops, there are also a number of estates known for their quality. Among the most outstanding are Esporão and JS Rosado Fernandes (José Maria da Fonseca Successores), both in Reguengos, and Quinta do Carmo, near Estremoz. This, like JS Rosado Fernandes, is a judicious blend of ancient and modern, all the crushing of the grapes being done by foot in magnificent palest pink marble *lagares* (Estremoz is, after all, the centre of the Portuguese marble industry), but the fermentation of the whites is in stainless steel vats.

Other wines worth mentioning are Tapada de Chaves, just outside Portalegre, Paço dos Infantes, from near Moura, Horta do Rocio, from Borba, and Mouchão, a little to the north-west of Estremoz.

ALGARVE

🍷 Negra Mole, Periquita

🍷 Crato Branco, Boal Branco

The Algarve, with its beaches, golf courses and hotels, makes a sterling contribution to the Portuguese economy. Maybe this is why the wine-growers of the region were given their own RD in 1980. Maybe the reason was political. Whatever the motive, it had little to do with the quality of the wine, which is universally disappointing. All but three per cent of the wine is red, although it's a pretty feeble red, high in alcohol and low in colour and flavour.

The latest development in the wine life of the Algarve is that the region has been sub-divided into four separate RDs: Lagoa, Lagos, Portimão and Tavira. So, out of only 14 RDs in Portugal, four are in the Algarve, easily the least-distinguished wine region. As things stand at the moment, the Algarve is one region of Portugal in which we unhesitatingly suggest that you make no effort to find out about the local wines if you go there on holiday. And you won't meet them elsewhere.

CAVES ALIANÇA
Bairrada RD, Dão RD, Douro RD, Vinho Verde RD
BEIRA LITORAL

🍷 Bairrada: Baga, Tinta Pinheira, Moreto

🍷 Baga, Tinta Pinheira, Moreto

🍷 Bairrada: Bical, Fernão Pires (Maria Gomes), Cerceal
Espumante: Loureiro, Bical, Fernão Pires, Cerceal

Caves Aliança, still family-owned, is one of the largest wine companies in Portugal – both in sales and exports. Based in Bairrada, its main source of income is sparkling wine. It is also among the best producers of red Bairrada, however, because of a forward-looking approach to wine-making, and the own-label reds from Dão and Douro are both very good.

The white Bairradas get the full modern treatment. The juice is chilled and left in contact with the skins for up to 24 hours, to extract as much flavour as possible; it is then filtered and fermented at only 12°C. At that low temperature it sometimes takes six weeks to accomplish what could be done in one. The result is pleasant, but lacks character.

The red Bairradas can be even more revolutionary. The stalks are removed from the bunches of grapes (unusual in Bairrada). Some of the juice is macerated with the skins for about a day to extract red colour but not the bitter-flavoured tannins; this juice is then fermented separately to give a softer, more aromatic wine.

Many of these ideas come from the winemaker, Dido Mendes, who studied at the renowned University of California Davis College. Even the conventionally-made Aliança red Bairradas are fruity and easy to drink, though with plenty of ageing potential. The company makes all the white wine for its fizz, but does buy in red and white from other regions such as Dão, Douro and Vinho Verde to sell under the Aliança label.

ARINTO

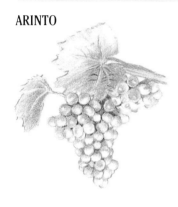

Two quite different grapes go under this name in Portugal, but the most common and distinctly the finer is the Arinto de Bucelas. It is the principal white grape of Bucelas – where it must make up at least 75 per cent of the white blends – but it also grows right down the length of Portugal from Vinho Verde country in the north (known here as Pedernã) to the Alentejo in the south. Arinto grapes are remarkable in being able to retain their acidity even in the hottest of climates – a wonderful asset in a country such as Portugal. Young wines made from the Arinto are often boring, with refreshingly high acidity but a very bland flavour; if well made, however, they can have a fresh, fruity, citrus character, and develop interesting and complex lemony-resiny flavours with up to five years' ageing. The high acidity makes the Arinto a good base for sparkling wines. Unfortunately, though it is a recommended grape in practically every Portuguese region (except Dão and the Algarve), growers tend to favour other higher-yielding and less rot-prone varieties.

In Dão, locals use the name 'Arinto' for a quite different vine. The Arinto do Dão makes rather alcoholic wines that lack the acidity and ageing potential of the other version.

ARRUDA IPR
ESTREMADURA

🍷 Camarate, Periquita, Tinta Miuda

🍷 Fernão Pires, Jampal, Vital

Arruda, 40km (25 miles) north of Lisbon, is one of the districts in line for RD status, provided it comes through its probationary period satisfactorily. Like Alenquer, Arruda is shielded from the damper Atlantic climate by mountains to the north and west. Many of its 7000 or so hectares (approximately 17,000 acres) are planted on softly rolling hills, topped by windmills formerly used to grind corn, now disconsolately abandoned.

So far, no wine from the impressive manor houses that stand in undulating vineyards has escaped outside the region, but this can only be a matter of time. One-third of the region's vineyards are farmed by members of the co-op, so their wines dominate Arruda's production. Facilities at the co-op are not particularly modern – fermentation is in cement vats, uncooled – but the red wines are light and plummily fruity, best young as they do not improve much beyond three years old. White wines are not inspiring.

ALENTEJO

It would be inaccurate to describe the Alentejo as flat, but it's not exactly mountainous, either. As you drive across the gently undulating plains, it feels more like riding the rollers of a boundless inland ocean than exploring the countryside of southern Portugal. Scattered, whitewashed farmhouses survey the surrounding land from the brows of small hills – with enough of a vista to watch protectively over flocks of sheep, herds of cattle, olive plantations or vines.

The best-run farms of the Alentejo make as much money out of olive oil, cork, cereals and livestock as they do out of wine. And around the towns of Estremoz, Borba and Vila Viçosa, vineyard owners find it hard to attract locals to do the seasonal work vines demand: they are all gainfully employed in the traditional, and profitable, local marble industry.

Add to this a reputation for indolence, and it is hard to understand how any wine gets made in this vast, remote region. Summers are hot enough for work to come to a standstill towards midday. Dogs seek any precious patch of shade, and lie there, tongues lolling and panting. Human activity slows to the point at which crossing a road to greet an acquaintance becomes a major expedition. Yet most of the area's wine regions, in the more northerly Alto Alentejo province, are at a high enough altitude for spring and autumn nights to become distinctly chilly.

In this climate, you might expect the region's reputation to be based on its red wines. Few white grape varieties escape unscathed from such sweltering daytime heat, but many red varieties can cope, especially with the benefits of cool nights to help them retain some of their aromas. However, historically, this has not been the case. Even now, the reputation of Vidigueira is specifically founded on its whites, though recent improvements in wine-making facilities should bring the reds up to scratch as well as consolidating the position of the whites. The advantage Alentejo whites enjoy comes principally from the characterful Roupeiro grape variety, capable of retaining a decent level of acidity through the hot Alentejo summers.

Most experts would agree, however, that the Alentejo is red wine country, producing rich, long-lived reds that need some years to develop their full potential. The brightest hopes are from the countryside around the busy town of Portalegre, the furthest north of the five current IPR areas. The vineyards are on higher ground than most of the Alentejo, sheltered from the continental heat of central Spain by the granite mountains of São Mamede immediately to the east. Consequently, the weather is cooler, acidity levels are higher, and the wines finer. José Maria da Fonseca Successores have already released a richly fleshy, oaky, rather New-World style red called Morgado de Reguengo, fermented in stainless steel and aged (briefly) in new Limousin oak barrels, from an estate near Portalegre.

In addition, red wines from Borba and Reguengos are already showing the potential of their regions, and the new João Pires estate at Moura and the Cartuxa wines from Évora make good cases for creating yet more demarcated regions in the Alentejo – the most rapidly developing and exciting table wine area of Portugal.

Red and white wines

1. Portalegre
2. Borba
3. Redondo
4. Reguengos
5. Vidigueira

GRAPE ENTRIES
Arinto
Baga
Fernão Pires
Periquita
Roupeiro

WINE ENTRIES
Alentejo
Reguengos

WINERY ENTRIES
Esporão
Fonseca Successores
João Pires

◀ Vines and cornfields near Serpa in the Baixo Alentejo. So far, the Baixo Alentejo has only one IPR region, Vidigueira, but there is plenty of wine-making potential in this southerly province.

BAGA

This grape is pronounced 'bugger', and historically it has lived up to its name! Baga grapes are thick-skinned and rich in colour and tannins, giving dense red wines that can be bitterly astringent; this is especially true if, in line with tradition, skins *and* stalks are left in for a week or more with the fermenting juice. It is a fairly late variety and depends very much on a hot, sunny September to ripen to perfection. In less than optimum conditions, the resulting wines can be high in acidity, which adds to their astringency (but can make for good fizz – sparkling red Baga is a wonderful foil to roast sucking pig, *leitão*). Portuguese producers have been known to complain that Baga produces wines too low in alcohol, but we drinkers are more likely to breathe a sigh of relief.

However, modern methods of wine-making have revealed the true potential of this grape. Given the removal of stalks before fermentation, shorter fermentations on the skins, and new techniques for extracting colour without too much tannin, the Baga can turn out deliciously rich, fruity and duskily fragrant wines, still generally with a firm structure of tannin and acidity, but in a few cases quite soft and approachable.

The Baga is Portugal's most planted red grape variety and is widespread. Its principal habitat is Bairrada, where it covers 90 per cent of the vineyards, but it also accounts for about half of all red Dão and is the predominant grape of some of the Dão sub-areas. It is grown in the Minho (*vinho verde* country up in the north), the Douro (where it is known as Tinta Bairrada), and is also found in the centre and south, in the Ribatejo and Alentejo. It is a vigorous vine, and yields prolifically.

BAIRRADA RD
BEIRA LITORAL

Winery entries: Aliança, Fonseca Successores, Pato, São João, Sogrape, Velhas

🍷 Baga, Periquita, Tinta Pinheira

🍷 Bical, Fernão Pires (Maria Gomes), Rabo de Ovelha

Luis Pato, Bairrada's best known grower and winemaker, compares the soils of his region to those of Champagne and Saint-Émilion: 20 to 40cm (8 to 16 inches) of clay on the surface, and limestone underneath; however, less than a quarter of the Bairrada region lies on this ideal soil.

Most of Bairrada's vineyards are about 80km (50 miles) south of Oporto, between the coast and Portugal's main north-south road. Bairrada achieved demarcation only in 1979, though its red wines, principally from the Baga grape, have been used for years to make some of Portugal's most expensive *garrafeiras*. These red wines, with startlingly rich flavours of raspberry, plum, strawberry, tobacco and cedar, are undoubtedly Bairrada's finest, yet demand for white Bairrada has risen so much recently that growers have started to graft white vines on to red. The most hopeful prospects for increasing quality in white Bairrada are probably founded on grapes more interesting than Maria Gomes, the main variety: Luis Pato is experimenting with Cercealinho, a cross between Cerceal and Alvarinho.

In the making of red Bairradas, there are two camps, ancient and modern. Typically, much of the region's wine is made in co-ops, whose equipment is not up to much. They leave the stalks in during fermentation, or remove them in such a rough way that the bitter flavours they are trying to avoid are released into the juice. There is not a lot of stainless steel or refrigeration, and the results are usually rough, tough wines, over-balanced by tannin and acidity. Given the right choice of wine, careful blending, and adequate ageing, this approach *can* work, as the rich, traditionally made wines of Caves São João show.

The modernists (Luis Pato, Aliança and Sogrape) insist that removal of grape-stalks before fermentation is the first essential. Thereafter, techniques differ – whether to macerate before or after fermentation, or not at all – but somehow the naturally high acidity of the Baga has to be tamed to make its wines acceptable to international markets. Then, perhaps with a hint of new oak ageing, Bairrada has the potential to rival any red wine in the world for flavour and complexity.

BEIRAS

🍷 Marufo, Rufete, Periquita and others

🍷 Pérola, Arinto do Dão, Arinto Gordo and others

The inland Beira provinces occupy the upper-middle portion of Portugal on the map, below the River Douro but above Estremadura, Ribatejo and Alentejo. The area's six new wine regions – Pinhel IPR, Castelo Rodrigo IPR, Cova da Beira IPR, Varosa IPR, Encostas da Nave IPR and Lafoёs IPR – are located in the Beira Alta and Beira Baixa. Both these inland provinces are at highish altitudes – up to 1000 metres (3280 feet) above sea level for the Beira Alta, and 500 metres (1640 feet) for the Beira Baixa – and as capable of experiencing snow in winter as of having intensely hot summers.

It has been unusual to see wines from either of these provinces identified on a label as coming from Beira, but this may change with the new demarcations. Essentially, although red wines outnumber whites by five to one, Pinhel and Castelo Rodrigo (in Beira Alta) are best known as providers of base wine for white sparkling wine. Yet some of Portugal's best winemakers, such as Peter Bright of João Pires, are convinced of the potential of the red wines from Cova da Beira (in Beira Baixa).

BORRADO DAS MOSCAS

'Fly droppings' is the appetizing translation of this white grape variety, which, despite its name, is a *quality* grape making wine with a fine, fruity aroma, good acidity and interesting flavour. It becomes very ripe and sweet, however, unless picked early, and can make very alcoholic wines. Its main habitat nowadays is Dão. It is also an official variety of Bairrada, where it goes by the name of Bical, but it is now losing ground there to the bland Maria Gomes (Fernão Pires). This is sad, as wines made from Bical can be full of subtle and intriguing flavours, such as marzipan, butter, mushroom and spice.

BUÇACO PALACE HOTEL
BEIRA LITORAL

🍷 Baga, Bastardo, Castelão Nacional, Mortagua

🍷 Bical, Fernão Pires (Maria Gomes), Moscatel, Rabo de Ovelha

Some of Portugal's finest wines, both red and white, are made at this large and extravagantly ornate, nineteenth-century castle-hotel – set amid gardens, lakes and a magnificent forest just outside Luso.

Wine has been made at the Buçaco Palace Hotel since 1913 – but from bought-in grapes as the hotel owns no vineyards (Buçaco lies between Bairrada and Dão). Traditional methods prevail. Grapes for both red and white wines are still pressed underfoot in shallow stone *lagares*. After fermentation the whites spend 12 to 18 months in barrel, the reds about three years; they are then bottled, without any filtration, and laid down for long ageing. When released for sale, both red and white are rich, well-balanced, complex wines – but they are sold only to guests at the hotel, and at four other hotels in the same group.

BUCELAS RD
ESTREMADURA

Winery entry: Velhas

🍷 Arinto, Cerceal, Esgana Cão, Rabo de Ovelha

It could be argued that Bucelas wine – from an area not far north of Lisbon – has more of an historic reputation than a present-day one. It was mentioned by Shakespeare as 'Charneca' (one of the nine Bucelas villages), and made fashionable at the British Court by Wellington after his Peninsular War campaign. Today however, its piercing acidity and need of long ageing are making it less popular.

Caves Velhas is the main producer of Bucelas – and for years was the only one; but since 1982, a small estate, Quinta do Avelar, has also been making Bucelas.

The most recent entrant to the limited circle of Bucelas producers is a Portuguese subsidiary of the sugar company Tate & Lyle, Alcantara, which owns a 135-hectare (336-acre) estate, Quinta da Romeira. Quinta da Romeira produced the wine Wellington sent back to England, so it will be fascinating to see what Alcantara can achieve when it makes Bucelas for the first time in 1993.

CÁLEM
Port RD
DOURO

🍷 Tinta Roriz, Tinta Barroca, Tinta Cão and others

🍷 Arinto, Malvasia Fina, Viosinho and others

Cálem – one of the Portuguese port houses (as opposed to British) – still belongs to the family that founded it in 1859. Now the largest family-owned port house, it has seven different *quintas* or farms totalling 182 hectares (nearly 450 acres). Four of the *quintas*, Foz, Santo António, Sagrado and Vedial, are interconnecting properties on the Douro and Pinhão rivers, forming an unusually large vineyard unit. There has been a lot of replanting and additional planting in recent years, mostly on new, wide terraces. Quinta da Foz has been sold since 1982 as a single *quinta* port in off-vintage years, an unsubtle but pleasant wine, rich, sweet and rather meaty-bloody. Two other *quintas*, Carvalheira and Sagrado, are now also being sold as single *quintas*.

Cálem's original maturation lodges, still in use, are down beside the famous double-decker bridge that spans the river between Oporto and Vila Nova de Gaia. The rickety floors are made of ancient barrel staves, and worrying chalk marks on the walls show the flood levels of years gone by. Elsewhere in the lodges, however, stainless steel and glistening white tiles provide a modern contrast, as does the industrial-looking vinification centre at Santo Martinho de Anta.

Best-seller is the tawny Old Friends (Tres Velhotes), the leading brand in Portugal itself, and in the important French market. Aged tawnies (from 10 to 40 years old) and *colheitas* are a speciality. The *colheita* wines can be wonderful, witness the delicate, nutty-pruny 1962. Vintage ports can be very good, stylishly sweet, raisiny, cedary and minty.

CARCAVELOS RD
ESTREMADURA

Winery entry: Pires

🍷 Espadeiro, Negra Mole, Preto Martinho, Periquita

🍷 Boais, Cerceal, Rabo de Ovelha

Until recently, the most notable feature of Carcavelos was a cricket pitch, an area of grass lovingly tended by the Lisbon Casuals Cricket Club. The fact that Carcavelos was home to one of Portugal's 14 RDs was incidental to the rest of life in this fashionable little seaside town. And if you had actually tasted the only wine made in this tiny region, you would have henceforth concentrated on the cricket. Quinta do Barão makes a sweet fortified wine vaguely similar to a five- to eight-year-old tawny port but with none of the style. The alcohol is coarse, the flavour has a hint of aged nuttiness but a rough, peppery taste dominates.

Not a lot to remind the discriminating drinker of the days when Carcavelos wines were good enough to be sent by the King of Portugal as gifts to the Court of Peking (or maybe the wines were never any good, but the Chinese were too polite to refuse them). But hope may be in sight, thanks to a newly-planted estate, Quinta dos Pesos. Its wines, first released at the end of 1990, could revitalize this flagging RD.

CHURCHILL GRAHAM
Port RD
DOURO

🍷 Touriga Nacional, Tinta Roriz, Mourisco Semente, Tinta Barroca

🍷 Malvasia Fina, Malvasia Rei

'A boutique-type vintage house' is what Johnny Graham set out to establish when he founded Churchill Graham in 1981 (Churchill is his wife's maiden name). It was the first port business to start up from scratch in 50 years: local regulations demanding that shippers hold substantial stocks of wine deter most hopefuls. For Johnny Graham (a member of the old port family), it was all made possible by a long-term agreement with an elderly and wealthy farmer, Jorges Borges de Sousa. The deal gives Churchill Graham access to de Sousa's substantial stocks of port wine, plus grapes from his six *quintas*, which all rate 'A' on the official quality scale. The wines are traditionally made, with the grapes crushed underfoot then fermented in old *lagares* – shallow, granite troughs. Though this sounds worryingly archaic, the results for the red wines are very good.

The wines go simply by the name of Churchill and are generally first-class, from the rich, much more complex than usual Vintage Character and Crusted Ports, to the stylish, cedary Vintage.

The vintage wines are blended from the three top *quintas*, Agua Alta, Manuela and Fojo; Agua Alta has also been sold as a single *quinta* port from the 1983 and '87 vintages. The 1987 is a much more successful wine than the '83, needing at least five years' further maturation. The white port is a very traditional, golden, nutty style.

COCKBURN-SMITHES
Port RD
DOURO

♟ Touriga Nacional, Tinta Roriz, Tinta Barroca and others

♀ Malvasia Fina, Rabigato, Ramisco (Codega)

Cockburn, one of the oldest port companies, sells more port in the UK than any other shipper and much of that is its famous Special Reserve, a fairly fruity, plummy-sweet aged ruby. Special Reserve has been so successful that Cockburn has occasionally refrained from making vintage port in order to use the extra wine for Special Reserve.

It was partly with this shortage of raw materials in mind that during the last two decades, Cockburn has extended its planting at Vilariça. At the moment, only 15 per cent of the grapes used come from its own vineyards. Another 50 per cent come from farms where Cockburn's experts supervise the work, and the remaining grapes are bought on the open market. The company has five wineries, some ancient, some very modern, which make about 60 per cent of the wine it uses. The rest is bought in as ready-made young wine from farmers whose wine-making is closely vetted by Cockburn.

Cockburn's up-market wines are very good. Vintages tend to be dense, chunky, minty-cedary wines, and the 10- and 20-year old tawnies are very attractive, creamy and nutty. The Quinta da Eira Velha single *quinta* vintage is best drunk soon after release, since it seems to thin out with further maturation, and Cockburn's Crusted Port is raw and ungainly in its youth, yet probably too light to develop much with age. Among the cheaper ports, the LBV is light, soft and raisiny, and the superior ruby Special Reserve fairly fruity, sweet and plummy. The white ports are unimpressive, though the Fine White Port is pleasantly raisiny.

▼ *Barcos rabelos*, now moored as pretty advertisements on the river at Vila Nova de Gaia, were once the main means of transporting barrels of young port down from the mountains.

COLARES RD
ESTREMADURA

🍷 Ramisco, Molar, Parreira Matias, Periquita

🍶 Malvasia, Arinto, Galego Dourado, Janapal

Colares is one of the most extraordinary wine regions in the world, a cliff-top plateau overlooking the Atlantic, where you have to search hard to find the occasional vineyard among the windswept pine groves, campsites and other features of a holiday coastline. It is yet another historic Portuguese wine area being strangled by its position and its failure to keep up with the times.

That the vines grow there at all is surprising enough. They have to be planted through the sand (several metres deep) into the ground beneath. Then, to escape the wind, vines are left to trail along the sand for much of the season, and only raised up on short bamboo sticks when grapes have begun to form and there is a danger that they might scorch on the sand in the burning summer months.

After all this, the grapes that have struggled into existence are treated in a very cavalier fashion. Taken to the Colares co-op, they are crushed and fermented, stalks and all, in large wooden vats. Three days later the juice has become wine and is run off into cement vats to wait for three or four years before anything more is done. Then the owners of the vineyards receive wine in proportion to the weight of grapes they originally delivered, and it is up to them to make something out of this young, terrifyingly tannic liquid. Given all these handicaps, it is hard to see how this fascinating RD will survive into the twenty-first century.

CONDE DE SANTAR
Dão RD
BEIRA ALTA

🍷 Touriga Nacional, Alfrocheiro Preto, Jaen and others

🍶 Encruzado, Cerceal, Verdelho, Arinto

Things are changing very much for the better on this beautiful Dão estate since the son of the family, Pedro de Vasconcellos, returned recently with a wine degree from Montpellier and fresh from work experience in Bordeaux. With his father, Pedro is building a new winery on the estate – the old winery was a dismal, basic affair, and the wines correspondingly disappointing. The raw materials from the old vineyards are good, however, and Pedro plans even better things for the future. At the moment, all the wine leaves the winery in bulk, and is bottled by the port company Cálem, who have a contract to market it until 1994. Since they bottle it as and when they receive orders, the wine can vary considerably from batch to batch. Until very recently, Conde de Santar was the only Dão estate to make its own wine.

Up in the hills near Viseu, Conde de Santar is centred on a big and beautiful eighteenth-century manor house – adorned with a spectacular array of traditional blue and white tiles, and surrounded by formal gardens and fountains. The estate has olive groves and orchards, but grapes are the main crop: 100 hectares (nearly 250 acres) of vines for white wines and 80 hectares (nearly 200 acres) for reds. Conde de Santar is a name to watch.

CROFT
Port RD
DOURO

🍷 Touriga Nacional, Touriga Francesca, Tinta Barroca and others

🍶 Malvasia Fina, Verdelho, Esgana Cão and others

Croft is one of the oldest British port firms, having been founded in the late 1600s as Phayre & Bradley – the first Croft joined the firm in 1736. The large and beautiful Quinta da Roêda, known as 'the diamond of the Douro', has belonged to the Croft family since the end of the nineteenth century. There is a big, modern wine-making centre on the estate. Sold as a single *quinta* wine in 'off' vintages, Roêda forms the backbone of Croft vintage ports. However, in recent vintages, Roêda has failed to work its old magic, and both the single *quinta* wine and the Croft Vintage ports have been disappointing. As a result, we would relegate this shipper – once an automatic member of port's 'first division' – to the second-liners. Croft Distinction, historically a reliable eight-year-old tawny, is apparently going to become less important in the corporate scheme of things, in favour of a new good, soft, nutty 10-year-old tawny. Croft also owns two other port companies, Delaforce and Morgan.

DÃO RD
BEIRA ALTA

Winery entries: Aliança, Conde de Santar, Fonseca Successores, São João, Sogrape, Velhas

⚑ Touriga Nacional, Alfrocheiro Preto, Bastardo and others

♀ Encruzado, Assario Branco, Barcelo and others

Dão is the perfect example of a well-known Portuguese wine region struggling to come to terms with the modern world. We can remember bottles of Dão (usually red) on British shelves in the mid-1980s that had nothing to recommend them except a low price. And yet when we visited this lovely, pine-forested region, and tasted the young wines from barrel, they were magnificent, full of rich, blackberry and blackcurrant fruit. What had gone wrong?

There's nothing wrong with the place. The Dão region has enormous potential for grape-growing and wine-making. Sheltered by mountains on every side except the south-west, Dão enjoys a climate of hot, dry summers and very cold winters, with plenty of rainfall. The soil is mainly granite in the hillier north-east, and the sloping vineyards here produce full, rich reds; whereas the sandier soils in the centre and more westerly parts make lighter wines. Many vineyards are planted on south-facing slopes to maximize the ripening effect of the sun.

Where Dão's problems started was with the making of the wines. There was a rule that commercial companies were not allowed to buy grapes, which in practice meant that nearly all the wine was made in co-ops – with antiquated equipment. The companies had to buy ready-made wine for blending and ageing. Occasionally they came up with good results: Caves São João's Porta dos Cavaleiros has consistently been one of the best Dão reds. But most Dão has always been short of fruitiness, and poorly made. There were minimum ageing requirements as well, imposed on all Dão wines, that prevented any of the glorious fruit in the young wines ever surviving into a bottle.

But now a lot of that has changed. EC legislation has meant the end of the co-ops' monopoly on wine-making, and the Dão Vinegrowers Association has new, more forward-looking people in charge. The giant Sogrape company is in the lead. It recently bought an enormous 100-hectare (247-acre) Dão estate, Quinta dos Carvalhais and built a brand new winery big enough·to produce all the base wine for Grão Vasco, its Dão brand. Eventually, when newly-planted vines come into full production, the estate should provide all the grapes needed for Grão Vasco, as well as for an individual estate wine.

José Maria da Fonseca Successores are also in the Dão region, making the wine for Casa da Insua. However, unless the rules change even further, Casa da Insua will not be released as Dão, because 30 per cent of the red wine is made from Cabernet Sauvignon, not one of the permitted grapes (even though it has been in the Insua vineyards since the last century). They also make a white from Sauvignon Blanc, Sémillon and some of the permitted white Dão varieties.

Things, long overdue, are finally happening at Conde de Santar, until very recently the only Dão estate to make its own wines. Other estates bottling and selling their own wine are Quinta do Serrado (Carvalho, Ribeiro & Ferreira) and Sete Torres.

DELAFORCE
Port RD
DOURO

⚑ Touriga Francesa, Touriga Nacional, Tinta Roriz and others

♀ Malvasia Fina, Rabigato

Though Delaforce is owned by Croft, it is run quite separately and members of the Delaforce family are still actively involved in the business. The company itself owns no vineyards, but has exclusive agreements with a number of farms, including, since the late seventies, the beautiful Quinta da Corte, perched above a deep bend in the Rio Torto. Delaforce's main brand is an old tawny, His Eminence's Choice, pleasantly soft, figgy and nutty, a blend of tawny ports of between six and 30 years old. Special White is pleasant, sweet and not very characterful. Delaforce Vintage ports can be very good, like the 1985, which is softly sweet, flowery and minty. But the light, brown-sugary 1982 is disappointing.

DOURO

After the Tagus, the Douro is the most important river in Portugal (and its importance continues over the border into Spain, where it becomes the Duero). It is not surprising, then, that the wine region takes its name from the river, as, without this waterway, Douro wines might never have reached the outside world. The Douro is a wild and beautiful part of Portugal. Its very poverty of natural resources has driven the inhabitants to ingenious extremes in order to wrest a living out of what can only just be called soil. The part of the Douro where port can be made has the poorest soil – slate-like schist that must be broken up by digging or even dynamiting before vines can be planted. Where the slate gives way to granite, the permission to make port is withheld, limiting production to Douro table wine.

Man's hand is everywhere evident in the look of the region. In order to plant vines on the steep slopes plunging down to the Douro and its tributaries, terraces have been carved out of the slate rock. Traditional terraces are narrow, and supported by dry stone walls (one of the few ways of disposing of large boulders before the advent of proper roads and tractors). More recent experiments include plantations 'up and down' the hillsides and wide terraces known as *patamares*, both enabling the vineyards to be cultivated by tractor.

The river has changed, too, no longer a fast-flowing waterway where every journey taking wine down to Oporto was an adventure. A series of dams started in the late 1950s has tamed the Douro's roar to a placid gurgle. Now no pipes of port travel by boat: large tankers make the twisting road between Oporto and the Douro region hell for other motorists as they grind slowly up and down the steep gradients.

The climate in the Douro becomes hotter as you travel from west to east. The wet coastal climate that envelops Oporto never penetrates to the Douro wine region, stopped by the 1400-metre (4600-feet) peaks of the Serra do Marão mountains. But there is more rainfall between Mesão Frio and Régua (the Baixa Corgo) than is good for really high quality port, and not enough in the very hot, eastern Douro Superior, stretching 50km (30 miles) in from the Spanish border. The prime port zone is the Cima Corgo, centred on Pinhão, an area where many of the famous port houses have their *quintas* (estates).

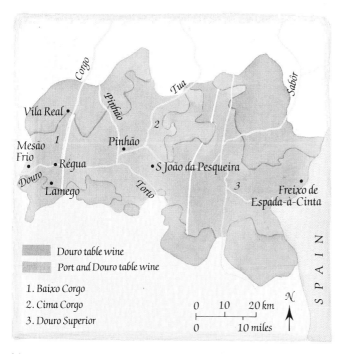

Douro table wine
Port and Douro table wine

1. Baixo Corgo
2. Cima Corgo
3. Douro Superior

▲ Taylor's Quinta de Vargellas, high in the Douro valley, is the source of one of the best single *quinta* ports.

GRAPE ENTRIES
Arinto
Baga (Tinta Bairrada)
Fernão Pires
Moscatel
Roupeiro (Codega)
Touriga Nacional

WINE ENTRIES
Douro
Port

WINERY ENTRIES
Aliança
Cálem
Churchill Graham
Cockburn-Smithes
Croft
Delaforce
Dow
Ferreira
Fonseca Guimaraens
Graham
Niepoort
Offley Forrester
Quinta da Pacheca

Quinta do Côtto
Quinta do Noval
Ramos Pinto
Real Companhia Vinícola
Sandeman
Smith Woodhouse
Sogrape
Taylor, Fladgate & Yeatman
Caves Velhas
Warre

DOURO RD
DOURO

Winery entries: Aliança, Ferreira, Quinta da Pacheca, Quinta do Côtto, Sogrape, Velhas

🍷 Touriga Nacional, Touriga Francesa, Tinta Roriz and others

🍾 Esgana Cão, Malvasia Fina, Rabigato and others

Most people think of the Douro only in terms of port, but it is probably the most under-estimated source of table wine in Portugal. Mark you, the Portuguese pay serious money to get hold of Barca Velha – Portugal's answer to First Growth claret, in price if not always in quality. As well as the famous brands, such as Barca Velha, Reserva Especial and Planalto, many of Portugal's best *garrafeira* wines have a shot of wine from a carefully chosen Douro estate.

The Douro region has a lot of potential for table wines. It is a hilly to downright mountainous part of the world, and variations in altitude can produce marked differences in grape ripening: the best port vineyards tend to be at fairly low altitudes, while higher vineyards – yielding less super-ripe grapes – are more suitable for table wines. There's a bigger range of grape varieties here than almost anywhere else in Portugal, from the excellent Tinta Roriz through almost every other red grape Portugal has to offer, and most of the white ones too. Climate and rainfall vary tremendously from the damper Baixo Corgo in the west to the baking Douro Superior along the border with Spain. Even the soil varies: mostly slaty schists but also granite-based.

And it is worth remembering that the original exports of Douro wine, in the late 1600s, were *unfortified*. It was not until well into the eighteenth century that it became standard to stop the fermentation with brandy and make a wine similar to the port we know today.

Many port producers are now experimenting with table wines. Ferreira, Real Vinícola, Cockburn and Borges already sell table wines, as do the co-ops at Régua, São João da Pesqueira and Mesão Frio. And there are good wines from farms like Quinta do Côtto and Quinta da Pacheca, and large non-port companies such as Sogrape.

The Douro even has its makers of sparkling wine. Raposeira, owned by multi-national giant Seagrams, is the largest, with its plant in Lamego. Another interesting venture is by the California sparkling wine producer Schramsberg who has gone into partnership with four co-ops near Vila Real to grow grapes for top-quality fizz. The next entrant in the search for Portugal's perfect sparkler could be Champagne Roederer, who have just bought into port producer Ramos-Pinto. And when the French start making table or sparkling wines outside France, the time has come to take notice.

DOW
Port RD
DOURO

🍷 Tinta Roriz, Touriga Francesa, Touriga Nacional and others

🍾 Esgana Cão, Folgosão, Verdelho and others

It is always assumed that Dow is one of the top shippers of port. Well, it isn't. 'Dow' is actually a brand name used by the shippers Silva & Cosens, part of the Symington family empire, Symington Port Shippers. However, it is certainly one of the most respected brands of port, making vintage wines regularly ranked among the top six best.

Symington Port Shippers have their main base in the Douro at Quinta do Bomfim, just east of Pinhão. Here they make about half the wine required by the companies in the group, and the grapes from the 76-hectare (187-acre) vineyard on the estate are principally used for top Dow wines. From 1978 onwards, Quinta do Bomfim has been released as a single *quinta* wine in years when a Dow vintage is not declared. At Bomfim, facing south over the Douro, high summer temperatures often cause the grapes to become slightly baked and raisined, and Dow vintage ports sometimes have a hint of this, though grapes for the top wines also come from Quinta do Macedos and Quinta do Zimbro.

The Dow vintage ports are excellent, and the off-vintage 1978 Quinta do Bomfim also reflects the dry, cedary style for which Dow is renowned. Among the aged tawnies, the 30-year-old is a particularly fine wine, full of nutty, creamy flavour, and the Dow Vintage Character has more vintage character than most.

ESPORÃO
Reguengos IPR
ALENTEJO

♂ Periquita, Trincadeira, Moreto and others

♀ Roupeiro, Perrum, Traça Blanca and others

Herdade do Esporão has a chequered history. The 2000-hectare (4940-acre) estate was bought in 1973 by the present owners to be turned into a vineyard. Two years later it was expropriated in the left-wing fervour following the revolution. In 1979 one-third of the estate was returned, and the struggle to create the vineyard began.

Esporão is just outside Reguengos de Monsaraz, and was, until 1986, the largest member of the local co-op. The owners, by now a publicly-quoted company called Finagra, wanted to start making their own wine, but to do it little by little. The co-op said all or nothing, so Esporão built its own winery in time for the 1987 vintage – just!

The vineyard – Portugal's single largest – is planted with local grapes and Cabernet Sauvignon, and the wines, red and white, have been rapturously received in Portugal. They are both very good, but so far their price has deterred most overseas buyers.

FERNÃO PIRES

Portugal's most cultivated white variety produces small, highly flavoured grapes that turn into distinctive grapy-peppery wines. Unless picked early, the grapes become very sweet and low in acidity, so the resultant wines taste alcoholic and flat. Picked early and carefully made, the wines can be quite fruity. Though the Fernão Pires is to be found in most areas of Portugal and is a heavy cropper, it is rarely planted extensively. It is, however, the main white grape variety of Bairrada, where the locals call it Maria Gomes, and is relatively widespread in the Ribatejo and Oeste. Apart from Bairrada, it is an official variety in Arruda, Alenquer, Torres Vedras, Douro, Setúbal, Alentejo and Cartaxo, and is grown in Dão though not officially permitted in the demarcated wines.

FERREIRA
Port RD, Douro RD
DOURO

♂ Port: Touriga Nacional, Touriga Francesa, Tinta Cão and others
Douro: Tinta Roriz, Tinta Barroca, Touriga Nacional

♀ Port: Esgana Cão, Folgosão, Verdelho and others

Ferreira ports are excellent, and much of this is thanks to ceaseless experimentation in vineyards and wineries. Quinta do Seixo, the more modern of Ferreira's two wineries in the Douro, offers a glorious contrast between the large, old barrels where the young wine is stored and the temperature-controlled stainless steel tanks used for fermentation. Almost all Ferreira's top port is made here (the vintage and the best tawnies), and so is Esteva, their least expensive table wine. This is light and stylish, with a scent slightly reminiscent of port and an attractive, cherry flavour.

But the glory of the Ferreira table wine range is Barca Velha, Portugal's most expensive and sought-after red. It is made from Tinta Roriz, with some Tinta Barroca and Touriga Nacional, and was first created in the fifties. Originally fermented in small oak vats with ice packed round them, Barca Velha is now made in stainless steel tanks. But what has not changed over the years is the maturation of the young wine in new Portuguese oak barrels for about 18 months. Then the best barrels are set aside to become Barca Velha – a very serious wine, starting out strongly oaky and developing rich, complex fruit flavours. Unsuccessful candidates (or wines from lesser vintages) are bottled as Ferreira's Reserva Especial, which can often be very fine.

The ports are lighter in style than those from some of the 'British' houses – the vintage wines made in an elegant, blackcurrant and cedar style, the LBV with more chocolaty richness than most, and glorious aged tawnies. Dona Antonia's Personal Reserve (about eight years old) is softly nutty; Quinta do Porto 10-year-old has lovely, plummy, creamy flavour as well as the nuttiness; and Duque de Braganza 20-year-old is richly nutty, with strong pruny fruit, still fresh and lively, and one of the best 20-year-old ports we have tasted. Ferreira is the top port brand in Portugal but is hardly known overseas.

FONSECA GUIMARAENS
Port RD
DOURO

🍷 Touriga Francesa, Tinta Roriz, Tinto Cão and others

🍶 Malvasia Fina, Esgana Cão, Folgosão and others

Guimaraens – with its brand name Fonseca (inherited from the company's pre-1822 owners) – was taken over in 1948 by Taylor, Fladgate and Yeatman. Fonseca ports, however, are made completely separately from those of Taylor's, using different premises to store wines in Vila Nova de Gaia, and different farms in the Douro to provide the grapes (the principal Fonseca *quintas* are called Cruzeiro, Santo Antonio and Panascal).

Fonseca ports are characterized above all by a sweet, plummy flavour reminiscent of the sugared plums known in Portugal as 'Elvas plums'. Made in a lush, opulent style, they are sweeter and more seductive than the ports from Taylor, their sister company. This applies throughout the range, from the sweet, plum and cedar concentration of the Vintage (regularly among the top six) and the Fonseca Guimaraens (Fonseca's off-vintage release substitute for a single *quinta* port), to the sweetly nutty aged tawnies (the Fonseca 40-year-old is possibly the best aged tawny available). The traditional style Late Bottled Vintage is an unfiltered, substantial wine that throws a crust if left to develop in bottle and needs decanting, but is one of the best. Fonseca Bin 27 is merely superior ruby, and Quinta do Panascal has so far been disappointing.

FONSECA INTERNACIONAL
ESTREMADURA

🍷 Periquita

🍶 Fernão Pires, Moscatel de Setúbal

The Lancers brand may not be very familiar on the eastern side of the Atlantic, but in the USA it has long been a household name. A decade ago, this pale, gently fizzy, sweetish pink wine in its distinctive crock-like bottle used to sell a million cases a year. And although the popularity of this style of wine has been declining, and sales are now down to 540,000 cases, this is still a massive figure, putting Lancers sixth on the best-seller list for imported wine in the USA, ahead of Mateus.

Lancers belongs to JM da Fonseca Internacional (now owned by IDV, the wine and spirits arm of the international giant Grand Metropolitan). The new red-brick winery for the production of Lancers, surrounded by a whole village of glistening white storage igloos, was built in 1970, and has been kept right up to date ever since. Attractive white-arched cellars below the winery house an impressive array of new oak barrels for ageing wines for other companies. But production of the crock-bottled Lancers, which still accounts for 60 per cent of Internacional's output, is a much more industrial affair. The base wines (mostly pink and made predominantly with Periquita grapes from the Palmela region) are prepared in a commendably sterile and modern way by the nearby firm of João Pires. For the USA, Africa and Asia, the wines are then injected with fizz on the bottling line, but Europe gets a superior version – thanks to a unique system that Fonseca installed a few years ago. This was actually designed for fully sparkling wines like Lancers Brut Sparkling. For 21 days, wine passes at a rate of 50 litres per hour through a series of tanks filled with sterile wood-shavings on which yeast cells have been deposited. This is supposed to provide the sort of intimate wine-to-yeast contact that Champagne gets inside the bottle, and hence the sought-after yeasty aromas and flavours. Yet, although Lancers Brut Sparkling is pleasant and clean, little yeasty character is detectable, and no one expects the even cheaper brands to pick up any flavour in their shorter trip through the equipment.

The inexpensive sparkling wine was one product the company developed in the hope of recouping the American market once the Lancers trade started to decline. Others, on a small scale, were a simple still red, and an equally inoffensive, still, off-dry Blush (very much paler and drier than Lancers), as well as a Lancers *vinho verde*. They also sell Lancers-style wines under the brand name Faisca, and for own-label wines to supermarkets.

▶ This ornate cellar is a complete contrast with the modern, industrial winery of Fonseca Internacional above its tiled vaults. It is used to mature the finest wines of João Pires, who rent space for bottles and casks, and to entertain visitors.

FONSECA SUCCESSORES
Bairrada RD, Dão RD,
Moscatel de Setúbal RD,
Portalegre IPR,
Reguengos IPR
ESTREMADURA

🍷 Bairrada: Baga
Dão: Touriga Nacional, Tinta
Pinheira, Bastardo
Portalegre: Tinta Roriz, Periquita,
Trincadeira, Tinta Francesa
Reguengos: Periquita, Trincadeira
Preta, Moreto, Tinta Roriz

🍷 Dão: Arinto, Encruzado, Barcelo
Moscatel de Setúbal: Moscatel,
Arinto, Boais and others
Portalegre: Arinto, Assario, Vale
Grosso, Alva

José Maria da Fonseca Successores is one of the most traditional yet innovative wine companies in Portugal. Domingos Soares Franco, one of the owners, trained at the famous University of California Davis wine-making school, and this gives him the know-how and confidence to use the most modern methods where appropriate, but draw on the better aspects of Portugal's tradition if they will give positive results.

The company is based very firmly in the Setúbal peninsula, where it owns 350 hectares (865 acres) of vineyard. However, none of its wines will be eligible to use the names of the two new IPR regions, Arrábida and Palmela, as the grape blends are too adventurous for the rather staid rules imposed by the regional committees. This despite the fact that José Maria da Fonseca Successores is the second largest vineyard owner in Palmela, and sells 55 per cent of all the wine made in Arrábida.

Since May 1986 the company has also owned an estate in Reguengos de Monsaraz, the JS Rosado Fernandes vineyard and winery – one of the most famous Alentejo properties. Domingos Soares Franco did add some stainless steel tanks in 1988, to replace the old stone *lagares*, but still ferments most of the wine in huge clay amphorae. The result, after several years' ageing, is a rich, densely fruity Tinto Velho of great quality.

The latest projects are the making and distribution of the Casa da Insua wine in the Dão region, and of the Morgado de Reguengo estate wines in Portalegre, at the very northern end of the Alentejo.

José Maria da Fonseca Successores is the largest producer of Moscatel de Setúbal but, as its wines contain only about two-thirds Moscatel grapes (thus inadmissible as Moscatel de Setúbal under EC rules), it is phasing out the word 'Moscatel' from the labels. As to the other Setúbal peninsula wines, Quinta de Camarate is the most attractive of the reds, with stylish, ripe Cabernet Sauvignon fruit. Pasmados (no foreign grapes) has a penetrating, fig and strawberry flavour, and Periquita is tougher, more traditionally Portuguese.

GRAHAM
Port RD
DOURO

🍷 Touriga Nacional, Touriga Francesa, Tinta Roriz and others

🍸 Esgana Cão, Folgosão, Verdelho and others

Anyone standing on the terrace at Quinta dos Malvedos, looking downstream along the Douro, might be forgiven for wondering whether this was some sort of earthly paradise. The river curves away to the left in a view of unparalleled tranquillity, steep hills plunging to the water. No wonder that this *quinta* was a glittering prize for the Symingtons when they bought Graham's in 1970.

The house at Malvedos has been gradually restored, room by room, and latterly the vineyard has been cleared and replanted and a new winery built. Top Graham ports are also made from Quinta dos Lages.

The off-vintage wine that Graham produces is named after Malvedos, but the company has been careful *not* to market it as a single *quinta* wine, since in the past not all the grapes have come from the Malvedos estate. When the replanted Malvedos vineyard is in full production, however, it will produce more than enough grapes for a true single *quinta* wine, to be labelled Quinta dos Malvedos. Malvedos wine echoes the Graham vintage ports by being sweeter, softer and more florally scented than Dow's and Warre's, always more approachable when young, though surviving just as well as its tougher brothers.

HENRIQUES & HENRIQUES
Madeira RD
MADEIRA

🍸 Tinta Negra Mole, Boal, Malmsey and others

Henriques & Henriques, the second largest Madeira company, owns important vineyards in Câmara de Lobos and Estreito de Câmara, and has recently modernized its cellars and wineries. It also owns a number of other firms, including Belem, Carmo, Casa dos Vinhos da Madeira and António Eduardo Henriques Successores; in addition, the company supplies Madeiras for the Sandeman and Harveys labels.

We don't think much of their cheaper wines, except for the medium-dry Verdelho, which has good, savoury, honeyed and salty-tangy flavour. The older wines are much better. The dry Sercial 10-year-old is really complex – nutty-cheesy-grapy, tangy and pleasantly woody; the Malmsey 10-year-old is tangy, salty, raisiny and nutty, good but not great. Brand names include Monte Seco and Century Malmsey. Right at the top of the quality scale, they sell some fine old vintage and *solera* Madeiras.

LOUREIRO

This is the most aromatic of the *vinho verde* grapes, grapily reminiscent of Muscat, but with an added musky quality and far greater delicacy and complexity. In very recent years, since the *vinho verde* producers have begun to be more selective about grape varieties, it has been possible to find pure Loureiro *vinhos verdes*. These are intensely aromatic and flavourful, but even a small proportion of Loureiro in a blend leaves its musky-grapy mark. It is all the better for its pronounced acidity, which it keeps even if left hanging on the vines until quite late in the year. Dourado ('golden') is an alternative name, after the lovely golden shade of the ripe grapes. The variety is found throughout the Vinho Verde region, but especially in the centre, around the town of Braga.

MADEIRA RD
MADEIRA

Winery entries: Henriques & Henriques, Madeira Wine Company

🍸 Tinta Negra Mole, Bual, Sercial, Verdelho, Malvasia (Malmsey)

Old Madeira must be the safest possible bet for anyone who dabbles in buying venerable wines at auction. There's always the risk that an aged port or claret may have snuffed it. But fine Madeira can be relied upon to survive for centuries, preserving layer upon layer of complex flavour.

The trouble in recent times has been that not much of the island's production can be classified as 'fine' as it has mostly been made from the dull Tinta Negra Mole grape, rather than the four traditional top-quality grapes, Sercial, Bual, Verdelho and Malmsey. However, EC regulations require that wine labelled with a grape name should contain

at least 85 per cent of that variety – so the Tinta Negra Mole can no longer masquerade as a top-quality grape.

By tradition, good Sercial is pale, dryish wine with lightish body and good acidity, ageing to austere, cheesy-nutty-appley flavour and a medium-dark colour. Verdelho starts out in life golden coloured, medium bodied and medium-dry, also with good acidity and, at best, apricotty, nutty flavour, tasting drier with age. Bual is medium to dark brown, fuller bodied, more fragrant and fairly sweet, and Malmsey, the darkest, is raisiny-fruity, full-bodied, fragrant, very rich and sweet.

The best Madeiras are aged for many years in 650-litre casks of oak, satinwood or mahogany, stored in sun-baked attics; (even the cheapest wines must spend a minimum of 18 months in casks). In rooms below are the huge, sealed heating-vats used to 'cook' the lesser wines; fortified and concentrated grape juices are then blended in to achieve the final effects. All this heating and ageing before bottling means that exposure to air is unlikely to damage your bottle of Madeira once it is opened – Madeira is one wine you can enjoy, glass by glass, for months.

Few of the Madeira producers own any vineyards to speak of. The grapes come from a myriad of tiny smallholdings whose owners also grow bananas, willow for tourist baskets, avocados, lemons and other crops. The leading producer, the Madeira Wine Company, handles half of all Madeira wine exports. Next largest is Henriques & Henriques. Good smaller producers include d'Oliveira and Artur Barros e Souza.

MADEIRA WINE COMPANY
Madeira RD
MADEIRA

♀ Tinta Negra Mole, Complexa, Malmsey and others

The Madeira Wine Company (which controls most of the making and selling of the island's wines) now groups 26 companies, including Blandy Brothers, Leacock, Miles, Rutherford & Miles, Cossart Gordon and Lomelino. Many of the brand names from these companies still appear on Madeira Wine Company bottles, though it would be idle to search for distinguishing differences – all the wines are made at the same premises, in modern, temperature-controlled, stainless steel equipment. Importantly for quality, the company buys only grapes – no juice or ready-made wine – and so ferments everything itself.

Affordable highlights include Blandy's 10-year-old Malmsey, a rich, pungent, exotically flavoured sweet wine with refreshing acidity; the salty-nutty-cheesy, slightly sweet Verdelho Special Reserve of Cossart Gordon; Cossart's Duo Centenary Celebration Sercial, with concentrated nutty-salty flavours; Leacock's Special Reserve Malmsey, a complex, rich, treacly-salty wine; and Rutherford & Miles' Special Reserve Malmsey, concentrated, raisiny, treacly and spicy. The simpler Reserve wines of Cossart Gordon are good value. Right at the top of the scale, Blandy's Solera wines are wonderfully concentrated and complex.

MARGARIDE
Almeirim IPR
RIBATEJO

♥ Merlot, Cabernet Franc, Alicante Bouschet and others

♥ Trincadeira, Baga

♀ Fernão Pires, Rabo de Ovelha, Boal

As its full name might suggest – Herdeiros de Dom Luis de Margaride – this Ribatejo estate is dominated by the memory of Dom Luis de Margaride (who died in 1966), father of the current owners. It was he who established the vineyards on the two family farms: the Convento da Serra and the Casal do Monteiro ou Alamo.

Dom Luis's main work was in studying the soils of the two estates and experimenting with different grape varieties. Not content just to grow the local Periquita for reds and Fernão Pires for whites, he tried others, such as the Bordeaux trio of Cabernet Sauvignon, Cabernet Franc and Merlot. Fernão Pires turned out best for the whites in the end, but the Margaride reds incorporate the Bordeaux threesome.

The wines are made in a low, barn-like winery built in 1956. The top whites get the full modern treatment of centrifugation, cool fermenta-

MOSCATEL

tion in stainless steel and ultra-sophisticated filtration, whereas the reds have to make do with autovinificators to start fermentation which then continues in stainless steel tanks. Only about half the production is bottled (the rest is sold in bulk).

The wines are stunningly consistent, the Fernão Pires proving a star performer for the whites, with fresh, minty-grassy flavours and a hint of marmaladey Muscat-like character. The rosé is refreshingly dry, with delicious, rosehip fruit; reds range from the light, attractively plummy Convento da Serra Tinto to the complex Dom Hermano Garrafeira.

The majority of Portugal's Moscatel, Moscatel de Setúbal, is none other than the Muscat of Alexandria, the least fine of the Muscat family. Grown on the Setúbal peninsula, it makes very sweet, grapy-raisiny wines, which are usually partially fermented and then 'stopped' by the addition of flavourless grape spirit. Sometimes the skins are then macerated in the wine to extract more aroma and flavour. The firm of João Pires on the Setúbal peninsula is unusual in making a light, dry, grapy-aromatic Moscatel table wine from the same type of grapes. Portugal has more of the finer variety of Moscatel (Muscat à Petits Grains) than Spain. Here this is called Moscatel do Douro or Moscatel Galego and there is also a pinky-red version, Moscatel Roxo (Muscat Rose à Petits Grains). Moscatel do Douro and Moscatel Roxo also grow, to a lesser extent, on the Setúbal peninsula, and Moscatel do Douro is a permitted minority grape for white Douro table wines.

MOSCATEL DE SETÚBAL RD
ESTREMADURA

Winery entries: Fonseca
Successores, Pires

♀ Moscatel de Setúbal, Moscatel
Roxo, Moscatel do Douro and
others

These sweet, grapy-raisiny fortified wines have had their own demarcated region – about 48km (30 miles) south of Lisbon, on the Setúbal peninsula – since 1907. However, Moscatel grapes represent only a fraction of the grapes planted here: there are just over 100 hectares (247 acres) of Moscatel vines, and more than a hundred times as much vineyard land growing other grapes to make dry wines, red and white.

One-tenth of all Moscatel de Setúbal is made by the co-operative, and apart from a few small-scale producers, such as the Quinta de São Francisco, the rest comes from the top-quality firms of José Maria da Fonseca Successores and João Pires – with grapes supplied by local growers. In fact, only two-thirds of the grapes José Maria da Fonseca use are Moscatel; this means that their wines do not qualify under EC regulations as 'Moscatel de Setúbal' since any wine labelled with a grape variety must be 85 per cent of that variety.

After partially fermenting the juice, both companies add grape spirit to stop fermentation, then leave the skins macerating in the fortified wine until February or March to extract more aromas and flavours. It is then pressed and aged, first in large wooden vats, next in small barrels.

The José Maria da Fonseca wines used to be released at two ages, five or six years and 20 or 25 years, but recently they have been sold with a vintage. The younger wine has been about four years old when first sold, fresh, sweet, grapy and delicious, if rather spirity. The older wines are kept topped up with grape spirit as the alcohol evaporates during storage, and they, too, have a spirity edge, but also a rich, raisiny intensity, fresh acidity and a long, grapy finish. João Pires have been making Moscatel de Setúbal only since 1983, and released their first vintage in 1988. It is a deliciously marmaladey five-year-old wine, even down to the hint of bitterness you might get from chunks of peel, with butterscotch and nut flavours as well.

NIEPOORT
Port DO
DOURO

♟ Touriga Nacional, Tinta Roriz,
Tinta Barroca and others

♀ Malvasia Fina, Rabigato, Gouveio
and others

This old-fashioned Dutch port company, founded in 1842, is one of the smallest and is still family run – by Rolf Niepoort and his son Dirk. After more than a century of buying all their grapes from farmers, they recently bought two *quintas* of their own, which will give them 45 hectares (111 acres) of vineyard when fully planted.

The company specializes in tawny ports, particularly the elegant, aromatic *colheita* wines (single vintage tawnies), which spend many years maturing in barrel before being bottled and sold. *Garrafeira* ports are another speciality, wood-aged for five years, then transferred to glass demijohns for perhaps another 20, and finally into bottles. They also have aged tawnies at 10, 20 and 30 years. The vintage wines are often made in the elegant, blackcurrant style that seems the norm with Portuguese (rather than the British) port shippers. The Late Bottled Vintage is good value, sweet, elegant, soft and pleasantly medicinal.

OESTE

♟ Periquita, Castelão Nacional,
Tinta Miuda and others

♀ Fernão Pires, Vital, Arinto and
others

◀ Immaculate vineyards near Arruda
in the Oeste, belonging to a member
of the excellent Arruda co-operative.

The Oeste is a loose, unofficial grouping of the wine regions along the western, coastal side of Portugal north of Lisbon and south of Bairrada. There are six of them trying to attain full RD status: Alcobaça IPR, Alenquer IPR, Arruda IPR, Encostas de Aire IPR, Obidos IPR, Torres IPR. Frankly, only Arruda, Alenquer and Torres should qualify on any objective assessment of wine quality. The usual reason for inclusion in the proposed list of future RDs is the presence of a large co-op in the region. This is certainly a rule that works for Torres, Arruda, Obidos and Alcobaça. More than once has there been the suggestion that the votes of hundreds of co-op members count for more in the proposing of a new wine region than the wine that comes out of the bottle.

OFFLEY FORRESTER
Port RD
DOURO

🍷 Tinta Roriz, Malvasia Preta, Souzão and others

🍷 Malvasia Corada, Rabigato, Malvasia Fina

One of the oldest port companies (founded in 1737) and today one of the ten biggest, Offley Forrester make stylish ports – rather sweeter than those from other 'British' companies. Their vintage wines and some others are made principally from grapes from Boa Vista, a conglomeration of four adjoining *quintas* (including Quinta de Boa Vista itself) that together make up 125 hectares (over 300 acres).

Offley Forrester's main vintage port, Offley Boa Vista, is made in more years than most companies' vintage ports, and frequently ignores the unwritten rule of the 'British' port shippers that they never declare vintages from two consecutive years. It is a distinctive style of vintage port, less tough than most, often cedary in flavour, and a good keeper despite its lightness. We prefer vintages of the sixties and eighties to those of the seventies. They are good value, being cheaper than the big name vintage ports (Taylor, Cockburn, Dow, Warre, Croft, Graham and Fonseca). There is also a pleasant, sweet, raisiny, spirity Boa Vista LBV, Boa Vista Special Reserve, a young (around five years) tawny style, and Baron de Forrester, decent but not great tawny. Big-volume brands include the fresh, cough-syrupy Duke of Oporto Ruby and Porto Rei Tawny. The white ports, of which there are four, are unimpressive. Offley Forrester is now wholly owned by Martini & Rossi.

LUIS PATO
Bairrada RD
BEIRA LITORAL

🍷 Baga

🍷 Baga

🍷 Fernão Pires (Maria Gomes), Bical, Cerceal, Cercealinho

Luis Pato is one of the very few exceptions to the Portuguese rule that good wines are made only by large companies. His wines are excellent, produced since 1980 from family-owned vineyards on the Quinta do Ribeirinho and at Ois do Bairro. These wines include a deliciously rich, creamy-chocolaty rosé from cool-fermented Baga, really reminiscent of Pinot Noir, a pleasant dry white fizz, and a pink sparkler, with a lovely, honeyed, chocolaty flavour that could lay claim to being Portugal's best fizz. When it comes to white Bairrada, Luis Pato finds the Cerceal and Cercealinho grapes particularly interesting, especially if some of the skins are added back to the fermenting juice to give extra flavour. But Fernão Pires and Bical are still important in his blend.

However, the reds (some sold under his father's name, João Pato) are his *serious* wines. Luis Pato believes there are only two things holding Bairrada back from assuming its rightful place among the world's great wines – fermenting the wine with the stalks still on the bunches, and not using new oak barrels for ageing. As a radical, he removes the stalks from his wines, and has a few Limousin oak barrels. The results have gone from good to tremendous in the space of a decade. The reds from the 1988 vintage are especially good, with rich flavours of buttery, raspberry fruit and hints of mint, wines to hang on to in confident expectation of joys to come.

PERIQUITA

This productive, early-ripening vine grows all over the southern half of Portugal (Oeste, Ribatejo, Setúbal Peninsula and the Alentejo), and does especially well along the coasts, where it thrives on sandy soil. There is some in Bairrada, and in the Algarve it tends to be blended with the characterless Tinta Negra Mole. North of the Algarve, the wines have reasonable colour, average alcohol and a pleasant, strawberry fruitiness when young. In the fuller-bodied examples, wines made from the Periquita can be rather harsh for the first few years, though they are good keepers and soften with time to give mature, figgy flavours and a firm structure. The Portuguese enjoy this variety as table grapes, and used to export them to Britain. It has several synonyms: Castelão Frances, João de Santarém, Trincadeira Preta and Mortagua. (The latter, confusingly, is also a synonym in Bairrada for the Touriga Nacional.)

JOÃO PIRES
Carcavelos RD, Moscatel de Setúbal RD, Vinho Verde RD, Arrábida IPR, Palmela IPR, Redondo IPR
ESTREMADURA

♍ Carcavelos: Trincadeira, Periquita, Goulego Dourado and others
Arrábida: Periquita, Merlot, Zinfandel
Redondo: Periquita, Alfrocheiro, Trincadeira

♀ Moscatel de Setúbal: Moscatel
Vinho Verde: Loureiro
Palmela: Fernão Pires

▲ An impressive balancing act by one of the pickers in the Alentejo vineyards that supply grapes for João Pires's most traditional-style red wine, Tinto da Anfora.

The least visible part of the João Pires operation is the most important: this super-modern winery produces all the base wine for JM da Fonseca Internacional, the Grand Met-owned makers of Lancers (a rosé 'pop' wine that sells particularly well in the USA). That accounts for over 90 per cent of the wine turned out by João Pires, provides the bread and butter, and enables the company to indulge in smaller-scale, but higher profile, wine-making, often using grapes from individual estates. This is supervised by one of Portugal's best winemakers, Australian Peter Bright (as is the Lancers base wine). Under his guidance, some fascinating projects have come into being. Best known of these is probably Quinta da Bacalhôa, a Cabernet/Merlot wine from an estate near Azeitão. In the white corner, the João Pires Branco is equally successful, a light, dry Muscat made with grapes from Arrábida, Palmela and the Ribatejo – fresh, aromatic and extremely popular.

João Pires own nearly 500 hectares (1235 acres) of vineyard, so are able to grow grapes for the Lancers base wine as well as favourites such as Tinto da Anfora, the tough, figgy, traditionally Portuguese red, and Catarina, a grassy, honeyed, minty Palmela white made from Fernão Pires, with a few months' ageing in new oak. Paço do Cardido Vinho Verde, almost entirely made from Loureiro, is one of the best single-estate *vinhos verdes*, perfumed, lemony and exciting, and their Chardonnay is easily the best from Portugal, rich, soft and buttery. The Australian know-how shows in the João Pires Moscatel de Setúbal, a real Aussie Muscat look-alike, and also in the mixture of traditional fermentation and carbonic maceration (the kind used to make Beaujolais) for the light red Quinta de Santo Amaro (Arrábida).

New projects include the revival of Carcavelos with the wine from Quinta dos Pesos; a magnificently fruity, rich Merlot called Má Partilha from Arrábida (but not admissible as such because Merlot is not a permitted grape variety); and two wines from the Alentejo, Santa Marta Branco and Terra do Xisto. These may not all escape from Portugal, as the João Pires wines are immensely popular there.

PORT RD
DOURO

Winery entries: Cálem, Churchill Graham, Cockburn-Smithes, Croft, Delaforce, Dow, Ferreira, Fonseca Guimaraens, Graham, Nicpoort, Offley Forrester, Quinta do Côtto, Quinta do Noval, Ramos Pinto, Real Companhia Vinícola, Sandeman, Smith Woodhouse, Sogrape, Taylor, Warre

♀ Touriga Nacional, Touriga Francesa, Tinta Roriz and others

♀ Esgana Cão, Folgosão, Verdelho and others

Port is such a famous wine that, like sherry, it has the dubious privilege of having its name borrowed by producers of 'port' wines all over the wine-making world. The world regards it as a wine style, but the Portuguese are the originators and still the masters.

Port starts its life on the steep slopes of the Douro region, well inland – from Mesão Frio eastwards to the Spanish border. The vineyards can be found perched high above the River Douro and many of its tributaries, and the wines are made here as well, in modern wineries attached to the principal *quintas* owned by big companies and co-ops, or in more primitive conditions on little farms throughout the region. But most port leaves the Douro in the spring following the vintage, and travels by tanker to the lodges (warehouses) in Vila Nova de Gaia, across the river from the city of Oporto (which gives port its name).

Ports fall into three categories: white, bottle-matured red and cask-matured red; it is the reds that have made port's reputation.

Cask-aged ports run the gamut from the youngest, cheapest ruby to the finest, oldest, scented tawnies. All are matured in large, wooden casks, possibly for only the minimum three years in the case of young rubies, whereas old tawnies are released at 10, 20, 30 and even 40 years of age. *Colheita* ports, single vintage tawnies (usually from the Portuguese shippers), can be among the Douro's most delicious wines. Cheap tawnies are simply blends of white and ruby port.

The finest of the bottle-aged ports is vintage port, 'declared' only in the best years, and only two years after the actual harvest, when individual shippers have had time to make up their minds. It is aged in cask for two years only, then spends 10 to 20 years in bottle. In 'off'-years, some shippers make vintage wines out of the grapes from their top vineyard. These are known as single *quinta* ports, and can offer a glimpse of vintage port, but will probably mature faster and cost less.

Another good alternative is crusted, or crusting, port. It is usually a blend of wines from two or three goodish years, aged in cask for three or four years, then bottled. There is also the traditional style of Late Bottled Vintage port – aged for four to six years in cask before bottling.

That leaves modern Late Bottled Vintage (LBV) and Vintage Character ports: although pleasant, neither tastes remotely like proper vintage port, so the word 'vintage' on the labels is somewhat confusing!

QUINTA DA BACALHÔA
ESTREMADURA

♀ Cabernet Sauvignon, Merlot

Quinta da Bacalhôa, near Azeitão on the Setúbal peninsula, is known for its fine red wines – first produced in the 1980 vintage. There is a decided French influence. The 12·5-hectare (31-acre) vineyard is planted with Cabernet Sauvignon (90 per cent) plus some Merlot. The wines are fermented, Bordeaux style, for a much shorter time than is traditional in Portugal, and then aged in Bordeaux-size Portuguese oak barrels. Results are delicious: meaty, blackcurrant Cabernet flavour overlaid with oak, and ageing well for six or so years. Vintages vary: 1982 and '83 were excellent, '87 very good and '88 is fabulous.

QUINTA DA PACHECA
Douro RD
DOURO

♀ Tinta Roriz, Tinta Barroca, Touriga Francesa and others

♀ Malvasia Fina, Verdelho, Rabo de Ovelha and others

Eduardo Serpa Pimentel's Quinta da Pacheca makes good red Douro wine. It also makes white wine, but this is entirely untypical because of the grape varieties used: Riesling, Sauvignon Blanc and Gewürztraminer. The results, however, are not inspiring. Even so, in Portugal the white wines have a snob appeal that finds them a ready market. To an outsider, they have little varietal character and little real quality.

The reds are an entirely different matter, however. Trodden by foot in old stone *lagares*, they are among the best red table wines made in the Douro – rich and cedary, with touches of honey, tobacco and figs.

QUINTA DE ABRIGADA
Alenquer IPR
ESTREMADURA

🍷 Periquita (João de Santarém)

🍷 Arinto, Vital, Fernão Pires

The best wines we have so far tasted from the Alenquer region – some 35km (20 miles) north of Lisbon – come from Quinta de Abrigada: both red and white wines are light, fresh and modern. Of the 400-hectare (988-acre) estate, only 35 hectares (86 acres) are currently planted with vines, but there are plans to plant another 15 hectares (37 acres) soon.

This is not one of the new wave of single estate Portuguese wines: Quinta de Abrigada wines were bottled in their own right as long ago as 1972. The reds are made in a modern way in lined concrete tanks, the whites cool-fermented in stainless steel. Results: a light, stylish, cherry-fruity red (with a richer, oakier *garrafeira* version in the best years such as 1976, '80, '85 and '89), and two qualities of white – the fresh, light, creamy Quinta de Abrigada Branco, made since 1989 only from Arinto and Vital, and the cheaper Terras do Rio, which also contains Fernão Pires grapes.

QUINTA DO CÔTTO
Douro RD, Port RD
DOURO

🍷 Tinta Roriz, Touriga Francesa, Touriga Nacional and others

🍷 Avesso, Malvasia Fina, Malvasia Rei

Miguel Champalimaud has made ports but these were not very successful. His table wines, on the other hand, are good. Quinta do Côtto – 15-hectare (37-acre) – lies near the border with the Vinho Verde region, and the family owns a *vinho verde* estate called Passo (Paço) do Teixero, which makes a clean, savoury, lemony wine. But the Douro wines from Quinta do Côtto are the really impressive ones. Even the white wines (fermented cool) are good when drunk young, and the reds can be excellent. Champalimaud makes two qualities of red wine: ordinary Quinta do Côtto Tinto and, in the best years, Côtto Grande Escolha. Red wines are fermented in autovinificators, then aged in wooden vats. Côtto Grande Escolha spends only a short time in these before being run into new Douro oak barrels for 18 to 24 months.

Older vintages of the Quinta do Côtto Tinto have evolved well, showing lovely tastes of cedar and tobacco. Côtto Grande Escolha can seem a bit unwieldy and oaky when it is young, but develops delicious flavours with age, and is excellent at nine or ten years – blackcurrant plus cedar with a sweet, savoury character. The 1987 Côtto Grande Escolha was entirely sold in Portugal, and Champalimaud did not make one in 1988 or '89, but when the next vintage appears, it will be worth looking out for.

QUINTA DO NOVAL
Port RD, Vinho Verde RD
DOURO

🍷 Touriga Nacional, Touriga Francesa, Tinta Roriz and others

🍷 Port: Rabigato, Malvasia Fina
Vinho Verde: Loureiro, Trajadura

Quinta do Noval is both an estate and the name of the company that owns the estate. The only port actually made in total from the Quinta do Noval estate – at Pinhão, in the heart of the Douro – is the vintage. Other ports sold by the company are sold under the 'Noval' brand, indicating that not all the grapes come from Quinta do Noval itself.

The company (until 1973, called AJ da Silva) is best known for two things. In the 1950s, it pioneered Late Bottled Vintage port, and Noval LB – now no longer from a single vintage, but a straight vintage character – is still very successful. But Noval's principal claim to fame is that one of its wines, the 1931 Nacional vintage, is the most expensive bottle of port ever sold, for £3470 in a restaurant in the Bahamas. The Quinta do Noval Nacional vintage ports are a real curiosity, made from ungrafted vines grown on the estate. Darker in colour, tougher and with a much more powerful flavour, Noval Nacional is probably the greatest vintage port made.

However, if Nacional is the greatest, the same cannot be said about the ordinary vintage wines. They are attractive, with a muscovado sugar sweetness to them, and seem to come to maturity faster than many other brands. This is not necessarily a bad thing, but prevents Noval being ranked with the very top shippers for vintage port.

In an entirely different region, Quinta do Noval bought Solar das Bouças, one of the finest single *quinta vinhos verdes*, in 1989. The wine is made mainly from Loureiro, with about 30 per cent Trajadura. It is magnificently aromatic, overflowing with peach, strawberry and grape scents – not typical but, to our non-Portuguese tastes, much better!

RAMOS PINTO
Port RD
DOURO

♟ Touriga Nacional, Tinta Roriz, Tinta Barroca and others

♟ Malvasia Fina

Apart from the unimpressive whites, Ramos Pinto ports are good right across the range, from the minty-plummy, medicinal Vintage Character and lovely, complex Late Bottled Vintage to the actual vintage wines, which are light but very fruity and stylish with rich, minty, blackcurranty flavours. Their classic old tawnies, also excellent, are unusual in being single *quinta* wines. Quinta Ervamoira 10-year-old Tawny is delicious, soft, walnutty wine, and Quinta Bom Retiro 20-year-old, darker and richer, has lovely raisiny-minty, savoury character.

Bom Retiro is Ramos Pinto's main base in the Douro, site of their winery and research lab. They also have two other *quintas* right up in the remote eastern Douro Superior: Ervamoira and Bons Ares. The latter does not qualify to make port, but will soon be producing table wines – 30 hectares (74 acres) are already planted with Douro varieties plus Cabernet Sauvignon, Cabernet Franc, Riesling and Sauvignon.

RAPOSEIRA
DOURO

♟ Chardonnay, Pinot Noir, Malvasia, Cerceal

♟ Chardonnay, Pinot Noir, Cerceal and others

Raposeira is Portugal's largest sparkling wine producer, and deservedly the best seller. Even at the time of its foundation, at the end of the nineteenth century, the company was experimenting with foreign grape varieties, and Chardonnay and Pinot Noir are today an important part of the blends. Top of the range is Velha Reserve Brut, made only from Pinot Noir and Chardonnay, but the other wines, blends of these with local grapes, are also good, fresh and fruity, inexpensive and lacking the earthiness that mars most Portuguese sparkling wines. Super Reserva comes in white and rosé, ranging from dry to sweet. Even the simple Raposeira Reserva, the best seller, contains some Chardonnay and is simple, fresh and attractive. All wines are 'Champagne method'.

REAL COMPANHIA VINÍCOLA (ROYAL OPORTO)
Bairrada RD, Colares RD, Dão RD, Douro RD, Port RD, Vinho Verde RD
DOURO

🍷 Port/Douro: Tinta Francisca, Tinta Carvalha, Tinta Roriz and others

🍷 Port: Donzelinho, Malvasia Fina, Esgana Cão and others
Vinho Verde: Loureiro, Trajadura, Pedernã and others

Royal Oporto/Real Vinícola wines are not great, but then they are cheap. Some are sold under supermarket own labels. Nine out of ten bottles of the company's ports are tawnies, but in fact only one-tenth of this is real old tawny, the remainder being simple, light-coloured young ports. Of the up-market tawnies, the 10-year-old is best, a fairly good, nutty wine. The 20-year-old is rather coarse, but some of the *colheita* wines are good. The single *quinta* tawnies from Quinta das Carvalhas and Quinta do Sibio are decent but not special. There's a pleasant, lightweight, nutty-figgy Late Bottled Vintage and an unattractive white port. Vintages (produced in every year possible) are always quick-maturing and tend to have a chocolaty, muscovado-like flavour, to lack concentration – and display an alarming variation between bottles!

Royal Oporto is the second-largest of the port producers yet about half its output is, in fact, not port but table wine. There is nothing very impressive, though one of the *vinho verde* brands, Agulha, is clean and simple (Lagosta is less good).

REGUENGOS IPR
ALENTEJO

Winery entries: Esporão, Fonseca Successores

🍷 Tinta Roriz, Moreto, Periquita, Trincadeira

🍷 Manteudo, Perrum, Rabo de Ovelha, Roupeiro

Of the five areas within the Alentejo striving for demarcation, Reguengos was one of the fastest to organize itself. There is nothing extraordinary about the land round Reguengos de Monsaraz: stony, undulating plains haphazardly dotted with olive trees plus a few fields of stumpy vines. What distinguishes Reguengos from the rest of the Alentejo is that it has three heavyweight wine producers: Finagra at Esporão, José Maria da Fonseca Successores at the JS Rosado Fernandes winery – and the local co-operative. There are now some 600 vineyard owners in the co-op; between them they own around 4000 hectares (9880 acres), with a production potential of 15 million tonnes of grapes a year. They are now planting and replanting, training their vines along wires so that the vineyards may be mechanically cultivated.

Reguengos reds are better than whites (with the exception of the Esporão white). Indeed, *only* red wine is made on the JS Rosado Fernandes estate. The reds from the Reguengos co-op are generous, cherry-flavoured wines. Older co-op wines we have tasted date from before 1986, when Esporão was still a member, and were excellent. What will happen when the *reservas* and *garrafeiras* are made from post-1986 wine we can only surmise. But, given the quality production of JS Rosado Fernandes and Esporão, wine from the Reguengos co-op could represent an inexpensive way to sample one of Portugal's most up-and-coming wine regions.

RIBATEJO

Winery entry: Margaride

🍷 Periquita, Castelão Nacional, Trincadeira Preta and others

🍷 Fernão Pires, Trincadeira das Pratas, Arinto and others

◀ The village of Azambujeira in the Ribatejo. These vineyards on the wide, fertile valley of the Tagus have great potential, but few winemakers are as yet exploiting it.

Taken together, the wine regions of the Ribatejo – Almeirim IPR, Cartaxo IPR, Chamusca IPR, Coruche IPR, Santarém IPR and Tomar IPR – are second only to the Oeste in the amount of wine they produce.

The whole of the Ribatejo region is fertile, and lies in the wide, flattish valley of the River Tagus. Only when you get as far north as Tomar does the ground get any higher, although Chamusca stands on the edge of hills to the east of the valley floor. The weather is very mild, for the Tagus exerts a moderating influence on the naturally harsh continental climate, and the river is tidal even as far as Almeirim.

Most of the wines come from co-ops – the one at Almeirim being the region's largest. About twelve times as much white is made as red. It is not wildly exciting stuff (except for the wines of the Margaride estate), but it is widely used by merchants from other parts of Portugal to make up their blends. The reds can be as good as most in Portugal, with generous, plum and cherry fruit, and the whites honeyed and minty. But these are the highlights; the generality, for the time being, is dull.

ROUPEIRO

This high quality white grape is much more common than it might first appear, because it goes by all sorts of different names in different parts of Portugal. It is called the Roupeiro in the Alentejo and Setúbal peninsula, but Codega in the Douro and Tras-os-Montes (where it is very widespread); what's more, vine boffins think that the Tamarez, Crato and Alva Branco, all from the Algarve, are the same grape, likewise the Codo Siria of Pinhel and the Malvasia Grossa. The Roupeiro's tightly packed bunches ripen early, and if not picked promptly they can turn into dull, flat wine, lacking the freshness of acidity. Early picked and well made, however, Roupeiro can yield quite characterful, honeyed, lemony wines for drinking young. They lose fruitiness and freshness with age.

SANDEMAN
Port RD
DOURO

🍷 Touriga Nacional, Touriga Francesa, Tinta Roriz and others

🍇 Malvasia Rei, Verdelho, Esgana Cão and others

Founded in 1790 simultaneously with the sherry firm, this port branch remained in Sandeman hands until 1979, and is still run by the family even though now owned by international drinks company Seagram. Sandeman vintage ports made before 1970 were often very fine indeed, but quality has slipped since then – partly because a number of important *quintas* stopped supplying grapes. Sandeman traditionally owned no vineyards, but has latterly bought three *quintas* to guarantee future supplies of top-quality grapes, two at Pinhão and one right up in the east by the Spanish border.

The unimpressive cheaper ports are matured in Régua, at the warm western limits of the Douro vineyards. The rest are taken to Vila Nova de Gaia for ageing. These include the pleasant but spirity Founder's Reserve Vintage Character, a medicinal, ruby-style Late Bottled Vintage and two aged tawnies, the best of the range: 10-year-old Royal and 20-year-old Imperial – both made in a dry, woody style but with good concentration of minty-nutty flavour. The white ports, including the dry Apitiv brand, are coarse, and vintages from 1970 onwards are variable.

In 1989 Sandeman was the largest-selling port brand in the world, but the company's new policy is to cut volume, and raise quality and prices.

SÃO JOÃO
Bairrada RD, Dão RD
BEIRA LITORAL

🍷 Bairrada: Baga, Periquita, Moreto
Dão: Touriga Nacional, Jaen, Bastardo

🍇 Bairrada: Fernão Pires (Maria Gomes), Bical
Dão: Arinto, Dona Branca, Barcelo

Caves São João is very much a family affair – sometimes a little too much so, as there are internal disagreements as to wine-making styles! But Luis da Costa seems to get his way on most things, and continues to make the Caves São João wines among the best in both Bairrada and Dão. There are some aspects of the company that are completely traditional (like buying three-quarters of the wine they need direct from co-ops), and others as modern as anyone else in Portugal (such as planting and making pure Cabernet Sauvignon, aged in French oak).

In the matter of white Bairrada, Luis da Costa was well ahead of his time, creating a fresh, young style back in 1959 – 20 years before Bairrada was denominated. Now all the wines that Caves São João produces (as opposed to buying ready-made) are made in stainless steel. Their 30-hectare (74-acre) vineyard, Poço do Lobo, planted in 1983, is destined to supply grapes for the Cabernet Sauvignon and a single estate red Bairrada. The 1986, '87 and '89 Cabernets are rich, creamy and blackcurranty.

The Poço do Lobo red Bairrada will undoubtedly be sensational when it is finally released, but what is hard to understand is just why the Frei João Bairrada and Porta dos Cavalheiros Dão reds are so good. These come from the same co-ops whose wines seem boring in most other merchants' hands, and yet turn out far superior. The solution may lie in the 20 per cent Caves São João buy as grapes and make into wine themselves. Whatever the reason, both are rich and complex, the Reservas particularly so, and develop impressively with age.

SETÚBAL PENINSULA

Winery entries: Fonseca
Successores, Pires

🍷 Periquita, Alfrocheiro,
Espadeiro and others

🥂 Fernão Pires, Arinto, Moscatel
de Setúbal and others

▲ Moscatel vines in a vineyard
belonging to João Pires near Azeitão
on the Setúbal peninsula. Most
Moscatel grapes here are made into
sweet fortified wines, but João Pires
make a delicious dry Moscatel, as well
as a Moscatel de Setúbal.

Apart from the long-established Moscatel de Setúbal RD, the Setúbal
penisula – to the south of Lisbon – contains two new wine regions:
Arrábida IPR and Palmela IPR. That these regions produce some of the
best red wines in Portugal, however, is thanks to the quality of the wines
made by José Maria da Fonseca Successores and João Pires, two
extremely innovative producers, rather than to particular qualities of the
area itself. Yet the new regions have been laid out in spite of, or more
accurately, to spite these two important companies. (The local co-ops
had a major say in the drawing up of boundaries and choice of
authorized grape varieties!)

One of José Maria da Fonseca's leading brands is called Quinta de
Camarate, named after the vineyard from which the grapes come. The
new boundary between Arrábida and Palmela goes straight through the
middle of the *quinta* which means – frustratingly – they can call their
wine neither Arrábida nor Palmela.

Both José Maria da Fonseca and João Pires are keen to discover
which are the best grapes for the regions. So they grow Cabernet
Sauvignon, Merlot, Sémillon, Chardonnay, Riesling and Gewürztraminer
as well as native Portuguese varieties. Cabernet and Chardonnay are
among those suggested for the new regions, but no mention is made in
the new rules of the others, nor of some high-quality Portuguese grapes
such as the Touriga Nacional and Tinta Aragonez, both of which José
Maria da Fonseca would like to try.

However, there is no doubt that Arrábida and Palmela do have the
potential on their gently sloping limestone hills and sandier plains to
produce fine wines. At present, José Maria da Fonseca Successores and
João Pires are way ahead of the field in terms of quality, and Fonseca
Successores own the second largest vineyard in Palmela and sell over
half the wine made in Arrábida. But, as one of Fonseca Successores's
owners says, 'People think that producing a wine with the region's name
on the label is enough to improve the quality.' Experience the world over
suggests otherwise.

SMITH WOODHOUSE
Port RD
DOURO

♟ Touriga Nacional, Touriga Francesa, Tinta Roriz and others

♀ Esgana Cão, Folgosão, Verdelho and others

Smith Woodhouse is a name mostly seen in small print on bottles of own-label supermarket and wine merchant port. But you shouldn't underrate it because of this: Smith Woodhouse is one of the few standard-bearers for a style of port that has all but disappeared. Smith Woodhouse Late Bottled Vintage Port is the *traditional*, late-bottled style, unfiltered before bottling so that all the flavour stays in the wine. OK, so it throws a crust and needs decanting, but that's a lot better than having a so-called late bottled vintage that's had the guts ripped out of it by filtration and tastes of very little as a result.

Smith Woodhouse, though now part of the Symington group, has a long and distinguished history of its own dating back to 1784 when it was founded by Christopher Smith, a future Lord Mayor of London.

The two most important *quintas* for Smith Woodhouse's top wines are Quinta do Vale de Dona Maria and Quinta do Monte Bravo, but the Symington group has agreements with many top *quintas*, particularly in the valley of the River Torto, and there is no shortage of good wine. This is clearly demonstrated by some of the vintage ports: the 1980 Smith Woodhouse is among the best wines of this much underrated vintage, rich and sweet, with hints of walnut and thyme.

Smith Woodhouse also make the Gould Campbell wines.

SOGRAPE
Bairrada RD, Dão RD, Douro RD, Port RD, Vinho Verde RD

♟ Bairrada: Baga,
Dão: Touriga Nacional, Tinta Pinheira,
Douro: Tinta Roriz, Tinta Francesa, Touriga Nacional

♟ Mateus Rosé: Bastardo, Touriga, Alvarelhão, Tinta Pinheira

♀ Bairrada: Fernão Pires (Maria Gomes), Rabo de Ovelha, Cerceal
Dão: Cerceal, Rabigato
Douro: Viosinho, Malvasia, Gouveira
Mateus White: Malvasia, Arinto, Esgana Cão, Cerceal
Vinho Verde: Pedernã

This huge wine company, owned by a branch of the wealthy Guedes family, made its fortune with Mateus Rosé, which still accounts for 93 per cent of its wine sales. Mateus is made in a super-modern winery at the small village of São Mateus, in the Bairrada region. Nowadays it is clean and fruity enough, varying in sweetness and fizz according to the whims of different markets, but Sogrape's other, more recent wines are far more interesting.

When demand for Mateus started to decline a few years ago, Sogrape decided to develop a range of finer wines, and applied Mateus capital and technology to some of Portugal's old established RDs. In 1982 they began to buy vineyards. The first was Solar Honra de Azevedo in the Vinho Verde RD and this now provides much of the raw material for three Sogrape *vinho verde* brands: fresh, fruity, off-dry Gazela, Chello, an authentically dry *vinho verde*, and the soft, grapy-flavoured Quinta de Azevedo.

Also in the eighties, Sogrape began developing new styles of Bairrada wines at the Mateus plant, which happens to be in Bairrada. They now have 70 hectares (173 acres) of vineyard there, and have recently launched an unusual range of modern, light, fruity Bairradas under the brand name Terra Franca. The reds are particularly amazing – not great, but different. The simple red Terra Franca is remarkably light, but with deep, subdued red-fruits aroma and flavour and soft, gentle tannin. The *garrafeira* is still fairly traditional and astringent, though more fruity than most. The basic white is not up to much, but the Reserva is good.

Sogrape had had a winery in the Douro since the early forties (another source of Mateus Rosé). In addition, they recently equipped a small estate in Vila Real and, in the late eighties, launched two new Douro wines, branded Vila Regia. The red is fragrant, strawberry-fruity wine with some tannin, the white fresh, simple and lightly fruity. There is also a richer but still simple white Planalto Reserva and a good, rich, slightly oaky white Sogrape Douro Reserva.

At the moment, the Dão wines, under the brand name Grão Vasco, are the least impressive of the range (though excellent by Dão standards). But in 1989 Sogrape bought a 100-hectare (247-acre) Dão property called Quinta dos Carvalhais, and completed a new winery there in time for the 1990 vintage. So things should be improving.

TAYLOR, FLADGATE & YEATMAN
Port RD
DOURO

🍷 Touriga Nacional, Touriga Francesa, Tinta Barroca and others

🍷 Malvasia, Arinto, Boal and others

Taylor's vintage ports justifiably fetch the highest prices at auction, and the superb quality extends most of the way down the price scale. Our ecstatic tasting notes first falter with First Estate, a pleasant but spirity ruby not up to the standard of the rest of the Taylor's range, and the Chip Dry White Port, rather coarse (like most white ports). And tawnies are not a strong point: the 10-year old is fairly sweet, pleasant but not distinguished, the 20-year-old rather good and very nutty, though rather austere, and the 'Over 40 Years' Tawny is too old for our tastes. Those reservations apart, the rest of the wines are consistently excellent. The Late Bottled Vintage – a style of port pioneered by Taylor – is the biggest seller on the market, a cedary, figgy, minty, quite complex wine for the price, not too heavy and not too sweet.

The top wines are based on grapes from two *quintas* in the Douro Superior, not far from the Spanish border: the beautiful Vargellas and nearby Terra Feita. The famous Quinta de Vargellas has belonged to the company since the end of the last century, so remote that until recently the only way to reach it was by a narrow-gauge railway (Vargellas had its own station). Its wines, big, fragrant, very fruity and extremely dark and tannic in their youth, maturing to lovely, elegant, cedary flavours, are very often the region's best off-vintage single *quinta* wines. Vines cover 40 per cent of the 100-hectare (247-acre) estate. The other *quinta*, Terra Feita, was bought by Taylor only in 1973, though it had long been managed by them. The recent acquisition of a neighbouring farm has brought the Terra Feita vineyard up to 50.5 hectares (125 acres), a size at which Taylor may well release a single *quinta* wine before long. The vintage wines themselves, from the finest years, are also made principally from the grapes of these two estates. Taylor vintages are stylish, concentrated, elegant wines – dark and tannic when young, maturing to cedary, minty complexity. They tend to be very long-lived.

Taylor, founded in 1692, is under the same ownership as Fonseca Guimaraens (though their wines are made completely separately) and a company specializing in 'own label', Romariz.

TORRES IPR
ESTREMADURA

🍷 Periquita, Castelão Nacional (Camarate), Tinta Miuda and others

🍷 Fernão Pires, Vital, Arinto and others `

The town of Torres Vedras is probably better known to foreigners as the point where Wellington halted the advance of the French army during the Peninsular War than as a wine region. However, it does have a huge co-op capable of making good young red wine, though their mature reds are too hit-and-miss to be reliably recommendable. The Torres Vedras climate, and that of the region surrounding it, is distinctly influenced by the proximity of the Atlantic Ocean, making it cooler and damper than Arruda and Alenquer. This, combined with perfectly decent grape varieties, should mean wines as good as anywhere in the Oeste, but the wine-making needs to improve. At present, the co-op bottles only about one-third of its production, and almost all exports are in bulk, principally to Switzerland, Luxembourg and ex-Portuguese colonies.

However, Torres Vedras seems determined to raise its international profile, and the fuss over the proposed name of the region looks as if it may achieve what the region's wine cannot. Although the town is called Torres Vedras, and the co-op writes 'Adega Cooperativa Torres Vedras' clearly on its labels, the name chosen for the new region has been just 'Torres'. Heard the name anywhere before? It looks to the outside eye as if a large but internationally insignificant Portuguese wine region is trying to cash in on the success of a well-known Spanish wine producer (Miguel Torres of Penedés). As EC law stands, producers are not allowed to use the names of demarcated regions, but whether an established producer can stop a new region from pinching his name and the goodwill that goes with it remains to be seen!

VINHO VERDE

Both red and white *vinhos verdes* come from the top left-hand corner of Portugal, between Oporto and the Spanish border. The Vinho Verde region (sometimes known as the Minho region, after the river that forms the border with Spain) is damp and temperate, with no mountain ranges to shield it from the mild influence of the Atlantic. So damp is it, in fact, that vine growers are forced to train their vines high off the ground to avoid fungal infections aggravated by the wet weather. Although in recently-planted vineyards vines are trained along wires up to two metres above the ground or along double rows of wires with wooden cross-piece supports, the traditional way to grow vines was up trellises around the borders of fields, or, even more primitively, up trees. This way of training can produce huge yields as the foliage rampages along overhanging supports or up into the highest branches.

Hence the strange sight of harvesters picking grapes up tall ladders at vintage-time, still a common spectacle in the Vinho Verde region. This traditional way of cultivating vines was encouraged by legislation – still in force as recently as the 1974 revolution – which dated from the introduction of maize into Portugal during the sixteenth century. Vineyards were then forbidden in favour of the new cereal, the only dispensation being that vines might be grown round the edges of fields as 'decoration'. The fields themselves contained maize or cows, the maize providing feed for the cows, and the cows providing fertilizer for the maize (and vines). In the many small farms that crowd the Minho region this is still the mix, the grapes being delivered to the local merchant or co-op to be made into wine. The only change is that kiwi fruit is beginning to supplant maize.

To give the idea that the Vinho Verde region is entirely agricultural would be wrong, however, as it is also the centre of Portugal's textile industry. In the heart of *vinho verde* country, too, is Guimarães, the ancient capital of Portugal, which still has a ruined tenth-century castle overlooking the town, a splendid fourteenth-century ducal palace, and old houses built in indestructible local granite flanking narrow, cobbled streets.

There are vines around almost every corner of the roads that wind through the lush countryside, and almost every family with a plot of land grows grapes to sell or turn into wine. There is a multiplicity of different grape varieties used for *vinho verde*, and certain of these predominate in certain parts of the region. The north, around Monção, is the home of the Alvarinho, as highly prized in Portugal as it is over the border in Spain. Further south, the aromatic Loureiro and Trajadura dominate, succeeded by the relatively neutral, acid Azal around Guimarães, and the savoury, tangy Avesso where the region borders the Douro.

The best and most aromatic Loureiro-based wines come from Solar das Bouças, Paço do Cardido, Quinta do Tamariz, Casa dos Cunhas, Quinta da Quintão and the Ponte de Lima co-op. Good Azal-based wines are to be found from Casa de Cabanelas, Casa de Compostela, Paço d'Anha and Quinta da Portela, while the Tormes and Passo (Paço) de Teixeró wines show well the savoury character of southern Avesso-based wines.

◄ The damp weather of the Minho region means that vines have to be trained well off the ground to avoid catching fungal diseases. This small patch of domestic vineyard is typical of the way most grapes are grown for *vinho verde*, in among the flowers and vegetables.

GRAPE ENTRIES
Arinto (Perdernã)
Baga
Loureiro

WINE ENTRIES
Vinho Verde

WINERY ENTRIES
Aliança
João Pires
Quinta do Noval
Sogrape
Caves Velhas

Red and white wines

TOURIGA NACIONAL

This superlative red grape is the best of the port varieties. It grows mainly in the Douro, where it is used both for table wines and for port. It is also found, under the name Tourigo, in Dão, where it must make up at least 20 per cent of the blend, though plantings here have declined in the last 50 years. Some grows in the Setúbal peninsula and in Bairrada (alias Mortagua – confusingly, Mortagua is elsewhere a synonym for the Periquita), but it extends no further into the centre and south.

The grapes are very rich indeed in colour as well as tannin, but the wines have the fullness, fruitiness, aroma and flavour to back up this youthful toughness, and the balance and the guts to keep and improve for years. The young wines have a powerful aroma of blackcurrants, liquorice and ripe berry fruits.

The only problem with the Touriga Nacional is its tiny yield – a single vine in its favourite habitat, the Upper Douro, will produce no more than 300g of grapes, while another variety alongside might produce 2kg. The port producers began a 15-year programme of clonal selection at the end of the seventies in the hope of improving yields, and heavier-bearing Touriga Nacional vines should soon be available.

TRAS-OS-MONTES

♥ Bastardo, Tinta Amarela, Tinta Carvalha and others

♀ Gouveio, Malvasia Fina, Codega and others

Tras-os-Montes ('behind the mountains'), hard up against the north-east Spanish border, is a region that has turned from agriculture to tourism. Its mountainous slopes offer more to walkers than to farmers, and its spa resorts have been attracting Portuguese visitors for many years.

Nevertheless, Tras-os-Montes has three wine regions on probation: Valpaços IPR, Chaves IPR and Planalto-Mirandês IPR; and, true to form, the estate currently producing the best wine in the region is in none of them. Valle Pradinhos is at Macedo de Cavaleiros, bang in between Valpaços and Planalto-Mirandês; the wine is red, rich and magnificently fruity. But in general, it's the old Portuguese story of growers sending their grapes to be made into mediocre wine at the co-op.

Mind you, the local co-op at Valpaços has made some very decent reds in the last few years, the best of which have creamy, sour cherry fruitiness and considerable concentration. The most noticeable product of the rest of the region, however, is the sort of rosé that comes in funny-shaped bottles and is best avoided.

CAVES VELHAS
Bairrada RD, Bucelas RD, Dão RD, Douro RD, Vinho Verde RD
ESTREMADURA

♥ Bairrada: Baga, Periquita, Tinta Pinheira
Dão: Touriga Nacional, Tinta Pinheira
Douro: Touriga Nacional, Touriga Francesa, Tinta Barroca and others

♀ Bairrada: Bical, Fernão Pires, Bucelas: Arinto, Esgana Cão
Dão: Arinto, Dona Branca
Douro: Gouveio, Malvasia, Rabigato
Vinho Verde: Loureiro, Trajadura, Azal

Most of Caves Velhas's business, like that of several other large Portuguese wine merchants, consists of buying wines from all over the country, and selling them under its own label. They sell *vinho verde*, under the Arca Nova label, and red and white wines from the Douro, Dão and Bairrada with their own Caves Velhas label. Best of these are the red Bairrada and Dão; the rest are adequate rather than exciting. Caves Velhas also sell a very successful brand, Romeira, blended from Ribatejo wines. This is a reliably fruity Portuguese red, not too heavy on the tannin. The Caves Velhas Clarete and Garrafeira, also from the Ribatejo, are also worth seeking out when in Portugal.

However, perhaps Caves Velhas's most significant role in the Portuguese wine scene is that, almost single-handedly, they have preserved the Bucelas RD from extinction. For some years until 1982, they were the only company selling Bucelas, one of Portugal's most historic white wines. Although there are now two new companies making Bucelas, Caves Velhas is still the largest producer in the area, and sells about three-quarters of all Bucelas available. As well as their own 70 hectares (173 acres) of Bucelas vineyard, Caves Velhas buy in grapes from other growers, and are working on the release of a single *quinta* wine, Quinta do Boição.

Confusingly, the younger of the two Bucelas wines they make is called Bucellas Velho (old Bucelas); fermented in stainless steel, it is strongly lemony with a hint of pine. The Bucelas Garrafeira, mostly drunk in Portugal, is made in a more traditional way and is richer, fatter and fuller than the young wine – which perhaps indicates that you might improve the young wine by giving it more age in bottle.

VINHO VERDE RD
MINHO, DOURO LITORAL

Winery entries: Aliança, Pires, Quinta do Noval, Sogrape, Velhas

♥ Azal Tinto, Borraçal, Espadeiro and others

♀ Azal, Loureiro, Trajadura and others

Outside Portugal *vinho verde* may conjure up visions of vaguely fizzy white wine, usually sweetish, and often sold in a dumpy Mateus-shaped bottle, but to the average Portuguese it means young wine. Not green wine (the literal translation), but young, fresh, wine-of-the-year wine – best drunk before the foam has barely subsided on the fermentation. And, as such, it is a description that can apply to white *and* red wine. The secondary meaning of the word applies to wine (red or white) that conforms to the rules of the Vinho Verde RD region, which stretches from just south of Oporto right up to the border with Spain.

About half of all *vinho verde* (pronounced 'veenyo vaird') *is* red, but that proportion is decreasing. Sour and raspingly acidic, it's drunk only in the north of Portugal, and finds no takers elsewhere.

The white version is a lot more fun, although it still has the same high acidity. The climate in the Vinho Verde region is so mild and wet that it takes an unusually hot summer to ripen all the grapes, and this results in low-sugar, high-acid grapes. Almost all *vinho verde* is made by large companies or co-ops. Much of the technology in these wineries is brilliantly up-to-date – it needs to be with the motley mixture of grapes that comes in. Clouds of rot rising from overripe grapes are not uncommon, while many other bunches contain only acid, green berries. The problem arises because of the number of different grapes grown for *vinho verde*, not all of which ripen at the same time. Yet when the decision to harvest is taken, the whole family and some of the neighbours lend a hand, and everything goes into the baskets.

Things are done more efficiently at a small handful of estates who grow their own grapes, make their own wine and bottle it. Most of these formed an association in 1985, of which there are now 33 members. These estates plant grapes in blocks by variety, so they can be harvested at optimum ripeness, and most have ultra-modern wineries. The resulting wines are authentic *vinhos verdes*, a far cry from the cheap, sweetish wines in the dumpy bottles. They are bone-dry, either with a muscatty fragrance or a piercing, lemony flavour.

WARRE
Port RD
DOURO

♥ Touriga Nacional, Touriga Francesa, Tinta Roriz, Tinta Barroca

♀ Esgana Cão, Folgosão, Verdelho and others

Warre – the oldest British port shipper, founded in 1670 – is now part of the Symington group. For several years, Warre's vintage ports have been based on grapes from two *quintas*, Warre's own Quinta da Cavadinha and half of the Quinta do Bom Retiro owned by the Serôdio family. The result is usually one of the toughest, longest-lived vintage ports, sweet and tannic, often combining the herby character of Dow with some of the sweetness of Graham.

In 1987 Warre released the first single *quinta* wine from Cavadinha, which has 35 hectares (87 acres) of vineyard. It was a 1978, followed in due course by a 1979, and immediately established Cavadinha in the front rank of single *quinta* wines.

Warre sell an excellent tawny, Nimrod, between 15 and 20 years old, as well as the oldest brand of port registered, Warrior, now a Vintage Character. Other high points of their range are their Crusted and traditional Late Bottled Vintage wines, both tremendously characterful, unfiltered ports that need treating with due reverence and care.

BOTTLES, CORKS AND LABELS

Another way of saying 'Champagne method'.

Mushroom-shaped Champagne cork, wired down to withstand the pressure of the fizz.

A capsule keeps the cork clean, helps prevent it drying out, and protects it from weevils.

Only a small proportion of sparkling wines are labelled with a vintage.

Being such an important international seller, Torres sprinkles its labels liberally with English.

Name of the producer, probably the most famous in Spain.

Name of the producer, the largest in Sanlúcar.

Denomination of origin.

Manzanilla is a light, delicate sherry, exclusive to Sanlúcar.

Brand name.

Alcoholic strength; 15.5 per cent is the minimum for *fino* and *manzanilla* sherries.

Official indication of how long the wine has been matured in tanks, wooden barrels and in bottle before sale.

Stopper cork typically used for fortified wines, topped by the official seal of Jerez's Consejo Regulador.

Cava is Catalan (and now, by adoption, Spanish) for 'Champagne–method' fizz.

Denomination of origin.

There's nothing much to learn simply from looking at the colour or shape of a Spanish or Portuguese bottle. Portuguese wine *labels* can be pretty unrevealing, too, often making no mention of a region of origin, but most will give you the producer's name, a brand name and the vintage (plus address, volume and alcohol content, which are legally required in the EC). A few years ago we would have warned you to beware of bogus vintages – Iberian drinkers have traditionally been impressed by historical dates. Now they are more likely to be genuine.

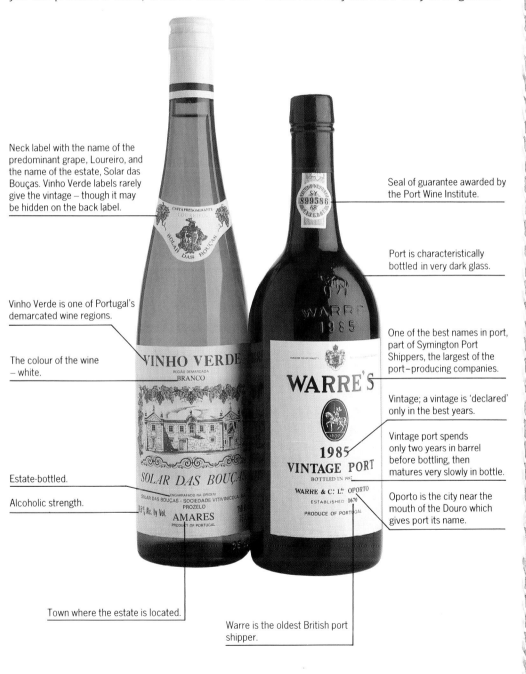

Neck label with the name of the predominant grape, Loureiro, and the name of the estate, Solar das Bouças. Vinho Verde labels rarely give the vintage – though it may be hidden on the back label.

Vinho Verde is one of Portugal's demarcated wine regions.

The colour of the wine – white.

Estate-bottled.

Alcoholic strength.

Town where the estate is located.

Seal of guarantee awarded by the Port Wine Institute.

Port is characteristically bottled in very dark glass.

One of the best names in port, part of Symington Port Shippers, the largest of the port–producing companies.

Vintage; a vintage is 'declared' only in the best years.

Vintage port spends only two years in barrel before bottling, then matures very slowly in bottle.

Oporto is the city near the mouth of the Douro which gives port its name.

Warre is the oldest British port shipper.

STORING
AND
SERVING WINES

STORING There are lots of substitutes for a cool, underground cellar – but none as good. We know, we don't have one. We store our wines in two small rooms, one with fitted wine racks screwed to the walls for wines from opened cases, the other for unbroached cases.

The essential conditions for successful wine storage are that your chosen spot should be as cool, airy, dark and vibration-free as possible. Where matters not a jot: it could be in the garage, a spare room, under the stairs, or in a shed at the bottom of the garden. Our 'cellar' isn't as cool as we'd like it, nor as airy, but at least it doesn't have violent changes in temperature, just gentle fluctuations with the seasons. One thing is important, though, wherever you keep your wines: the bottles should always lie flat. That way the liquid stays in contact with the bottom of the cork and prevents it drying out. If a bottle is left upright, and the cork does dry out, air will seep in and spoil the wine.

However, most wine doesn't *need* to sit in a cellar for years to mature. This is particularly true of wines from Spain and Portugal, which are generally sold ready to drink: the systems of *reservas*, *gran reservas* and *garrafeiras* are meant to ensure this. Only in a very few cases will they positively benefit from extended ageing – vintage port is the chief example. Iberian white wines should be drunk as young as you can get hold of them. The traditional, oak-aged whites are getting rarer, and these will have done most of their useful ageing in barrel at the winery, before they get anywhere near a bottle. Neither should young, less expensive reds be left hanging around for too long in your cellar. The fruitiness, their chief attraction, is all too quick to fade into dullness.

SERVING A lot of nonsense is talked about serving wines. Last summer, in a London *tapas* bar, we ordered a bottle of young Navarra red. It came well-nigh lukewarm, no fun on a hot summer's evening. The waitress was shocked when we asked her to put it in the freezer, but it came back five minutes later much more attractive for its brisk cooling.

Likewise, white wine is often served too cold. If a wine is heavily chilled, it smells of little, and hits the inside of your mouth with all the allure of an ice-lolly. And you taste very little until the wine has warmed up in your mouth. A couple of hours' chilling in the bottom of a fridge is enough, or, if you've left things too late for that, put the bottle in an ice-bucket (or any other sort of bucket), empty in as much ice as you can spare, and fill up with water. That works faster than ice alone, as water is a more efficient conductor than air. *Fino* and *manzanilla* sherry, by the way, are much better served chilled than warm, and you should always try to finish an opened bottle within the week, as they deteriorate rapidly after that.

It's a waste of time taking out a cork to let a

wine 'breathe'. If a red wine really tastes a bit too tough, slosh it from the bottle into a decanter or jug, and then back again through a funnel. The violent encounter with air might soften it. Apart from this, the main purpose of decanting a wine is to remove any sludgy sediment. However, few Spanish or Portuguese reds form a sediment in bottle – with the exception of some kinds of port – because most mature Iberian wines are bottled later than wines from elsewhere, and so have already lost any sediment. Vintage, single *quinta*, crusted and the traditional style of LBV port should all be decanted. Stand the bottle upright for 24 hours beforehand to let the looser bits of sediment sink to the bottom. Pundits say you should decant through muslin. We usually use a clean handkerchief, or even coffee filter papers.

TASTING The first thing worth remembering about tasting is that it's almost all done by smell. The tongue is a relatively blunt instrument, capable of discerning only sweetness, saltiness, sourness and bitterness. Everything else happens in the nose. So if you've got a stinking cold, you won't taste – or smell – very much at all.

Use good, big glasses to taste from. It's nice to swirl the wine around before sniffing it (which gives you a sneak preview of what you will 'taste' in your mouth later), and the bigger the glass, the less likely it is that the wine will shoot out over your clothes.

Then take a good mouthful and rootle it around your mouth. If you can suck air noisily through the wine, so much the better because

that sends the message winging up the nasal cavity that much faster. Finally, if you're trying several wines without food, spit each wine out and go on to the next. You'll never survive the assault course otherwise! If you're really interested, make notes about what you notice.

FOOD AND WINE Certain combinations of wine and food are magic, but they're not always the ones you expect. Port and Stilton cheese is delicious, but it's the creamy, nutty flavour of aged *tawny* port that really works well, rather than the rich fruitiness of vintage or ruby. Matching food and wine is enormous fun, and there are two main rules to remember. Either go for a similar flavour in your food to that of your wine, or go for contrast (like the tawny port and Stilton - sweet and salty).

On the whole, dry white wines do go better with fish and seafood than reds. Spanish whites from Catalonia and Portuguese *vinhos verdes* are the obvious candidates. Perhaps surprisingly, chilled *fino* and *manzanilla* are brilliant with seafood as well. Reds are the usual Spanish and Portuguese partners for meat. Wines made from Tempranillo (or Tinta Roriz in Portugal) and Cabernet Sauvignon go very well with lamb, while beef is better with wines based on Garnacha. Port is drunk as an *aperitif* by the French, whilst the British tend to lump together port, Madeira and up-market dry *amontillados* and *olorosos* to drink *after* a meal. But be inventive and adventurous. We were given lunch once by a Portuguese wine producer who served us roast sucking pig and *sparkling red Bairrada*. It was magnificent.

VINTAGES

Until quite recently, many producers in Spain and Portugal didn't worry *too* much about the date on the label of their wines. We vividly remember the Spanish co-op manager who shrugged his shoulders when challenged that a fresh, fruity red seemed younger than its declared years. 'In Spain, people like to see old dates on labels, but like to drink fruity wine. So we oblige them.' Thankfully, this is an attitude that now seems to have changed.

Vintages *do* vary considerably in Portugal, because many of its main wine areas are influenced by coastal weather, whereas in Spain the climate is more stable, and wild swings in quality from year to year are less frequent. But

a vintage chart is only useful as a broad indicator of quality: there are so many variations in soil, micro-climate and wine-making that one man's 1988 red can be delicious, while his neighbour's is a disaster.

There's not much point having a chart that tells you how good the *vinho verde* was in 1980, either. By now it will certainly be dead and gone. In hottish countries such as Spain and Portugal, white wines are almost always best from the most recent vintage. Vintage charts are only *really* useful for wines that mature well – and ones that you can still buy. These are probably going to be red or fortified.

A good indicator in Spain and Portugal as to vintage quality is to see if there are any *gran reservas* or *garrafeiras*. These are produced only in the best years, so their very existence is a good sign.

SPAIN	90	89	88	87	86	85	84	83	82	81
La Mancha	8△	8△	4▽	6★	6▽	6▽	8▽	7▽	6▽	7▽
Navarra	8△	8△	6●	7△	6●	7★	7★	8★	9★	9★
Penedés	8△	7△	7△	8△	4★	7△	5▽	7★	7▽	8★
Ribera del Duero	8△	9△	6△	6△	9△	8△	3▽	8△	8★	9★
Rioja	8△	8△	6△	7△	6△	7△	5★	7★	9●	8★
Valdepeñas	8△	7△	5★	7△	6▽	5▽	9●	8▽	6▽	9★
PORTUGAL	90	89	88	87	86	85	84	83	82	81
Alenquer/Arruda	7△	7△	5★	6△	6★	9●	7★	6▽	6▽	5▽
Alentejo	7△	8△	7●	7△	7●	8★	7★	9★	7▽	4▽
Arrabida/Palmela	8△	7△	6★	7△	7★	10●	6★	7★	8★	5▽
Bairrada	7△	7△	5★	6△	5★	10●	4▽	7★	5▽	4▽
Dão	6△	6△	6★	7△	4★	8●	5▽	8★	5▽	4▽
Douro	6△	6△	5★	6△	6★	10●	4▽	8★	8★	7▽
Port	8△	6△	5△	6△	5△	10△	4★	9△	7●	5★
Ribatejo	7△	7△	6★	6△	7★	7★	7★	7★	5▽	5▽

HOW TO READ THE CHART   △ = not ready   ● = just ready   ★ = at peak   ▽ = past its best

The scores above are for the major wine regions in Spain and Portugal. The numerals represent an overall rating for each year, but

such measures can only ever be broad generalizations. There will be many variations with individual wines and producers.

GLOSSARY

SPAIN

BLANCO White.

BODEGA Winery, ageing cellar, wine-producing firm.

CAVA 'Champagne-method' sparkling wine.

CEPA Grape variety

CLARETE Pale red wine.

COSECHA Vintage.

CONSEJO REGULADOR Governing body of a *denominación de origen*. Each DO has one.

CRIANZA Used to describe both the process of ageing a wine and the youngest official category of matured wine. A *crianza* wine must have been aged in barrel, tank and/or bottle for at least two years.

DENOMINACIÓN DE ORIGEN (DO) Currently the top quality classification for Spanish wine. Rules specify each region's boundaries, grape varieties, vine-growing and wine-making methods.

DULCE Sweet.

EMBOTELLADO DE/EN ORIGEN Estate-bottled.

ESPUMOSO Fizzy.

FLOR A special yeast that grows on the surface of certain wines when in barrel, especially sherry. It protects the wine from air, and imparts a unique taste.

GENEROSO Wine of high alcoholic strength (over 15 per cent), whether fortified or naturally strong.

JOVEN Young.

GRAN RESERVA Top quality, mature wine from an especially good vintage, with at least five years' ageing (cask and bottle) for reds, and four years' for whites.

MISTELA Mix of grape juice and grape alcohol, sometimes drunk as it is, sometimes used for sweetening fortified wines.

RANCIO Style of wine that is deliberately oxidized; either naturally strong or fortified, it is aged in the sun in glass bottles, earthenware jars or wooden barrels.

RESERVA Quality wine from a good vintage with at least three years' ageing (cask and bottle) for reds, and two for whites.

ROSADO Rosé.

SECO Dry.

SOLERA Blending system used for sherry and some other fortified wines. When mature wine is run off a cask for bottling, only a quarter or so of the volume is taken, and the space is filled with similar but younger wine from another cask, which in turn is topped up from an even younger cask, and so on.

TINAJA Large, old-fashioned earthenware or concrete jar used for fermenting or storing wine.

TINTO Red.

VIÑA. Vineyard. Often loosely used in names of wines not actually from a vineyard of that name.

PORTUGAL

ADEGA Winery, ageing cellar, wine-producing firm.

AMFORA Equivalent of the Spanish *tinaja*.

BRANCO White.

COLHEITA Vintage.

COMMISSÃO Governing body of a *região demarcada*.

ENGARRAFADO NA ORIGEM Estate-bottled.

ESPUMANTE Sparkling.

ESTUFA Vessel in which Madeira wines are heated to produce a tangy, caramel flavour.

GARRAFEIRA High-quality vintage wine with at least half a per cent of alcohol higher than the required minimum, that has had at least three years' ageing (reds) and at least one years' ageing (whites).

INDICAÇÃO DE PROVENIÊNCIA REGULAMENTADA (IPR) Official category for wine regions aspiring to RD status. Sometimes known as *vinhos de qualidade produzides em região demarcada* (VQPRD).

LODGE Warehouse where port or Madeira is matured, blended and bottled.

PIPE Port cask.

QUINTA Farm or wine estate.

RESERVA Outstanding wine from a particular vintage that has an alcohol level at least half a per cent higher than the minimum for the region.

REGIÃO DEMARCADA (RD) Portugal's top quality classification. Rules specify each region's boundaries, grapes, vine-growing and wine-making methods.

ROSADO Rosé.

SELO DE GARANTIA Seal, over the cork on a bottle of RD wine, guaranteeing its authenticity.

TINTO Red.

VELHO Old.

INDEX

A page reference in *italics* indicates main entry.

ACKNOWLEDGEMENTS

Photographs All photographs supplied by Mick Rock/Cephas, except Michael Busselle *3*, *73*.
The authors and publishers would also like to thank the following: Peter Bright; Jaime Echávarri Olavarria (Grupo de Exportadores de Rioja); João Renano Henriques (Portuguese Government Trade Office); Graham Hines (Sherry Institute); Antonio Lopes Vieira; Richard Mayson; Miguel Merino Pastor; Mário Briosa Neves; Domingos Soares Franco; Jeremy Watson (Wines From Spain).

Editorial Director Sandy Carr; **Editor** Catherine Dell; **Art Editor** Alison Donovan; **Editorial Assistant** Siobhan Bremner; **Consultant** Wink Lorch; **Indexer** Naomi Good; **Maps** Stan North; **Illustrations** Peter Byatt, Robina Green.